A Bloodless Victory

JOHNS HOPKINS BOOKS ON THE WAR OF 1812

Donald R. Hickey, *Series Editor*

A BLOODLESS VICTORY

The Battle of New Orleans in History and Memory

JOSEPH F. STOLTZ III

Johns Hopkins University Press

Baltimore

Johns Hopkins University Press
2715 North Charles Street
Baltimore, Maryland 21218-4363
www.press.jhu.edu

Library of Congress Cataloging-in-Publication Data

Names: Stoltz, Joseph F., III (Joseph Frederick), author.
Title: A Bloodless Victory: The Battle of New Orleans in History and Memory /
    Joseph F. Stoltz III.
Description: Baltimore, Maryland : Johns Hopkins University Press, 2017. | Series:
    Johns Hopkins books on the War of 1812 | Includes bibliographical references and
    index.
Identifiers: LCCN 2017009947| ISBN 9781421423029 (hardcover : alk. paper) |
    ISBN 9781421423036 (electronic) | ISBN 1421423022 (hardcover : alk. paper) |
    ISBN 1421423030 (electronic)
Subjects: LCSH: New Orleans, Battle of, New Orleans, La., 1815. | Nationalism and
    collective memory—United States.
Classification: LCC E356.N5 S76 2017 | DDC 973.5/239—dc23
    LC record available at https://lccn.loc.gov/2017009947

A catalog record for this book is available from the British Library.

*Special discounts are available for bulk purchases of this book. For more information,
please contact Special Sales at 410-516-6936 or specialsales@press.jhu.edu.*

Johns Hopkins University Press uses environmentally friendly book materials,
including recycled text paper that is composed of at least 30 percent post-consumer
waste, whenever possible.

"A Correct Remembrance of Great Events"

On January 8, 1828, thirteen years to the day after Andrew Jackson's army famously defeated the British, the citizens of Concord, New Hampshire, met to commemorate the American victory. The residents of the state capital gathered around the speakers, who variously explained the importance of the battle and what it meant for the country. The Battle of New Orleans saved the western United States, one assured the audience. It "could not have been within the ordinary calculations of military results" for the British to return a city as important as New Orleans to the Americans. Another connected the battle to the impending presidential election of 1828, implying that Americans would have desperate need of Jackson's leadership in the future.[1]

The last speaker, though, used his time on stage to argue a different point. Nathan Felton implored the crowd that maintaining "a correct remembrance of great events, in which nations or individuals have been concerned, is important on many accounts." He reminded them that "accounts of such events are commonly preserved, and transmitted by history and tradition. History and tradition, however, in their ordinary forms, produce their effects but imperfectly, unless accompanied by other means, calculated to fix upon them our attention, and excite an interest in them." Felton explained that "among the means that have been used for these purposes, none have been more effectual than public celebrations."[2]

As Felton asserted, public celebrations and popular memory play an important role in how a society crafts its historical narrative. Historians certainly influence the shaping of this memory, but artists, playwrights, movie directors, and musicians often sway more people than historians. Each generation of these authors of public memory has retold the story of Jackson's victory in their own way. Some narratives focused on American martial spirit, and others on the multicultural nature of the American army.

One factor that makes such a popular historiography of the Battle of New Orleans challenging is that Americans have not always remembered the event with the same enthusiasm. During the early 1820s, Americans across the country celebrated the Battle of New Orleans as a national holiday on par with the Fourth of July. Two hundred years later, even the city of New Orleans had trouble commemorating the event. By examining the popular historiography of an event like the Battle of New Orleans across such a long span of time, we gain new insight into American culture and society across generations.[3]

Organizationally, this work consists of eight chapters. While in roughly chronological order, each chapter focuses on specific facets of the memory of the Battle of New Orleans. Especially in the chapters dealing with the twentieth century, though, topical discussion supersedes chronological organization, to aid the reader.

In order to properly understand the course of the memory of the Battle of New Orleans, one must first understand what really happened on the Plains of Chalmette. In American historical memory, many myths have clouded accounts of the battle and distorted the nation's understanding of it. Chapter 1 offers a brief survey of the New Orleans campaign and highlights the particular features that later mythology has distorted.

The ubiquitous cotton bale has long been a source of pride for many promoters of the Battle of New Orleans and a well of grief for historians of the engagement. Though Jackson's troops did briefly use cotton bales to raise the height of the rampart, they did so without orders from the military engineers directing the barrier's construction. When British artillery struck the cotton-filled section of the rampart, the white substance caught fire. The flames alerted the engineers to their troops' creative, yet foolish, construction method, and the engineering officers directed all cotton removed from the earthworks. The only cotton used in the preparation of Jackson's defensive position lay below the artillery emplacements. The cotton sopped up the moisture in the ground and provided a more stable firing platform for the cannons.[4]

Chapter 1 asserts that artillery played a far more important role than some histories of the battle have emphasized, especially those directed toward a popular audience. Jackson's defensive line had at least one cannon battery roughly every one hundred yards. Though some of these gun emplacements had only one cannon in them, they were often larger pieces of artillery than normally appeared on a battlefield. In an era when the Royal Artillery used a six-pounder as its standard field piece, Jackson's line possessed several twenty-four-pounders and one thirty-two-pounder.[5]

The last important myth involves the militia. Thanks to the Louisiana militia, Jackson had far more troops at his disposal than American popular histories have traditionally depicted. Though still outnumbered on the Chalmette battlefield on January 8, 1815, roughly three thousand Louisiana militiamen defended alternate paths to New Orleans, funneling the British toward Jackson's position. Furthermore, while the militia played an important role in the climactic January 8 battle, they did so as artillerymen rather than wielding long rifles. Chapter 1 challenges the mythical narrative of the frontier Kentuckian deftly felling his British opponents with aimed long rifle fire.[6]

Chapter 2 explores how the original facts of the battle evolved into the first myths and memories of the event. After the battle, Republican newspapers, playwrights, and artists depicted a Battle of New Orleans that represented their ideals for America. These popular cultural icons generated a myth of the battle which focused on the agrarian woodsman protecting hearth and home. They promoted a militia-based national defense force that decried a large standing army and kept martial power closer to state control than federal dominance. They depicted a battle that exulted in the western victories of the war while highlighting the struggles of the industrializing east. These accounts insinuated that the eastern United States had begun to grow soft.[7]

Republican political operatives found that the memory of the Battle of New Orleans could further their interests as well. The War of 1812 highlighted a number of flaws in Republican political ideology. The nation had a clear need for a national bank, the army could not remain as small as it had been before the war, and poor national infrastructure had doomed the American war effort from the start of the conflict. Banks, armies, and national roads long embodied Federalist policies, and many Republicans disliked the idea of publicly co-opting them. With attentions fixed on commemorating New Orleans and other victories, Republicans discovered a way to camouflage their policy changes. Even as many Republican politicians made speeches promoting the mythology of the Battle of New Orleans, they also adopted many policies that ran counter to the created memory of the battle.[8]

The memory of the Battle of New Orleans during the late 1810s and early 1820s also helped Republicans not only retain control of the federal government but also usher in the one-party "Era of Good Feelings." The War of 1812 had been a disaster for Republicans. By all rights, the American voters should have thrown out the War Hawks and brought back the Federalists. Indeed, voters began that process during the 1814 election season, but the Battle of New Orleans, the Hartford Convention, and the announcement in the United States of the signing of the Treaty of Ghent created the appearance that the Federalists had lost their momentum. The close chronological proximity of the three events gave the appearance and created the memory that the Battle of New Orleans ended a victorious war just as the Federalist-dominated New England states prepared to leave the Union and make a separate peace with England. Republicans pounced on the opportunity to embarrass their political opposition. The ability of Republicans to tie the Federalists to secession and connect the Battle of New Orleans to victory became so successful that within a few years the Federalists ceased to be a viable party on the national level.[9]

Chapter 3 moves the story of the memory of the Battle of New Orleans into the Jacksonian era. Republican efforts to use the battle as a promotional tool highlighting the ideology of frontier farmers and their rugged individualism aided Jackson in his goal to become president. The memory of the Battle of New Orleans made Jackson such a household name that he did far better in the 1824 presidential election than many professional politicians anticipated. During the next four years, urban political machines used the popularity of the Battle of New Orleans to run what many historians have called the United States' first modern presidential campaign.[10]

The fullness with which the newly founded Democratic Party harnessed the memory of the January 8 victory alienated many Americans. As January 8th commemorations transitioned to focusing the celebration on the man rather than the event, even some of the battle's veterans refused to participate in the ceremonies. By the height of Jackson's presidency, entire sections of the United States no longer participated in the national holiday. Some Whigs even publicly discredited the scale of the victory.[11]

By the time Jackson left office, "Jackson Day," as the Democratic Party had branded it, had become the birthday of the party. Spectacular celebrations in honor of the battle still occurred around the country, but the politicization of the events limited them to predominantly Democratic districts.[12]

Chapter 4 explores how sectionalism affected the memory of the Battle of New Orleans. Democratic support of the battle's memory fueled a sense of martial superiority in westerners. In the 1830s, on the United States–Mexican border, participation in the Battle of New Orleans instantly marked someone as an expert on military affairs. As several scholars of the Texas Revolution have asserted, many Texans argued that although the Mexican government had a large, professionally trained and well-equipped army, the rebels had little to fear. To them, since citizens of the Old Southwest had already beaten Wellington's Heroes, those warriors had little to fear from a Mexican army qualitatively inferior to the British veterans of Wellington's famed Peninsular campaigns during the Napoleonic Wars.[13]

That same martial confidence crept into the minds of the succeeding generation of Southerners. As the political issue of slavery became ever more divisive, Southerners further refined their memory of the Battle of New Orleans. Many of them insisted that the "westerners" so championed by the Jeffersonian Republicans and then the Democrats had predominantly, in fact, hailed from south of the Ohio River. Western frontiersmen had not defeated the British so much as Southerners had.[14]

On the eve of the Civil War, the South faced the prospect of a war against an industrial, quantitatively superior foe. According to a skewed memory of events, Andrew Jackson and his army of Southern troops faced the exact same situation against the British. The memory of the Battle of New Orleans encouraged the resolve of many Southerners to confront the long odds ahead of them.[15]

After the defeat of the Confederacy, the Democratic Party attempted to use the Battle of New Orleans as a way to heal the sectional wounds festering across the United States. The party once again organized spectacular Jackson Day balls across the country, but Southerners refused to attend when prominent former Union generals such as Philip Sheridan, George Meade, and Benjamin Butler showed up at the galas. Instead, Battle of New Orleans commemorations slowly withered around the South.[16]

Even in New Orleans, long the heartland of commemorating Jackson's victory, Southerners found the battle too painful to memorialize. During the Union occupation of the city, Benjamin Butler had ordered the words "The Union Must and Shall be Preserved" etched on the famous monument to Jackson and the victory. The base of the equestrian statue existed as a permanent source of doubt for many New Orleanians who questioned whether they had made the right decision in supporting the Confederacy.[17]

Southern men did eventually celebrate the Battle of New Orleans again, as chapter 5 reveals, but only thanks to the efforts of Southern women. The late nineteenth century witnessed the rise of numerous women's patriotic organizations, both ancestry based and otherwise, across the United States. Groups such as the Ladies Hermitage Association (LHA) and the Daughters of 1812 promoted the memory of the Battle of New Orleans as a way for Southerners to move past the embarrassment of the Civil War.

In Nashville, the LHA encouraged commemorative events focused on the Battle of New Orleans through their management of Andrew Jackson's old mansion. The Ladies organized Jackson Day balls like the ones witnessed earlier during the nineteenth century. They also leveraged their traditional feminine roles of educational supervision to ensure that schoolbooks in the South properly highlighted the martial glory attained by the students' predecessors. Finally, they organized reenactments of the 1815 battle which allowed Confederate veterans to play the part of Jackson's victorious troops.[18]

In New Orleans during the same period, the Daughters of 1812 rallied efforts to complete the long-forgotten Chalmette Monument that locals had started prior to the Civil War. The plight of the monument highlighted the grave situation the original battlefield faced. The Daughters strove to duplicate battlefield preservation efforts of groups such as the Daughters of the Confederacy and the Grand Army of the Republic. If the Daughters could keep the battlefield safe from development, they believed it would play a valuable part in promoting the memory of the Battle of New Orleans. The United States is unique in the sense that it is one of the few countries that has conserved battlefields from pre-twentieth-century conflicts. In Europe especially, land needed for the expansion of cities has limited the ability to preserve the landscape of the continent's most prominent military engagements. The process of conserving the Battle of New Orleans site was similar to what many American Civil War battlefields underwent in this same period.[19]

The United States' increasingly close relationship with Great Britain and the realities of the World War I battlefield affected the commemoration of Jackson's victory and consequently its memory. Across the United States from 1912 to 1915, War of 1812 memorialization promoted the idea of one hundred years of peace between the English-speaking nations of the Atlantic. As the "last battle" of the war, the Battle of New Orleans received special attention as the final place at which those nations had fired in anger at one another. Consequently, whereas in the nineteenth century the memorialization of the battle focused on the triumph over British arms, during the twentieth it symbolized friendship between those of a common language.[20]

Chapter 6 explores the twentieth century's reassessment of how the Americans won at New Orleans. Jean Laffite and his Baratarians played an ever-larger role in a narrative that had once focused exclusively on the successes of the frontier rifleman. Laffite had been a popular rogue of legend and myth throughout the nineteenth century, but the development of twentieth-century mass-market entertainment secured his and his men's place in the pantheon of Chalmette heroes.[21]

The movie industry's ability to alter popular understanding of events began to drastically shape Americans' knowledge of the past. Ceceil B. DeMille's 1938 *The Buccaneer* and its 1958 remake did not defy this trend. DeMille used Lyle Saxon's book *Laffite the Pirate* as the basis for his film rendition of the Battle of New Orleans. Because the film focused on the swashbuckling privateer, Americans left the theater convinced that the Gulf corsair played a central role in American success. The popularity of the films and the 1959 hit music single "The Battle of New Orleans" shaped the memory of the historical event in another way: they mobilized public support for the preservation of the original battlefield.[22]

Chapter 7 examines the troubles of creating a battlefield park in an urban landscape. The Daughters of 1812 managed the historic site for more than two decades, but the organization could not afford to compete against the commercial interests also desirous of the battlefield's land. Accordingly, the federal government, represented first by the War Department and then by the National Park Service (NPS), took on the role of battlefield preservation and interpretation. Thirty years of negotiation between the federal government, the state of Louisiana, and private businesses eventually resulted in the formation of the Chalmette National Historical Park.[23]

As tourism played an increasingly greater role in the economy of the city of New Orleans, business interests paid more attention to the Battle of New

Orleans and how its memory could be utilized for profit. The sesquicentennial celebrations in 1965 turned into a massive advertising campaign for the city and the region, paying little attention to historical accuracy. Commemoration focused on the traditional myths and stereotypes of the Battle of New Orleans because those facets encouraged tourism and commercial revenue.[24]

Race relations during the mid-twentieth century also affected the development of the Chalmette battlefield park and the memory of the battle. Completing the park required the removal of an entire African American neighborhood. Undereducated, the residents of the neighborhood did not understand the purpose of the battlefield park and had no tangible way to oppose their removal. The displacement of the residents crippled many of the families financially and further soured an already-tenuous relationship between African Americans in New Orleans and the battle's memory.[25]

The importance of the interpretation that occurred at the Chalmette battlefield and other New Orleans–area museums is the subject of chapter 8. By the 1960s, only a handful of cities in the country still had large-scale commemorations of the battle. As genealogical groups like the Daughters of 1812 began to play an increasingly less conspicuous role in promoting the memory of the battle, the NPS's efforts at memorialization took on added importance. Individual decisions the NPS made for institutional and financial reasons had dramatic consequences for the popular interpretation of the battle as that organization became one of the primary caretakers of the memory.[26]

During the late twentieth and early twenty-first centuries, organizations like the NPS struggled to find a meaning for the Battle of New Orleans which resonated with a modern audience. As the fields of historical interpretation and public history professionalized, the NPS increasingly focused on the culturally and ethnically diverse force that manned Jackson's ramparts. This interpretation not only was historically accurate but also served as a poignant rebuttal to the whitewashed version of the battle popular in the mid-twentieth century.[27]

Each generation of Americans made the history of the Battle of New Orleans their own and decided for themselves what the battle meant to them. Further, different segments of the population could have radically different interpretations of the same events by excluding certain actors or emphasizing particular actions. Exploring how people chose to commemorate history tells us a great deal about how they think of themselves and the people around them.

While only one name appears on the cover of this book, its completion is thanks to many people. I owe the editors at Johns Hopkins University Press a tremendous gratitude for the hard work they put in readying this piece for publication. Similarly, the peer reviewers did yeoman's work in making thoughtful and important suggestions that made the finished product better. Don Hickey is a legend in the field of War of 1812 studies, and I am humbled that he thought well enough of my project to include it in his series at Johns Hopkins.

Completing this book would not have been possible without the hardworking staffs of the Historic New Orleans Collection, the Louisiana State Museum, the Jean Laffite National Park and Preserve, the Hermitage, and the Tennessee Historical Society. Librarians, archivists, and curators do amazing work and never get told that enough.

My intellectual homes throughout the process of writing this book deserve tremendous praise. At the Fred W. Smith National Library for the Study of George Washington at Mount Vernon, I owe Douglas Bradburn and Mark Santagelo thanks for letting me indulge my occasional interest in the nation's seventh president in addition to my now full-time focus on its first. At the United States Military Academy, I must thank Col. Ty Seidule and Clifford Rogers for giving a freshly minted PhD a chance and all the support one could ask for. Many people from Texas Christian University will always hold a special place in my heart, but no person there more so than my dissertation advisor, Gene Smith.

Support on the "home front" and family are key to any grand endeavor. Both my mother and my aunt deserve particular commendation in supporting my education and interest in history over the years. Gumbo, my Yorkshire terrier, was essential in relieving the stress of copyediting, even if taking time out to throw his tiny tennis ball did make edits take longer. Finally, I must thank my soon-to-be wife, Julie. Your love over the years has been my greatest support, and I am thankful every day that you are willing to go on this adventure of life with me.

An earlier version of chapter 5 appeared as Joseph F. Stoltz III, "One Hundred Years of Old Hickory and Cotton Bales," in *The Battle of New Orleans in History and Memory*, ed. Laura Lyons McLemore (Baton Rouge: Louisiana State University Press, 2016).

CHAPTER ONE

"By the Eternal, They Shall Not Sleep on Our Soil"

The New Orleans Campaign

During the past two hundred years, the phrase "Battle of New Orleans" has generally referred to the single-day event on January 8, 1815. In each generation, Americans marvel at the scale of the British defeat and wonder how the United States achieved such a total victory against a qualitatively and quantitatively superior enemy. To comprehend Andrew Jackson's battlefield success requires an examination of the entire six-month campaign against the United States Gulf Coast, not just the incidents of a single day. Further, a proper understanding of the actions that occurred over the winter of 1814–15 is imperative to any investigation into the myths and memories of the battle.

Crown forces began preparing for their descent on New Orleans during the summer of 1814. British officials hoped to take advantage of the ethnically divided nature of the region. Aware that numerous minority groups lived under American rule, Crown officers approached Native Americans, runaway slaves, and the smugglers from Barataria Bay, all in hopes that these groups would lend assistance to the British invasion force. British sympathizers also approached the French- and Spanish-speaking populations along the US shore to gauge their support for the American government.[1]

Geographically speaking, New Orleans presented a nightmare to military strategists attempting to plan its defense and offered a plethora of challenges to any attacker. If an invader had access to naval resources, it could gain admittance to the city through numerous avenues of approach. Luckily for the British, they had the Royal Navy, "Mistress of the Seas." Just west of New Orleans, Barataria Bay allowed a seaborne invader access to the Mississippi River from the Gulf of Mexico by way of numerous bayous. Navigating this terrain required the use of skilled pilots. If the British could talk the Baratarians into helping them, the invasion force would have the necessary guides.[2]

Moving east, the next route for an attack lay directly up the Mississippi River. New Orleans rested ninety miles from the mouth of the Mississippi, making any attack up the river a slow affair for wind-powered vessels. The frequent turns required either cooperative weather or a significant amount of physical labor to pull the invasion fleet north against the current. The Americans could also fortify the most prominent bends in the river and rain fire down on the slow-moving naval force.[3]

A third path extended through the network of lakes east and north of New Orleans. Actually estuaries, Lake Borgne and, past it, Lake Pontchartrain offered water access to a number of land approaches to the city. The shallow waters of the lakes limited the flexibility of any attacker. Ocean-going vessels had too great a draft to access the lakes, necessitating the use of small boats. Once an invader picked one of the numerous approaches to the city which the lakes offered, the logistical feat of moving men and matériel along the axis of advance limited the ability to try a new route should the first fail.[4]

The last invasion corridor available to the British required them to first capture the city of Mobile, one hundred miles east of New Orleans. With Mobile in British hands, their forces would have access to a large harbor and overland routes to the Mississippi River. Their army could then march west and cut off New Orleans from the United States. At this point, the British would have the option to lay siege to the city and negotiate its surrender or attack it directly.

During the summer of 1814, the British explored all of these options. In August, Royal Navy officers approached Jean Laffite's Baratarians about joining the British cause, but the overtures fell on deaf ears. That same month, Royal Marine major Edward Nicholls landed in West Florida to coordinate and train Creek and Seminole warriors, as well as runaway slaves. Unfortunately for the British, Andrew Jackson had crushed the most militant faction of the Creek nation only a few months before at the Battle of Horseshoe Bend. In the wake of that battle and the subsequent Treaty of Fort Jackson, Nicholls could only raise a token force to assist British operations.[5]

Knowing that the main British force would soon arrive, Nicholls launched a preparatory attack on Mobile, attempting to gain the port for the invasion fleet's use. One hundred and twenty Royal Marines and Native Americans disembarked from their warships on September 16. The small force assailed Fort Bowyer from the land as five Royal Navy vessels bombarded the Americans from the water. The ships moved closer to shore, attempting to provide support to their land troops, and grounded in the shallow coastal waters. Fort Bowyer's artillery batteries opened up with renewed intensity, and eventually HMS *Hermes* exploded from the incessant barrage. The loss of the *Hermes* brought the British attack to a close, forcing the troops to return to Spanish Pensacola, where the British made a temporary base.[6]

With the arrival of the British on the coast, Jackson began to plan for the region's defense. The British had tipped their hand with the attack on Mobile, and Old Hickory raced south to thwart the invasion. In Jackson's mind, Spain forfeited its neutrality by harboring the British force in Pensacola. Accordingly, on November 7, Jackson invaded Spanish territory, flushing the British from the harbor and forcing them to operate without a land base from which to plan their assault on Louisiana.[7]

Jackson believed that the British would be foolish to attempt an attack on New Orleans without the use of a harbor and so became fixated on the idea of defending Mobile. The governor of Louisiana pleaded with the general to come to New Orleans and see to the city's defenses personally. President James Madison and Secretary of War James Monroe similarly pushed Old Hickory to attend to Mobile's defense remotely while directing his personal attention toward the Crescent City.[8]

These officials' concerns resulted from the destitute state of the city's fortifications, the previously unenthusiastic morale of the state militia, and the fear that, without some show of American military power, the foreign-born population of the city might aid the British. On November 22, Jackson left Mobile for New Orleans. Along the way, he made appeals to the city's population to ardently attend to the condition of the militia and began working with his military engineers to find maps of the region and plan a defense.[9]

Jackson arrived in New Orleans on December 1 to great fanfare. He and his engineers continued their efforts to understand the condition of the fortifications in the surrounding area. Personally inspecting the existing works defending New Orleans, Jackson also directed his engineers to build new strong points at various other strategic locations. In addition, the general boosted the confidence of the city's residents by conducting a military review of the local volunteer militia and the US regulars at his disposal.[10]

The parade took place in the Place d'Armes fronting the St. Louis Cathedral. Roughly seven hundred US Army infantry marched in crisp order to the sound of their field music. The battalion of Major Jean Baptiste Plauche followed the regular army soldiers. Composed predominately of French-speaking militiamen, Plauche's battalion numbered some 450 men, drawn from a variety of backgrounds. Most notably, a number of the unit had previous military experience in European service, especially the French army of Napoleon Bonaparte. Following Plauche's men marched many of the city's free men of color under the command of Majors Louis Daquin and Pierre La Coste. Heeding Jackson's call to arms, these men consisted of both native-born Louisiana Creoles and refugees from Saint-Domingue. In all, the tiny army consisted of no more than 2,500 men, but the parade in the small square located in the middle of the city accomplished its intended purchase—calming public nerves.[11]

The arrival of troops from across the Mississippi River Valley also buoyed the morale of the citizens of New Orleans. On December 20, eight hundred Tennessee volunteers under the command of Brigadier General John Coffee arrived in New Orleans. At roughly the same time, Major Thomas Hinds rode into town at the head of his Mississippi Dragoons, followed shortly after by the three thousand men of Brigadier General William Carroll's Tennesseans. With New Orleans critical to western commerce, the citizens of the Mississippi's tributaries rushed downriver to defend their livelihoods.[12]

By December, the British also had reinforcements in the Gulf theater as the main invasion force arrived off the coast of Louisiana. With advance forces failing to take Mobile or encourage support from the Baratarians, the British resigned themselves to attacking by way of the lakes north and east of New Orleans. The invasion fleet anchored off of the suitably named Ship Island and made preparations to disembark the army. Before any real landing could occur, the British first needed to gain control of the littoral waterways along the coast. US Navy lieutenant Thomas ap Catesby Jones and his fleet of gunboats intended to thwart the British fleet's plans.[13]

Jones's force had been observing the British fleet's movements ever since it had arrived in American waters. His orders gave Jones significant latitude in responding to the British threat, and Jones had stayed close to the enemy to keep his options open. By December 14, the British decided to chase off Jones's small fleet of seven gunboats. Becalmed by an easterly wind, the American force could not retreat; rather than scuttle his vessels, Jones decided to combat the British advance.[14]

The British attacked with a force of 1,200 sailors and marines divided across forty-two small boats each loaded with a carronade in the bow. The British stopped just outside of American cannon range to eat their lunch and then rowed against the current for an hour toward the American vessels. The whole affair lasted less than two hours and resulted in the capture of the American force. The British now possessed compete control of Lake Borgne.[15]

Admiral Cochrane ordered his sailors to begin ferrying the invasion force ashore to a small island, where the soldiers would be less crowded than in the ships. At the same time, army officers worked with their Royal Navy counterparts to scout the American coast and find a place to land. They contacted the residents of a small fishing village on the southern shore of Lake Borgne and paid for information concerning the water routes to the Mississippi River available through the swamps and bayous nearby.[16]

By December 22, satisfied with their preparations and reconnaissance, an advance guard of British troops set off in boats for Bayou Bienvenue with the balance of the invasion force following them. They advanced cautiously and managed to take the American militia guarding the mouth of the bayou by surprise. Next, the soldiers and sailors had to work together to navigate the narrow swamps ahead of them. Finally, around noon the British arrived at the Villeré plantation. Members of the elite Ninety-Fifth Regiment (Rifles) encircled the house and managed to capture all of the defending militiamen except for one, who fled off into the swamp.[17]

With the plantation captured as a base of operations, the commander of the advance guard, Colonel William Thorton, called a halt in order to await the balance of the invasion force. The serpentine bayou and the considerable distance to Pea Island made reinforcing the advance force a logistical nightmare. All through the night and following day, the Royal Navy worked to row the troops and supplies to shore.[18]

Jackson learned of the British landing only around noon on December 23. He ordered all available troops to concentrate on his position and march downriver, exclaiming to his staff, "By the eternal they will not sleep on our soil tonight!" From all around the city, soldiers prepared for the expedition down the Mississippi. Infantrymen sharpened their flints and gave their muskets a good cleaning. Caissons and artillery limbers rattled along at a gallop through the mud and cobblestone streets.[19]

Guarding Fort St. John on the shore of Lake Pontchartrain, Plauche's volunteer militia battalion learned of Jackson's call. Plauche and his French-speaking unit dashed off at a brisk jog, determined to get their chance at combating their people's ancient enemy. At around two o'clock, Jackson ordered his column down the river to face the British. Hearing a commotion off to his left, he sighted Plauche's unit running to join the formation. As the New Orleans militia came within earshot, Jackson bellowed, "Ah, here come my brave Creoles!"[20]

As Jackson rode south, he had with him the Seventh and Forty-Fourth US infantry regiments, Daquin's and Plauche's battalions of volunteer militia, Coffee's Tennesseans, and a handful of smaller company-size formations. To Jackson's northeast, Governor Claiborne commanded the First, Second, and Fourth regiments of Louisiana militia, totaling roughly 2,500 men. Downriver of the British, Brigadier General David Morgan commanded an additional force of some eight hundred Louisiana militiamen. Claiborne's and Morgan's forces protected Jackson's operational flanks by defending the other avenues of approach the British might take.[21]

By the afternoon, Jackson's troops began assembling into battle lines on the Rodriguez and Chalmette plantations. Less than two miles separated them from the British, and it was too dangerous to still be in column. The Americans sent scouts forward to reconnoiter the British position. Jackson's army waited until nightfall to attack.[22]

Shortly after sundown, British soldiers noticed the mast of a ship on the Mississippi River adjacent to their position. Believing it to be a vessel of the Royal Navy, the soldiers ran up onto the levee and began to hail the brig, cheering its arrival. As the guns of the USS *Carolina* opened fire, the soldiers realized they had made a fatal mistake.[23]

Jackson's army launched forward into the British camp as soon as they heard the naval vessel begin firing. The US regulars, as well as Plauche's and Daquin's battalions, attacked the British head-on. Coffee's Tennesseans and the New Orleans rifle company of Thomas Beale pressed the British right in an attempt to encircle the surprised army. Unfortunately for the enfilading force, they ran right into British reinforcements making their way from Bayou Bienvenue.[24]

The fighting soon degenerated from ordered combat to a close-fisted brawl, the inky darkness only broken by the flash of musket volleys or cannon blast from the *Carolina*. Before he lost complete control of his army in the nighttime melee, Jackson ordered a retreat back to the planation and the cover its canal offered. Falling back in reasonably good order, the American army took up its new defensive position and braced itself for any British counterassault. Still perplexed by the rapid American advance, the British commander found his force in no condition to pursue. Thorton ordered his men to take up their own defensive positions in case Jackson's army made another attempt.[25]

For the next few days the armies sat and stared at each other. The Royal Navy continued to ferry British troops to shore, and the army evacuated some of their wounded on the transport boats returning to the fleet. The Americans, after assessing their position, decided to dig in further along the Rodriguez Canal, and Jackson's engineers went about planning the new field fortifications.[26]

Jackson had a large and well-trained staff of military engineers on hand to direct the construction of the fortifications. The right (river) side of Jackson's line was proportionately stronger because the soldiers began on that end and had time to prepare more elaborate defenses. The whole line "as far as the woods, was proof against the enemy's cannon." To accomplish this level of fortifications, Jackson's engineers directed numerous cypress planks driven into the ground vertically, with the distance between planks increasing as the line continued north and the rate of construction increased. Horizontal crossbars then secured the vertical planks together and helped support the weight of the soil thrown up on the breastwork.[27]

On Christmas Day, Major General Sir Edward Pakenham finally arrived to take command of his army. Eager to discern exactly what lay in front of him, Pakenham directed that the army carry out a reconnaissance in force. As designed, this type of maneuver gave the appearance of a full attack by virtue of the number of men involved, but the individual unit commanders had orders not to bring on a general engagement. The threat of attack should cause Jackson to deploy his available forces and allow the British the chance to observe and assess their opponent's army.[28]

The reconnaissance commenced on December 28, and it went better than Pakenham could have hoped. With the rampart incomplete on the extreme left of Jackson's line, the militia defending it had almost no protection against the British formations approaching them. The American troops broke and ran, fearing that their chances of survival in a confrontation with the British in the open field were slim. Under instructions to conduct a reconnaissance, the British unit commanders failed to follow up on this good fortune, and Pakenham finished the day only with the knowledge that Jackson possessed a significant number of cannons.[29]

The British commander determined to deal with Jackson's artillery by using cannons of his own. He directed the Royal Navy to ferry the British army's artillery to shore and, if possible, also bring some of the navy vessels' cannons. The weight of the larger ships' cannons and their mounting on naval carriages made bringing them inland to the army a ponderous, labor-intensive affair. Still, Pakenham endeavored to mass as much artillery as he could and breach the American works before sending his men against them. The knowledge that every day his army delayed attacking offered the Americans time to make their rampart that much stronger troubled Pakenham all the more.[30]

On the morning of New Year's Day, Pakenham ordered his artillery to commence the greatest bombardment it could muster and attempt to breach Jackson's line. For hours the British and American cannons roared back and forth across the open plain belching fire at one another. Unable to assist, the American soldiers huddled behind the rampart, protecting themselves from the British fire. The soldiers in Pakenham's army stood by and watched as Royal Artillery rounds bounced fleetingly off of the American earthworks and the US guns slowly knocked the less protected British artillery out of action. Seeing that his cannonade had accomplished nothing, Pakenham ordered his guns to cease firing.[31]

Pakenham and his staff worked diligently on a way to assail Jackson's position, constantly aware that the American shovels continued to make the rampart stronger. Eventually they decided on a complex plan involving three coordinated assaults and a river crossing. To get to the other shore of the Mississippi required boats from the fleet, and British engineers went to work extending Bayou Bienvenue as close to the British position as possible and preparing to make a cut in the Mississippi's levee. British troops would then carry boats from the bayou to the river. Once they accumulated enough boats, a specially tasked force would cross the river, capture the American guns on the west bank, and turn the artillery on Jackson's position. While the army's engineers and the navy worked at the logistical feats needed for the plan, the infantrymen built the ladders and fascines necessary to surmount Jackson's rampart. For a week the British went about their tasks preparing for the attack. At the same time, Jackson's men awaited more reinforcements and improved their own defensive position.[32]

The Rodriguez Canal formed the basis for Jackson's defense. No longer in use as an irrigation source, the canal had a dry bottom with banks that had caved in by the time Jackson's engineers started fortifying it. The soldiers cut the levee, opening the canal to the Mississippi and flooding it along its length to a depth of five to six feet deep. Next, the soldiers began raising a parapet on the bank of the canal. As they dug into the ground and threw that dirt on the bank, they increasingly made the rampart thicker and higher in relation to their position behind it.[33]

Jackson's engineers also constructed a demibastion on the right of Jackson's line where the canal intersected the road along the river. "Two embrasures were constructed in its base to rake the Canal and plane [*sic*] in front of the line, and two others in its face for the purpose of raking the Levey [*sic*] & road. It was encircled by a [moat]." A bridge over the Rodriguez Canal connected the small fortification to the main American line. Inside the demibastion, Jackson placed two brass twelve-pounders and a six-inch howitzer mounted in field carriages so they could easily fire out of any of the available gun embrasures.[34]

Numerous other artillery pieces fortified Jackson's main line as well. Ninety feet to the left of the demibastion rested battery 2, consisting of a twenty-four-pounder manned by the navy. The Baratarians crewed the two twenty-four-pounders of battery 3 fifty yards down the line from battery 2. Next, only twenty yards away—continuing right to left—more sailors of the US Navy served the thirty-two-pounder of battery 4. US artillerymen manned battery 5 and its two six-pounders. Over two hundred yards separated batteries 4 and 5, but the range of the naval caliber artillery on Jackson's right meant that those pieces could more than assist against any assault on the American left. Just thirty-six yards from battery 5 rested a twelve-pounder crewed by French immigrants with prior service in Napoleon's army. Before Jackson's line entered the cypress swamp on the northern end of the American position, the US Army and a handful of Carroll's Tennesseans manned batteries 7 and 8, consisting of an eighteen-pound culverin, a six-pounder, and a small brass carronade. The soldiers compensated for the relatively small caliber of these weapons by loading them with grapeshot and hundreds of musket balls, turning them into enormous shotguns. Any assault against the American lines would face a considerable amount of cannon fire before the British even had a chance to scale Jackson's rampart.[35]

By January 7, Pakenham's plan finally seemed ready for execution. Colonel Thorton and his Eighty-Fifth Regiment of Foot, along with a contingent of Royal Marines, would cross the Mississippi River around midnight and take the American artillery on the west bank by surprise around dawn. Back on the east bank, a second force, under Brigadier General John Keane, would assail the American line along the riverbank. Pakenham intended Keane's brigade to demonstrate in front of the American line but not make a serious attack. These men would keep the Americans near the riverbank in place and prevent Jackson from reinforcing his left. There, on the northernmost portion of the battlefield, Major General Samuel Gibbs would lead the main attack.[36]

Pakenham's staff took deliberate care in preparing their attack force. The

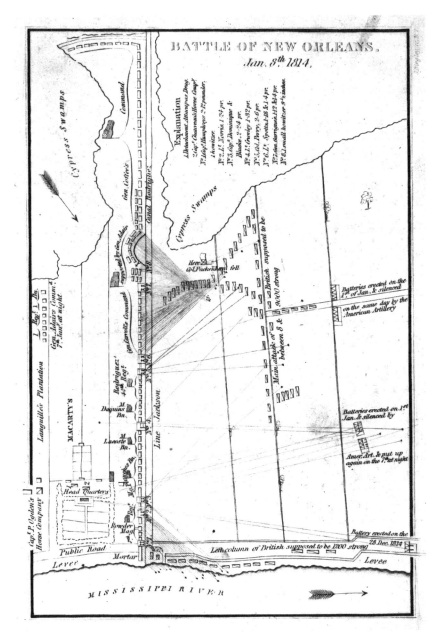

Illustration of the Battle of New Orleans, Jan. 8, [1815]. This early etching was one of the most accurate visual depictions of the culminating battle of the New Orleans campaign.

Ninety-Fifth Regiment of Foot would lead Gibbs's column. Armed with rifles and wearing specially designed dark green and black uniforms meant to blend into the terrain, the Ninety-Fifth represented the vanguard of nineteenth-century light infantry doctrine. Not only could the men of this regiment shoot as well as the American frontiersmen, but their organization as regular soldiers provided them a significant advantage in tactical flexibility and morale. When the attack began, the Ninety-Fifth would spread out across the field in front of the column and specifically target American officers and artillerymen. Under the protection of the Ninety-Fifth, Gibbs's force would advance on Jackson's position under the cover of the morning fog. When the column neared the American ramparts, the Forty-Fourth Regiment of Foot would rush forward and place the ladders and fascines necessary to scale Jackson's line. With those tools in place, the re-mainder of Gibbs's column would breach the American rampart and rout the US troops all the way back to New Orleans.[37]

Unfortunately for Pakenham, the plan began to fall apart almost as soon as his staff finished their meeting on the night of the seventh. Getting the boats for the river crossing into the water took far longer than expected. Pakenham went to sleep around midnight, but Keane's force still had not crossed the river. The current also proved far swifter than the British predicted, and the Mississippi carried the attack force significantly farther downriver than anticipated. By mid-morning, Keane's men continued to slog through thick mud up the Mississippi's western bank. Before they had gotten into position, they heard the battle open.[38]

Determined to make the attack on the east bank even if Keane's force had not taken out the batteries on the other shore, Pakenham gave the order to advance. Royal Artillery batteries commenced fire at around 8:00 a.m., with the American artillery responding moments later. Gibbs's force lurched forward and began their march somewhat protected from the American cannon fire by the morning fog and the curve of the cypress swamp. Just as the tree line began to turn back toward the American position, the fog also started to lift, exposing the British column to the full horrors of the American artillery. The carefully prepared charges in batteries 7 and 8 tore gaping maws into Gibbs's column, halting the men.[39]

The time had come for the Forty-Fourth to lay the fascines and place the ladders necessary to escape the hell in which the British found themselves. In the prebattle confusion, though, the Forty-Fourth could not find the scaling imple-ments, and its commander assumed that another regiment had taken the tools. The soldiers of the column stood in the open field under the withering America artillery fire as their officers tried to sort out the situation.[40]

Just under a mile to the left of Gibbs's column, Keane's men encountered far more success. Leading the way for Keane were the light infantry companies from across Pakenham's army. These men served much the same role as the Ninety-Fifth but had roughly the same uniforms as regular red-coated British infantrymen and only smoothbore muskets. Despite the material deficiencies, these light infantrymen had earned a reputation of tenacity and daring during their time under Wellington. The light companies not only kept Jackson from reinforcing his left but also had begun to breach the American line.[41]

Unaware of the success on his left, Pakenham rode forward toward Gibbs's column and ordered some troops from Keane's column to follow him. Abandoning the light infantrymen, and ruining any chance to take advantage of their success, the Ninety-Third Regiment of Foot marched to aid the faltering attack on the right. The Ninety-Third had garrisoned South Africa throughout the Napoleonic Wars, and its commander possessed little field experience. He led the unit diagonally across the American front, exposing his thousand-man regiment to every gun in Jackson's line. The unit presented such a large target that even Americans armed only with smoothbore muskets had little difficulty hitting it from one hundred yards away.[42]

The deaths of the Highland Scots in the Ninety-Third proved futile. Pakenham desperately tried to cajole his troops forward, but without the ladders and fascines, the attackers faced tremendous difficulty in surmounting Jackson's rampart. A few British soldiers did manage to claw their way up the embankment, but Americans either shot them dead immediately or forced their surrender. The British could not get enough men at once over the wall to overwhelm the Americans. His horse shot from under him, Pakenham remounted another, only to receive a piece of grapeshot in his thigh. Losing massive amounts of blood, his staff dragged Pakenham to the rear. Major General John Lambert, commander of the reserve brigade, then called off the attack, ordering all British troops to the rear.[43]

On the west bank, Keane's force managed to route the Americans and take their guns, but not before the defenders rendered the cannons inoperative, preventing their use against Jackson's force. With the main attack a disaster, and no idea how many American troops might be in front of them, Keane withdrew his men back across the Mississippi. The Americans soon returned to their position and began to fix the damaged artillery. From start to finish, the entire Battle of New Orleans had lasted only thirty minutes.[44]

Lambert, now the acting commander, petitioned Jackson for a temporary truce so that the British could attend to their wounded. For the next week, the Americans and British continued to stare across their lines at each other as both sides planned their next moves. Some Americans argued that Jackson should attack, but Old Hickory did not want to push his luck. He knew that fortune had smiled on his army many times already during the campaign. Further, it was one thing to fight the British from behind a strong earthwork; attacking them in an open-field engagement would be quite another.[45]

Eventually the British fled their camp during the night and retreated back to their fleet. Using a stronger force, they captured Fort Bowyer near Mobile and began preparations to take the city itself and continue operations against the United States' Gulf Coast. Before Lambert could start these actions, word arrived that diplomats had signed the Treaty of Ghent only a day after Jackson attacked the British on December 23.[46]

With the British fleet gone, Jackson and his army returned to New Orleans. The citizens held a spectacular celebration for the general in the square that now bears his name. He continued to hold the city under martial law until receiving definitive word of a peace treaty's signing. This action raised the ire of many citizens, but he continued to elicit the support of those who had fought alongside him on Line Jackson.[47]

The success during the campaign resulted from a number of factors. First, Jackson's force had the protection of a significant fortification. Soldiers worked on the rampart continuously from December 24 to January 7. For fourteen days they improved and refined the design under the direction of professional engineers, many of whom had training in military construction. Second, Jackson's line averaged more than one cannon every hundred yards, and many of the batteries mounted artillery larger than usual for service on a battlefield. In land engagements, twenty-four- and thirty-two-pounders typically only appeared during sieges and inside masonry forts. Possessing a significant amount of ordnance protected by strong earthworks offered Jackson an enormous advantage. Finally, the American troops operating around Jackson's position, but not on Jackson's main line, deserve special note. These militiamen, mostly Louisianans from the surrounding area, provided Jackson valuable intelligence and denied information to the British. The First, Second, and Fourth Regiments of Louisiana militia guarded the various alternative approaches Pakenham's force might take. The presence of these troops in significant numbers prevented British scouts from finding a way around Jackson's main position. Additionally, once it became clear that the British intended to try to hammer their way through his line, Jackson could concentrate on making the Rodriguez Canal fortifications even stronger. Jackson's victory did not occur out of sheer luck, providence, or frontier know-how. Rather, the Americans won because an American army guarded a strategic choke point and defended it with professionally designed fieldworks and artillery.

CHAPTER TWO

"Half a Horse and Half an Alligator"
The Battle of New Orleans in the Era of Good Feelings

In October of 1817, the *New York National Advocate* enticed its readers with the news that, at long last, they could visually perceive how the American victory at New Orleans came to pass. Jean-Hyacinthe Laclotte had finally completed his much-anticipated depiction of the battle, and it was now for sale in the United States. Laclotte served as one of Jackson's engineers throughout the campaign and made numerous sketches during the British assault on Louisiana. He prepared the print from his sketches, from his experience during the campaign, and from interviews with other veterans of the engagement. Now, Americans could own a depiction of the battle whose "accuracy [was] attested to by all the officers of the army who resided at New Orleans when the drawing was completed."[1]

The *National Advocate*'s article captured the imagination of the country, and word quickly spread from the Chesapeake to New England that Americans could now buy Laclotte's print. Many editors reprinted the *Advocate*'s story, telling their readers that from "a national point of view, [the print] merits encouragement," and assured their readers that they themselves already had a copy in their office. The battle had been "one of the greatest deed of arms yet known on the continent of America and which decided the fate of an important war." American interest grew even further when some newspapers reported the possibly apocryphal story that "the English *have taken so great a liking* to these engravings, that they do not allow them to remain in the print-shops, but buy them up as fast as they appear." The foreign correspondent to the *Albany Argus* assured the American audience, however, that "all [the British] efforts to prevent the circulation of them will be fruitless—some thousands are on their way to the United States, if not already arrived."[2]

During the decade following the Battle of New Orleans, Americans became enthralled with the "ardent love of country" and "enthusiasm" of the city's defenders. They relished the idea of understanding how the United States could go from getting its capital sacked and burned by an invading army to inflicting one of the most lopsided defeats in British military history until that time. How had an inexperienced American army bested British soldiers who had not once but twice put down the Corsican Ogre, Napoleon Bonaparte? A flurry of music, theater, and print media strove to answer this question for Americans,

Illustration of the defeat of the British army, by Jean-Hyacinthe Laclotte. Laclotte, an engineer on the staff of General Andrew Jackson, rendered one of the most famous early depictions of the Battle of New Orleans.

and sometimes to further the authors' own agenda in the process. In the case of snuffboxes sold with rather dubiously accurate depictions of the battle enameled on them, these were merely efforts to capitalize monetarily on the popularity of the event. Other times, artists and authors actively used the Battle of New Orleans to promote an ideological or political agenda. All of these efforts left an indelible mark on the national memory and a skewed understanding of the Battle of New Orleans, creating myths and legends of the event which continued well into the twenty-first century.[3]

One of the earliest pieces of popular culture which impacted the battle's memory appeared in American popular culture less than a year after the guns fell silent. Samuel Woodworth's "The Hunters of Kentucky; or, The Battle of New Orleans" rapidly became a standard feature of January 8th commemorations and patriotic events. The song recounts a fictionalized version of the battle in which Kentucky soldiers helped defeat "John Bull in [his] martial pomp" through the cunning use of "rifles ready cocked." These soldiers, "half a horse, and half an alligator," won because of their backwoods upbringing and willingness to protect hearth and home in the face of Britain's larger, more professional army.[4]

Explanations for the American victory like the one Samuel Woodworth provided appealed to many Americans, especially those of the Jeffersonian Republican persuasion. Republicans had always found comfort in the idea of the militia and a state-controlled military for the country. The fictionalized version of the Battle of New Orleans provided by Woodworth accentuated Republican Party ideology. Republican newspapermen, politicians, and activists found numerous opportunities to promote their beliefs through the idea that the Battle of New Orleans provided many lessons the young nation should learn and embrace. Their efforts to encourage their ideas by promoting the memory of the battle only reinforced many of the fictitious beliefs about the victory which developed during the first few years after the engagement. Those efforts also assisted in the demise of one political party and, eventually, the rise of another.[5]

Americans who lived in the wake of the war had an insatiable appetite for information regarding the battle. Across the country, newspapers carried stories about products and events related to the victory at New Orleans. The many new information sources available to Americans represented the vanguard of the communications revolution during the mid-nineteenth century. This burgeoning network provided a national forum for product distribution as newspapers reprinted advertisements for goods and services from across the country.[6]

Songs like Woodworth's "Hunters of Kentucky" were not the only performance pieces that took inspiration from the Battle of New Orleans. *The Triumph of Liberty; or, Louisiana Preserved* and *The Battle of New Orleans; or, Glory, Love, and Loyalty* both explored aspects of American nationalism and the battle's significance in American culture. These plays received considerable support from newspaper editors who provided advertising space and endorsements of the performances' quality. Dramatic pieces about the Battle of New Orleans emerged as some of the first works of the fledging American playwright community. In fact, Americans had previously frequented plays of British origin, but in the years following the War of 1812, American theater came into its own. *The Battle of New Orleans* and *The Triumph of Liberty* attracted American audiences both because of their nationalistic topics and because they helped define the future of American theater.[7]

Of all the various forms of popular culture which examined the Battle of New Orleans, editors promoted printed media the most. Writers flooded the early national period with written accounts of Jackson's victory told in works of poetry, autobiography, or fictionalized renditions of the Battle of New Orleans. Many editors suggested that these books helped Americans "see the history of [their] country's honor and virtue," and that reading the books would "infuse into the mind, the principles of liberty, virtue and patriotism." Others felt that the books about the battle would "make an impression on the memory" and that the popular topic might "lead [readers] to inquiry and more serious reading." For whatever reason, editors across the United States used their papers to distribute information and messages about the Battle of New Orleans.[8]

Thanks to the burgeoning new information network in the early nineteenth century, publicity for items and events relating to the Battle of New Orleans spread rapidly across the continent. The proliferation of newspapers and increasing rapidity of transportation allowed disparate regions of the country to discover quickly the latest methods of commemoration and also conduct a national conversation about those techniques. The publication of George Gleig's *A Narrative of the Campaigns of the British Army at Washington and New Orleans* aroused the attention of many Americans because it came from the perspective of a British army officer. The *New York Spectator* announced the book's printing in early May 1821, along with a brief preview of the work's contents. The next day, the *Baltimore Patriot* reprinted the *Spectator*'s story. By mid-June, the Danville, Vermont, *North Star* and the New Bern, North Carolina, *Carolina Centennial* had also repeated the original announcement and extract. The end of June witnessed the story's publication in the *Nashville Gazette*, and by July citizens of Missouri knew of Gleig's book, thanks to the *St. Louis Enquirer*.[9]

As fast as word had spread concerning the publication of Gleig's manuscript, news spread even more rapidly when the British residing in France began to buy up Laclotte's prints of the battle. On September 18, 1817, the *Albany Argus* first ran its story of British Battle of New Orleans art lovers. Overnight, the *Boston Independent Chronicle* repeated the *Albany Argus* story, and a day later the *Norfolk American Beacon and Commercial Diary* also reported the news to Virginians.

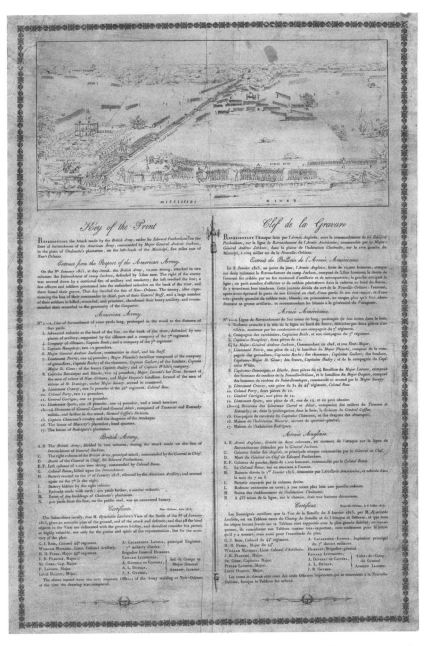

Illustration of the battle near the Chalmette plantation, Jan. 8, 1815, by Jean-Hyacinthe Laclotte. Laclotte included a guide to his famous depiction of the Battle of New Orleans to help explain the actions to the viewer.

Within eleven days of the story's first printing, Hallowell, Maine, could also read of the events in Paris thanks to the *American Advocate and Kennebec Advertiser*.[10]

Not all information was omnidirectional; frequently, regions of the country exchanged accounts about each other's methods of celebrating the Battle of New Orleans, providing a national forum of cultural exchange. In 1819, newspapers around the country carried stories of their city's battle anniversary celebrations alongside articles focusing on what other cities planned. The *New York Daily Advocate* informed its readership of a pithy toast delivered at a Dearing, New Hampshire, commemorative dinner which made light of the tremendously disproportionate casualties at the battle. In the same month, readers of the *Boston Patriot and Daily Chronicle* learned of the national flags displayed around New York Harbor on the eighth of January that year. Editors of the *American Mercury* in Hartford, Connecticut, expressed excitement at discovering that the Battle of New Orleans continued to receive considerable celebration throughout the country. All the while, newspapers up and down the Atlantic Seaboard carried news of the Louisiana legislature's decision to make the eighth of January a day of public thanksgiving and its mandate of an elaborate annual celebration.[11]

The interest shown by newspapers and their readership around the country in the commemoration of the Battle of New Orleans was at the time largely without precedent in US history. Previously, on a national scale, Americans had only celebrated events such as the Fourth of July or Washington's Birthday. These anniversaries transcended the regionalism the United States struggled with at the beginning of the nineteenth century. Indeed, sponsors of celebrations of the Battle of New Orleans should have faced the same struggles promoters of celebrations of American Revolution victories had faced. The nature of the American military system, with a reliance on the militia, meant that most battles would be regional encounters between an enemy and American troops drawn from that area. Accordingly, the states involved in the conflict took the most pride in the subsequent commemoration. The vast majority of troops who fought at the Battle of New Orleans came from the western states of Tennessee, Kentucky, and Louisiana. Even the two US Army regiments at the battle had recruited predominantly from western states. Still, citizens of the old Northwest Territory and Americans living in the Atlantic coastal states celebrated the Battle of New Orleans as if it had been their own regions' victory.[12]

That pride in the battle corresponded with an insatiable appetite for explanations of why the American army had achieved such a resounding victory. Put simply, some four thousand American militiamen should not have defeated ten thousand professional soldiers, especially George III's Peninsula veterans. Britain's troops, some of the finest in the world, had recently defeated the forces under the direct command of Napoleon Bonaparte himself. By the end of 1815, Americans knew that Britain's troops had defeated Napoleon yet again, this time at Waterloo. The Battle of Waterloo only added to the mystique of the Battle of New Orleans in Americans' eyes and made them that much more curious about how America had won.

A number of explanations emerged during the decade following the battle. Some argued that God himself had willed the Americans to victory, evidence that the divine being smiled on American fortune. Others felt that the success resulted from the political nature of the American government; people born outside the control of a king would value freedom more and fight harder to preserve it. Some even argued that Americans had become a hardier and more masculine race than the Anglo-Saxon stock from which many of them descended.

The "species of force that manned the ramparts of New Orleans" received considerable attention during the years following the battle, as Americans tried to understand exactly how they had won. For Samuel Woodworth and others, the answer clearly lay in the "hardy freeborn race" that slew the British lion. American men, especially those who fought the Battle of New Orleans, had grown up in the wilderness and along the frontier. They may not have possessed the "martial pomp" or training of the British soldier, but their background had prepared them for fierce conflict. Americans did not need military pageantry to fight; they did so naturally.[13]

Americans may have been naturally gifted fighters, but at the same time, they did not overtly seek a quarrel. Proper republican behavior dictated that American men only fought when necessary. Because peaceful negotiation and mutual understanding formed the cornerstone of republicanism, they used force only as a last resort. The unity of troops engaged against the British exhibited "pure American feelings—feelings which proved that a difference of opinion in relation to public men and public measures should never impair the claims of private worth or individual friendship." While American men may disagree at times, they would stand with one another in an hour of need despite their political differences.[14]

When Americans did fight, the heartiest of them would trade in their plows for muskets. The agricultural background of many of the American participants in the battle reinforced the Jeffersonian ideal that the country should consist of yeoman farmers, each possessing and working his little piece of Americana. The idea that "hardy woodsmen" defeated the mighty British army furthered this ideal by suggesting that the manly pursuits of rural life had instilled in Jackson's forces a virility that the urban men on the Eastern Seaboard lacked.

In the 1815 *Chronicles of Andrew*, the British held a council of war, following their first failed assault on the breastworks in front of New Orleans earlier in the campaign. As they deliberated, one British soldier remarked, "What kind of folks are those Tennesseans and Kentuckians? Surely they are not saltwater militia, such as those we found at Washington City. From what race did they spring?

Behold Andrew's army are all sharpshooters and strangers to fear." The authors, Joseph Dorris and Jesse Denson, felt that the rural upbringing of the Tennessee and Kentucky soldiers had led to their success. American men needed to remain "half a horse, and half an alligator," as Samuel Woodworth described it, so as not to become soft city dwellers like those who defended Washington, DC.[15]

Yet the most important reason for American men to remain stout and virile lay in their role as protectors of females. Protecting women, whether related to the man or not, easily overshadows any other suggestion of masculine behavior found in the media concerning the Battle of New Orleans during this period.

Writers often portrayed Englishmen's desire for American women in terms of a direct challenge. In Woodworth's "The Hunters of Kentucky," Pakenham declares, "he'd have their girls and cotton bags, in spite of old Kentucky." *The Chronicles of Andrew* depicted British soldiers taunting the Americans and pronouncing, "We will plunder your cities and embrace your wives and your sisters." If these allusions to what would happen in the event of a British victory were not clear enough, one poem went so far as to talk "of the foreign-vassal-vandal hordes," who were enticed "to murder, rape, and robbery." In the face of such rhetoric, American men could hardly shirk from the defense of their women.[16]

The alleged attitude of British soldiers stood in direct contradiction to the portrayal of American male interactions with women in many of the same sources. In the play *The Battle of New Orleans; or, Glory, Love, and Loyalty*, after an American army colonel captures a British woman and young boy, the officer brings the suspected female spy to General Jackson. In the course of the interview, the colonel pleads with Jackson to take pity on the woman and allow her to reside at the Ursuline convent in New Orleans for the duration of the battle rather than in the city jail. Jackson agrees and afterward makes sure to inform the colonel that he approved of his actions because "humanity in a soldier is but the common duty of a man; and he is unworthy of heaven's best gift indeed—who hesitates to give a woman honorable protection."[17]

Another reference to manly duty in the same scene occurs in relation to the young boy captured along with the women. Jackson jokingly asks the young boy if he would like to leave his mother's side. The boy gets excited about the idea of glory and adventure but solemnly informs Jackson that he will have to decline the offer. He has a duty to remain near his mother, to protect her until they find his father, lost to them for a number of years.

In a twist of plot, the audience learns that the boy's father is an American sailor the British impressed into Royal Navy service a few years before the battle. Serving begrudgingly for years, the sailor fortuitously arrives off the coast of Louisiana, along with the British invasion force. Realizing he is almost home, he dives overboard in an effort to desert. British soldiers on shore capture the sailor and take him to Pakenham for judgment. After a brief interview in which the sailor explains he is American, Pakenham threatens him. The sailor tells Pakenham that he will take "with heroic courage" whatever British officers trained in "remorseless butchery, cold-blooded assassination, [and] torture" choose to do to him because he knows that America is in the right. Eventually, a soldier, an American who joined the British army before the war, helps the sailor escape the camp and return to his wife and child.[18]

A variety of sources informed American men of how they should act. The proper republican American should be compassionate to women, loyal to his country, resolute in his cause, and primarily agrarian in his lifestyle. If American men followed these guidelines, they would ensure that no enemy could advance "into the heart of [their] land without meeting the punishment for their temerity." In return for these exertions, men in the United States would win "the smiles of the American fair."[19]

The United States' early playwrights and balladeers did not limit their discussions of women simply to terms of defenseless individuals in need of constant protection. While considerably fewer sources dealing with the Battle of New Orleans address the place and role of women in early American society, those that do offer a striking lens through which to examine the topic. As some historians have already discussed, in the early national period, "the ideal wife and mother devoted her life exclusively to domestic tasks; she was expected to run an efficient household, provide a cultured atmosphere within the home, rear moral sons and daughters, display social grace on public occasions, and offer her husband emotional support." When women did make an appearance in the memory of the battle, they did so frequently in support of these social values.[20]

Only a few weeks after the British army retreated to its ships and left the shores of Louisiana, Governor William C. C. Claiborne issued a proclamation reflecting on the campaign and urging his fellow citizens to remain vigilant and dutiful. Along with a number of other groups and organizations, Claiborne thanked the women of New Orleans for their service during the campaign. They had provided valuable assistance in caring for the wounded, as well as crafting clothing and supplies for the hastily raised volunteers from Louisiana, Tennessee, and Kentucky. Claiborne assured them that the men they aided would not forget the actions "of that tender sex, whose smiles soften the misfortunes of life and whose charms heighten the enjoyment of freedom."[21]

The contributions of women also received acclaim in *The Chronicles of Andrew.* The authors insisted that after the battle, "the delicate fair damsels crowneth [Jackson] with magnificent honor and exalteth him to the skies." Though flowery, this statement contains considerable historical basis. When American forces returned to New Orleans, an elaborate public ceremony occurred in the Place d'Armes in front of the city cathedral. As Jackson made his way through the square, rows of young women vested in the names of the various states of the Union flanked his passage. Two more women, attired as Justice and Liberty, occupied positions beneath a triumphal arch erected especially for Jackson to pass under. A final two young ladies rested atop pedestals under the arch in order to hold laurel wreaths over the victorious general. The exclusive role of women in the victory ceremony illustrates the importance Jeffersonian society placed on the need for women to emotionally support their men.[22]

The plays about the Battle of New Orleans provide perhaps the best examples of early American society's desired role for women. *The Battle of New Orleans; or, Glory, Love, and Loyalty* features two strong female characters from which women of the early national period could take example. The first is Louisa, a British woman captured at the beginning of the play. As one scene opens, Louisa is sitting in the Ursuline convent reading a book. Jeffersonian society expected American women to impart a sense of culture on their children and act as advisors or sounding boards for their husbands. Women could not fulfill this role if illiterate; therefore, early American society placed a premium on education for women. Openly showing Louisa reading made it clear to females in the audience that, despite previous generations' negative attitudes toward women's education, times had changed.[23]

Later, the audience learns that Louisa traveled to America in search of her husband, an American sailor impressed into the British navy. In her effort to reunite her family and defend her spouse, Louisa undertakes a quest across the ocean, a feat that playwrights of earlier times generally reserved for male characters.

The main female protagonist is Charlotte, the daughter of a wealthy New Orleanian and the romantic interest of Colonel Oakwood, the story's male protagonist. Despite the danger to those who remain in the city, Charlotte dutifully stays to protect the home while the rest of the family either flees to the countryside or defends the ramparts south of the city. As the final battle commences, the audience witnesses Oakwood leading his men during the engagement. At the climactic moment of the scene, the British take the American redoubt in front of the main works. As Oakwood leads a charge to recapture the position, he dashes forward into a melee with a British officer. Suddenly, Oakwood slips and falls. Then, just as the Englishman raises his sword to deliver a killing blow, an American soldier fires a shot into the British officer, saving the young colonel's life. The recoil of the musket knocks the volunteer's shako off, revealing Charlotte's hair falling from under the hat. Despite the danger to them both, they have time for a quick exchange of lines in which Charlotte explains to Oakwood that "in her dear country's cause, a woman's spirit towers above her sex—and heaven in this was ordinate." Charlotte then picks up a fallen American flag and helps Oakwood retire to the American lines.[24]

After the battle, as Jackson gives a booming closing speech to his troops, he

Sheet music cover for "The Heroe[s] of New Orleans Battle of the Memorable 8th of January 1815," composed by P. Laroque and printed by G. Willig. The Battle of New Orleans inspired many painters, dramatists, and musicians. This composition for the pianoforte was one of the earliest attempts to capture the enthusiasm for the American victory in song.

impresses on them the significance of a woman protecting the United States' colors. In the course of the monologue, Jackson reveals that Charlotte represents Columbia herself, the allegorical symbol of the United States, giving her actions even greater significance.

The public discourse surrounding the Battle of New Orleans further indicated the ideals of republican womanhood when exploring concepts such as the protection of family, the education of women, and the support of men. If American society dictated that men perform the fighting and strategic planning, it left to women the less glamorous but essential roles of logistics and staff work.

Charlotte's statements concerning the ordination of American roles and du-
ties by a higher power are not the only ones that appear in the depictions of
the battle. At the turn of the nineteenth century, Americans gained a newfound
interest in religion, culminating in the Second Great Awakening. Many of the
country's evangelical Protestant sects received their first initial boosts in membership at this time. In order to compete, many of the country's more traditional Protestant sects began efforts to reclaim devotees and gain conversions.
The situation became even more competitive with the appointment of the first
Catholic bishop to the United States, who placed Catholics under local control,
rather than under the direct rule of Rome. Fortunately, the vast open lands of
the United States, combined with the ever-expanding population and a common enemy in the form of belief systems such as deism and Unitarianism, allowed the various denominations to recruit and interact with only a modicum
of inter-religious animosity.[25]

Given the rising interest in religion during the early national period, it is
no surprise that the issue surfaced in discussions of the Battle of New Orleans.
Indeed, from the start, the works of art, journalism, and literature produced
about the battle depicted the event as a clash between the forces of good and
evil; one Massachusetts broadside went so far as to compare the British soldiers
to the minions of Lucifer himself.[26]

Making full use of biblical prose, *The Chronicles of Andrew* recounts the exploits of the "Madisonites" in their battle against the British. The book reveals
that Pakenham "came like a hailstorm with thunder and lightning and much
rain: and landed his furious host at the seaside" to make the Americans once
again the servants of King George. When the battle goes poorly, the British fear
that "surely the God of Israel fighteth" on the side of Jackson's forces.[27]

Even the soldiers who manned Jackson's ramparts in the face of real danger
had assurances that they fought on the spiritually correct side of the conflict.
Governor Claiborne himself appealed to the soldiers, claiming that "it has pleased
the almighty to look propitiously on our cause; it is one which he delights to
prosper: the cause of justice." The rhetoric concerning the Battle of New Orleans
bombarded Americans with the idea that God had been on their side and that
their cause and actions pleased him. These general notions of divine guidance
and support eventually led to continent-encompassing ideas such as Manifest
Destiny. In the meantime, Americans' interest in religion and the divineness of
their cause manifested in less grandiose ideas, but ones that nonetheless shaped
the fabric of early national society.[28]

A number of newspaper editors felt that *The Late War Between the United
States and Great Britain, From June 1812 to February 1815, Written in the Ancient
Historical Style* could prove quite useful in the promotion of both education
and spirituality. The *Vermont Gazette* informed its readers that the author main-

tained "the simplicity of the scriptural style . . . throughout," and that the briefness of the syntax was "calculated to make an impression on the reader." The paper's editors further informed their readers that it would be a "valuable book for schools," as the work contained "a faithful chronicle of events."[29]

The longest-lasting and most important interpretations of the Battle of New Orleans came from proponents of the Republican Party in their efforts to advance federal policy and their ideology. Jackson's army, almost entirely composed of militia, had not just beaten but decimated a force of, supposedly, the world's finest soldiers. Republicans latched onto Americans' interest in the victory and quickly put forward their message on how the United States had achieved success. This promotion allowed the Battle of New Orleans to transcend the localism of previous American military victories and provided Republicans the opportunity to use the battle as a vessel for advancing their ideology.

For Republican writers, the most important message to emphasize and sell to the American public was that the agrarian woodsman, defending hearth and home, had been the primary architect of American victory. While the majority of Jackson's force consisted of militiamen from across the western states and territories, later scholarship has revealed that the rural, rifle-armed militia of lore played only a minor role in the decisive final engagement. Rather, most British casualties resulted from the artillery manned by US Army and Navy artillerists, urban French-speaking militia from New Orleans, and former pirates. When the rifle-equipped militia did fire, they did so at close range without patched balls that could take advantage of their skill with a rifle. They simply fired as fast as they could at an enemy only a few dozen yards in front of them. The embellishment concerning the militia's role in the battle helped Republicans frame three significant policy arguments: the encouragement of an agrarian United States, the promotion of the militia as the primary method of national defense, and the idea that Federalists worked against a republican form of government.[30]

Thomas Jefferson and his Republicans had, since the founding of the nation, argued for a more agricultural way of life than the Federalists promoted. While Federalists vied for a national bank and an urban mercantile economy for the United States, many Republicans dreamed of a country of rural yeoman farmers. They believed that an agrarian lifestyle would cultivate a connection to the land, promote national defense, and generate self-interest in the region's improvement. Republican writers quickly latched onto the fact that the majority of troops at New Orleans led exactly the type of lifestyle encouraged by many Jeffersonians.[31]

In the immediate aftermath of the battle, even newspapers in the Federalist-dominated Northeast ran stories highlighting "the bravery of the Kentuckians, the Tennesseans, &c.," the "green back-woodsmen of America," and the "sons of the soil" as the reason the United States had won the battle. These metaphors were especially important in the context of the previous battles fought during the War of 1812. Time and again the American forces had squared off against the armies of Great Britain in Canada and the northern portions of the United States, and more times than not, the US troops had fallen back in disorder and disgrace. By the closing months of the war, Americans could point to only a handful of victories to encourage the American martial spirit.[32]

Then in 1815 at New Orleans, American westerners, each of whom was "half a horse, and half an alligator," stood "with rifles ready cocked" to "protect the ladies" and defend the national honor. Samuel Woodworth's famous song "The Hunters of Kentucky" may have been one of the first pieces of popular culture or opinion about the battle which promoted the western residence of the battle's victors, but it was far from the last. Many writers, especially in the West, rallied around the idea that rural Republican soldiers had been the defining cause of American victory. Northern troops from more urban Federalist regions of the country had consistently fled in the face of British arms, but westerners, often agrarian by trade, had stood firm with Andrew Jackson and mauled the largest British army of the war. As a result, the Battle of New Orleans "ought to fill every citizen of [the United States] with proud and glorious recollection" of "men freshly drawn from the pursuits of agriculture" defeating a force of regular soldiers.[33]

Some writers took so much artistic license that they argued that "hardy woodsmen" achieved a victory that had "never been more inspiration for firmness and strength" in history. Others were willing to admit that the battle *might* be less glorious than "the contest at the pass of Thermopylae," but the source of success clearly lay with "the gallant sons of the west." Though these cases represent the most embellished, one of the recurring themes linked to the Battle of New Orleans has always been the rural backwoodsman defending hearth and home. The industrializing North had numerous attempts to garner martial glory during the war, and it failed almost every time. Republicans argued that the cause of that limited success had been that many Northern soldiers, drawn from urban lifestyles, did not possess the ardor to defend their country because they had no vested stake in land or property. If the United States wanted to continue as a successful experiment in republicanism, the perpetuation and expansion of an agrarian lifestyle must occur.[34]

The reason Northerners had failed to achieve much success in the war, however, did not just fall to their urban lifestyles, argued some Republican writers. The problem occurred because many Northerners wanted to rely on paid hirelings to do their fighting for them. Republicans quickly held up the Battle of New Orleans as one of the militia system's crowning achievements and used it as propaganda to diminish Federalists' calls for a larger standing army.

Admittedly, in the eyes of many, the militia had earned a checkered reputation during the American Revolution. Federalist leaders profited from the militia's lackadaisical performance in open-field combat and built up the US Army during the presidential terms of George Washington and John Adams. Republican presidents Thomas Jefferson and James Madison had also expanded the army, but their party supporters consistently wrestled with what they thought might be a devil's bargain. Many Republican writers felt that the Battle of New Orleans offered an opportunity to bring new hope to the idea of the part-time citizen-soldier being the primary means of national defense. "If ever there was a stain upon 'raw militia,'" one writer opined, "it was wiped away on the 8th of January."[35]

Numerous Republicans in the early nineteenth century still harbored a deep fear and paranoia toward full-time soldiers, whether they wore British or American uniforms. Others simply resented the cost of supplying a standing army and felt that such an institution was a drain on national finances. The North American British colonies that became the United States had always defended themselves first and foremost by the militia (and, some argued, should continue to do so). Indeed, the British army that assaulted New Orleans had been a force of "veteran troops" fresh from the battlefields of Europe. An army of considerably smaller size composed of "freemen in arms" not only defeated Napoleon's conquerors but also gave them a thrashing that, captured British soldiers claimed, had been worse than they experienced while fighting in the Napoleonic Wars.[36]

Throughout the country, print shops exploded with endorsements of the militia system in the years following the Battle of New Orleans. Published works repeatedly emphasized that a green force of undisciplined militia halted "John Bull in martial pomp." Like their fathers before them in the Revolution, the men of the United States had beaten Britain, and they had done so, according to most newspapers, thanks to the militia. Some writers did point to the superiority of the artillery fire or the stoutness of the earthworks at New Orleans as the deciding factor, but there was no examination into who had been firing the artillery or who constructed the earthworks. The professional engineers who directed the construction, the trained artillerists who manned the cannons, and the labor of enslaved people who helped build the ramparts received no publicity in the popular tales of Jackson's victory.[37]

To Republican writers the Battle of New Orleans "proved the prowess and patriotism of those bands of undisciplined militia" at a "critical moment for the reputation of the republic." British "legions who had met and defeated the veteran soldiers of Europe" fled before "the firmness of freemen fighting for glory—for their country—and many of them, for the safety of that city which enclosed their wives, their children, and their property." When one's own house was at stake, many Republicans asked, what type of person would want to trust the defense of their wives and children to other people? They argued that if the Federalists had their way, they would put just such a system in place.[38]

By 1820, some writers in the Northeast, long a bastion of Federalist thought, had begun to repudiate the old ideologies of their region. They pleaded with northeastern voters to examine how the Federalist leadership had mismanaged the defense of their region at the local level. Federalists had refused to provide the militia the federal government requested. They had failed to provide adequate defenses for Maine and allowed British soldiers to invade New England. "Kentucky, with half the population of Massachusetts," had defended herself and had "sent her brave troops to Orleans." Tennessee had "fought and vanquished the Creeks, and under her unconquerable chief [Andrew Jackson] shrouded herself in glory at New Orleans." Massachusetts, "who boasted of her militia," had allowed the institution to fall into disrepair under the Federalists and "did not even protect herself" during the war. The state had even "permitted a faction to attempt in her name a separation of the Confederacy" at the Hartford Convention.[39]

The Battle of New Orleans and the Hartford Convention occupied the minds of many Republican writers in the months before the 1820 presidential election. A flurry of articles appeared across the United States extolling Republican success in the War of 1812 and the Federalists' supposed attempts to leave the Union in time of war. These authors sought to use the two events as dual examples of why Republicans should be in power and Federalists should not. The editor of the Republican *Boston Patriot and Daily Chronicle* went so far as to suggest that loyal Republicans should allow Federalist supporters the freedom to extol the virtues of the Hartford Convention long enough to make the critical error of supporting secession. Then the patriotic Republican could explain to the Federalist that they should be happy that Republicans had won at New Orleans because that victory distracted the Madison administration from prosecuting treasonous language such as that just spoken by the Federalist.[40]

The promotion of events like the Battle of New Orleans and the Hartford Convention reinforced the work James Monroe began during his goodwill tours of the country. When Monroe took the oath of office in 1816, the Federalist Party was on the ropes and Republicans sensed an opportunity to do away finally with party politics in the United States. While Monroe toured the country in his Revolutionary War regalia and acted as the charming face of the Republican Party, Republican writers worked tirelessly to sell their ideology to a politically receptive United States.[41]

Two of the biggest policy issues that Republicans and Federalists battled over in the early national period centered on the issue of the United States being agrarian or industrial and whether the army of the militia should be the primary means of national defense. With the Battle of New Orleans, Republican writers had access to an incredibly patriotic event that they could translate into a fable of Republican values. This positive reinforcement of Republican ideals, combined with a co-option of some Federalist policies, assisted the party in gaining support and tamping down the divisive politics that had plagued the United States for so long. By the 1820 election, Monroe ran virtually unopposed, and the Federalist Party did not even nominate a candidate. From that moment on, the Federalist Party ceased to play a role in national politics.[42]

Ironically, Republican writers, in their efforts to exorcise competing factions from the American political process, ended up advancing the very figure who would reintroduce faction to national politics. The promotion of the Battle of New Orleans as a seminal issue with lessons from which all Americans could draw was so successful that it allowed for the rise of popular politics in the form of the battle's architect, Andrew Jackson. If Americans should aspire to an agrarian lifestyle and militia service, then Jackson could argue that he met those qualifications far better than any other political figure at the national level. Jackson rode the battle's publicity into the national political spotlight and quickly made use of the promotional efforts Republican writers had first developed to combat the Federalist Party. In their effort to defeat one political party, Jeffersonian Republicans ended up creating an entirely new one.[43]

CHAPTER THREE

"Under the Command of a Plain Republican—an American Cincinnatus"

The Battle of New Orleans in the Age of Jefferson

On January 8, 1853, wind-chilled Americans huddled around each other in the streets of Washington, DC. They eagerly anticipated the unveiling of artist Clark Mills's newest work, the first equestrian statue produced in the United States. In Lafayette Square, across from the White House, Stephen A. Douglas gave an invigorating speech that slowly increased the crowd's emotions to a fever pitch. Finally, as Douglas's monologue ended, workers removed a large tarp covering the statue. There, above the assembled gatherers, stood a twenty-foot-tall edifice of the man the crowd adored, former president Andrew Jackson.[1]

Presumably, the onlookers had come to celebrate the old general's presidency more than his military career. By 1853, though, the two had become forever linked; it made complete sense that a statue to commemorate a popular president would take the form of a martial edifice. Indeed, Jackson and his political supporters had made a constant effort to connect Jackson the general with Jackson the political figure even as early as Old Hickory's 1824 run for the White House.

The Jacksonian period of American history left an indelible mark on the place of the Battle of New Orleans in US culture, as a fledgling political party used the event to build its base. As a result, that party's opposition downplayed and resented celebrations of the battle as nothing more than the political pandering of an organization that played to the basest emotions of American society. The polarization of feelings concerning Jackson's policies weakened the national celebration of the battle. Unlike the early political use of the battle by Jeffersonian Republicans, the Jacksonians' political agenda smacked more of personal advancement than of a sincere example of "lessons" for the United States. Unlike in the early national period, the Jacksonians' promotion of the battle occurred in a period of presumed party unity. As the factions of the old Jeffersonian Republicans grew increasingly divergent, both sides needed to develop an identity to differentiate themselves from their opponents. The Jacksonian supporters' repetitive use of the Battle of New Orleans to promote their candidate and policies made it a natural point of reaction and conflict. By the early 1850s, what had been a national point of celebration turned into a fractious time of commemoration for the Democratic Party.[2]

Old Hickory advertisement, by Thomas G. Little. Almost any commercial product could use the Battle of New Orleans as a marketing ploy, such as this Old Hickory brand of tobacco; notice the cotton bales depicted defending the American soldiers.

That Jackson became the primary candidate of the conservative wing of the old Jeffersonian Republicans is hardly surprising. He was a largely self-made man who found opportunity on the western frontier of the United States. Though a general and a plantation owner, at the time of the battle his house consisted of nothing more than a two-story log cabin. His political career had regularly favored the western agrarian farmer, and he had no tolerance for European interference in US expansion. In short, Jackson was the archetypal figure Republican media had lionized during the ten years following the Battle of New Orleans.[3]

With Jackson represented in Jeffersonian newspaper accounts and popular culture as an idyllic model of Republican sentiments, it is hardly a surprise that those enamored with the old general would stand him up for the presidency in 1824. Though the nomination amazed the more progressive factions of the party, the public interest in Jackson emerged as a logical outgrowth of the tactics used to cripple the Federalists as a viable national organization. Jackson became the candidate for Americans who wanted to scale back the adoption of some Federalist policies by the Republican Party after the War of 1812. In order to win the election, Jackson's supporters needed to find a way to highlight the reasons they felt their candidate represented the people of the United States better than his opposition. To that end, they looked to the already-established public interest in the Battle of New Orleans and the Republicans' previous efforts to highlight the battle as a symbol of their vision for the United States. These efforts provided ready-made platforms from which to launch only slightly revised messages about the battle which highlighted the central role Jackson played and symbolized how his success at New Orleans represented what he could do for the people of the nation if they elected him president.[4]

Ironically, one of the first uses of the Battle of New Orleans during the 1824 election attempted to lure Jackson away from running for the presidency. John Quincy Adams, looking for a regional balance to his presidential ticket, tried to woo Jackson into running as his vice presidential candidate. On January 8, 1824, Louisa Adams, John Quincy's wife, hosted a spectacular ball at the couple's home on F Street in Washington. Despite the more than one thousand people present to commemorate the ninth anniversary of Jackson's victory, the old general remained committed to the idea that, if he ran for president, he would do it as the main candidate and not as an appendage to a Washington insider.[5]

What many career politicians like John Quincy Adams, Henry Clay, and John Calhoun could not have known is that Jackson's candidacy heralded a new era of electoral politics. The American public loved Jackson despite him being what older statesmen like Thomas Jefferson considered "one of the most unfit men . . . for [the presidency]."[6] He was the hero of New Orleans, the savior of the country, the representation of the common citizen's aspirations. Unfortunately for Jackson and a plurality of the American voters, the general did not gain enough electoral votes to win the election outright, and the House of Representatives decided the outcome. There, Speaker of the House Henry Clay threw his support behind John Quincy Adams, who became the sixth president of the United States. In response to the usurpation of the people's will, supporters of Jackson began what amounted to a four-year-long political campaign for the 1828 presidential election. Throughout those years, the central tenet of Jackson's campaign focused on his leadership as a general. His supporters felt that he had best exemplified that commanding ability through his actions at the popularly known Battle of New Orleans.[7]

To promote Jackson for the presidency, his boosters borrowed heavily from the materials already popular in the United States concerning the Battle of New Orleans. Soon, rather than just singing "The Hunters of Kentucky" on the January anniversary, Jackson's supporters exposed Americans to the hymn year-round. The message was constantly the same: if you liked the United States winning the Battle of New Orleans, you liked Andrew Jackson.[8]

Making sure Americans understood that Old Hickory had been the primary reason that their nation succeeded at New Orleans became essential in this promotion of the battle and Jackson. Publicists and party boosters worked hard to direct the attention onto the man they supported for president. One point of contention that repeatedly emerged following the battle was who had the idea to defend the position known as Line Jackson on the Chalmette plantation six miles downriver of New Orleans. Numerous people claimed to have thought of fortifying the Rodriguez Canal, but by the 1820s, it could be politically dangerous to do so.[9]

One of the most heated incidents occurred when newspapers reported that John Adair, the commander of the Kentucky militia at the battle, implied that he had been the one to recommend the position along the Rodriguez Canal and the fortifications that the army dug. At first, many anti-Jackson newspapers repeated the story as a way to not only undermine Jackson's credit for the victory but also make fun of the old general's credentials. "As the victory of the 8th January had been thought to deserve the Presidency, we think if these facts are made to appear that in common justice, Adair and not Jackson ought to be made President."[10]

The Democratic Party political machine quickly swarmed into action. Newspaper editors across the country denounced Adair for trying to steal Jackson's glory and suggested that Adair showed great "magnanimity" in waiting more than ten years to set the record strait.[11] After all, "it [was] wonderful that during the contest between him and Gen. Jackson" surrounding "the credit due to the Kentucky troops, [Adair's] own gallantry in the field, and unrivalled wisdom in council, should never have been mentioned." Jackson newspapers assured their readership that stories of Jackson not being the sole architect of the victory were patently false.[12]

Eventually, Adair publicly addressed the outcry against him and assured the American people that all of Jackson's "measures for the defense of New Orleans, after [Adair] arrived there, were calculated to ensure success." Adair himself "did not reach [Jackson's] camps until the 3d of January, at which time his line of defense was nearly finished, and his men at their posts." He then went one step further and rebutted the general's detractors who claimed that Jackson's victory only meant he had guts and brawn, which hardly signaled one's fitness for the White House. "The Commander in Chief of an army, in a difficult and complicated service, must possess a cool, calculating head, a vigorous mind, a rapidity of reasoning, with clear perceptions, that will bring him, at once, to conclusions, upon which he is ready to act." Adair explained that he felt "there are fewer men, thus highly qualified to distinguish themselves at the head of an Army, than to fill any other station in any Government" and that "it would be unjust & illiberal to deny Genl. Jackson the possession of these qualifications."[13] What had started as an attempt by his detractors to undermine Andrew Jackson's qualifications for government office and take away his seminal role as the battle's hero quickly became an opportunity for Jackson supporters to finagle a ringing endorsement of the general from a man who had once been a political rival.

Adair was not the only public figure pressured into promoting the very individual they politically opposed; even Jackson's old presidential campaign opponents, John Quincy Adams and Henry Clay, felt compelled to support the battle and, by extension, Jackson. The first incident resulted from Adams's attempt to court Jackson in 1824 by celebrating the battle. Because Adams had thrown such a lavish January 8th celebration the year of the presidential election, proponents of Jackson immediately began to question the sitting president's failure to host the former general at another commemoration in 1825 at the White House. For a public figure like the president of the United States to not celebrate a major holiday such as January 8th concerned the Jackson supporters. They publicly warned the president that such oversight "may turn out to be as fatal to Adams as to Pakenham."[14] Surely, the president had chosen not to celebrate the battle out of base political animosity toward Jackson, and in the process, Adams sullied the name of the great general, the troops under Jackson's command, and the memory of the victory achieved some ten years earlier.

Jackson's other major campaign opponent in the 1824 election, Henry Clay, also felt the pressure to support the battle and the general. Yet Clay also asserted that support of the battle's memory did not necessarily equate to an endorsement of Jackson for president. "I take pleasure," Clay informed a Lexington, Kentucky, audience, "on every occasion to bestow upon [Jackson] merited praise for the glorious issue of the Battle of New Orleans. No American citizen enjoyed higher satisfaction than I did with that event . . . and felt grateful to him who had most contributed to the ever memorable victory." But Clay went on to explain that he "believed and yet believe him to have trampled upon the constitution of his country [during Jackson's conduct of the First Seminole War] and to have violated the principles of humanity. Entertaining these opinions, I did not and could not vote for him."[15]

Despite appeals to the American public by men like Henry Clay to separate commemorations of the Battle of New Orleans from celebrations and political endorsements of Andrew Jackson, the two subjects became increasingly fused together. The height of this melding occurred in 1828, as the three previous years' groundwork finally paid dividends during the presidential campaign.[16]

Jackson's supporters needed to use the Battle of New Orleans, because as Jackson's detractors later decried, the general had little record to run on. He was a folk hero who had risen in the ranks of public opinion through popular media. The 1824 election had proven that Jackson could come close to winning; indeed, he had gotten the majority of the popular and electoral votes. As the 1828 election drew nearer, Jackson supporters decided to use the popularity of the Battle of New Orleans to inflate the general's reputation even higher than it already had been in the minds of some voting Americans.[17]

For Jackson supporters, the most important region in which to try to build the general's reputation was the Northeast. Jackson already had considerable support in the South and the West, but in the old Federalist strongholds of the North, Jackson wielded less influence. In those decisive political battleground states, Jacksonians had to influence voters and subsequently altered the memory of the Battle of New Orleans. Groups like the Jacksonians of Merrick County, New Hampshire, staged votes for whether they should commemorate the Battle of New Orleans in 1828. Jackson supporters performed this political theater to show citizens' willingness to support Andrew Jackson in the coming election.[18]

Jackson-friendly newspapers reported on the votes and proclamations to celebrate what most Americans already commemorated as a national holiday. The news stories also regularly emphasized references to the great hero of the day by setting Jackson's name in full caps. These votes and their publication enhanced the notion of Jackson as the main feature of the battle and initiated the process of politicizing the Battle of New Orleans in a way that partisan politics had not done since the years immediately after the event, when Jeffersonian Republicans used the battle to weaken support for the Federalist Party in the Northeast.[19]

Unlike the Federalist Party, opponents of Andrew Jackson successfully fought the supporters of the general's message at times. Papers loyal to John Quincy Adams ran stories decrying the blatantly partisan attempts to politicize what should have been an apolitical national holiday. These papers reported the "prodigious efforts" by Jackson supporters to celebrate the battle and informed their readers that "there was more . . . electioneering than patriotism or gratitude in" the purpose of the January 8th celebrations organized in 1828.[20]

The debate concerning whether to celebrate the anniversary of the Battle of New Orleans in 1828 soon transitioned to a discussion surrounding how readers opposed to Andrew Jackson should commemorate the day if they still felt so inclined to take part in the patriotic activity. Residents of Hartford, Connecticut, decided that they should do so privately within the home. They felt that "certain ambitious and disappointed political aspirants have imprudently laid hold of the martial fame of General Jackson, and are seeking . . . their devious way to political power and place, and are striving, by means of 'Jackson dinners' . . . to turn the hearts of the people to gluttony." With no centralized national party apparatus, individuals or groups on the local level could use popular events like Jackson's election campaign and the popularity of the Battle of New Orleans for private gain with relative ease. These events created a distrust of those who supported the battle in a public way, and lack of public commemoration would diminish the influence and memory of the battle over time.[21]

Local Democratic Party organizations throughout the Northeast flooded newspapers with stories of Battle of New Orleans commemorations despite the protests of their political opponents. During the winter of 1828, numerous people's "hearts glow[ed] with gratitude to Gen. Jackson for his undeviating patriotism, and his victory at New Orleans." In Portsmouth, New Hampshire, "the anniversary of the victory of New Orleans was celebrated by the Democratic Republicans with great joy." Residents of Pittsfield, Massachusetts, "friendly to the election of ANDREW JACKSON to the presidency" celebrated the thirteenth anniversary of the Battle of New Orleans. The Bay Staters toasted "the glorious War of 1812—it taught Americans that ENEMIES were less dangerous than TRAITORS, and that Democrats might bid defiance to both." Furthermore, "Andrew Jackson—the hero—the patriot—the Man of the People [had] learned how to govern his country by learning how to save it."[22]

At the January 8th celebrations in Concord, New Hampshire, in 1828, a variety of speakers stood before the crowd and turned the Battle of New Orleans commemoration into a political rally for Jackson, just as many of the anti-Jackson newspapers had warned. Isaac Hill began the proceedings with a speech about the battle and its main protagonist. He explained to the crowd that victory at New Orleans "could not have been within the ordinary calculations of military results." The scale of the American success was too grand for history to attribute the success only to a well-placed mud banquette. No "mere military chieftain" could attain such a success. Only a leader and thinker of the highest order, like Jackson, could have won at New Orleans. Hill continued with an examination of Jackson's and John Quincy Adams's youth as an example of how the general's rural background and self-made successes rooted his hearty demeanor and rugged personality. J. B. Thornton then explained to the crowd how Adams and his ilk represented nothing more than Federalists in sheep's clothing, a theme later expounded on by the final speaker, Nathan Felton.[23]

Felton wooed the crowd, explaining that at the end of the war the country was "paralyzed by the existence of slaves in the South, and traitors in the North, who seemed ready to rise, and act in concert with one another, and with the savages upon our borders, on the first approach of a formidable force for their support." By linking the Hartford Convention attendees with British-recruited slave soldiers, hostile Native Americans, and invading redcoats, Felton allowed the audience to associate Federalists with each listener's greatest fear. Furthermore, he then identified Jackson as the country's savior from that fear.[24]

Allusions to Jackson's deity-like status could be even more explicit. Francis Yvonnet, speaking at a Troy, New York, Baptist church, explained to his audience that when Jackson arrived in New Orleans, "he found a population composed of the inhabitants of several nations, many of them disaffected towards our government, and others of such an abandoned character that the entrance of a hostile army would introduce into the city anarchy and confusion." Despite the warnings of an imminent attack, "no military force had been organized" before Jackson's appearance and "no arms provided for the few who might be disposed to use them; and [the locals], so little accustomed to the discipline of camp, that little reliance could be placed on them." Jackson worked tirelessly to prepare the city's defenses and denied himself sleep for four nights. Finally, the best he could show for his actions "was a small band, far inferior to their enemies' number, consisting of men, fresh from walks of life, the simple yeomanry of the West, who now, for the first time, wielded the destructive implements of death, and whose commander, like themselves, was little accustomed to war." Because the United States and Andrew Jackson had won that day despite everything going against them, "we are almost irresistibly led to the conviction, that not human agency, but a special interposition of Divine Providence, must have accomplished the victory." If God had worked through Jackson once to thwart the British in their efforts against Great Britain, why should voters not assume that the Divine Maker had similar plans for Jackson as president of the United States?[25]

The results of the 1828 election surpassed even the wildest dreams of many Jackson supporters, as the old general won by a more than two-to-one advantage in the Electoral College. The scale of the victory compared to James Monroe's defeat of the Federalist Party in 1816, with a few notable differences. Unlike Monroe, Jackson had not been able to sell his message to many people in New England, despite his supporters' tireless efforts. The rough-around-the-edges, British-killing, Indian-fighting general simply did not appeal to many northeasterners. Few New Englanders felt they could ignore Jackson's lack of education, especially when the alternative candidate was a well-educated individual like John Quincy Adams.[26]

Jackson did continue to do well out west, though, and every state added to the Union west of the Appalachians tilted in the general's favor during the election. Jackson's campaign message brought forth through the promotion of the Battle of New Orleans highlighted ideals valued by rural westerners or urban eastern laborers, many of whom dreamed of being able to move out west some day. To retain this support during his first term, and to prepare for the 1832 presidential campaign, the newly styled Democratic Party continued to play to its base and held Battle of New Orleans celebrations throughout the presidency of Andrew Jackson. In time, January 8th became not only an occasion to cel-

The Ball at Tammany Hall, New York, on January 8, 1860, in Commemoration of the Anniversary of the Battle of New Orleans. January 8 was an important day for the Democratic Party throughout the nineteenth century, which contributed greatly to the alienation of Whigs and Republicans from the event's memorialization.

ebrate the Battle of New Orleans and the architect of its success but also a day of celebration for the Democratic Party in general.

Even in the Northeast, Jackson supporters championed the cause of their hero and maintained that Jackson's opponents represented nothing more than Federalists in disguise. Charles Gordon Atherton pleaded with his listeners on January 8, 1829, to notice that "the states, without any exception, which voted for the first Adams, have now voted for the second." People from those states in 1828 used "the same methods . . . the same system of detraction and slander . . . as by those who formerly opposed the great and illustrious Jefferson" in 1796 and 1800. Then, when the failures of the Federalist Party became clear after the War of 1812, the same people who decried Jefferson at the turn of the century "shrank from all imputations of hostility" and "before [Jefferson's] death, went on pious pilgrimages to his residence, and now weep tears of shame and contrition over his grave." Atherton assured his assembled congregation that "so it will be hereafter with those who have so insidiously reviled the Hero of New Orleans." Democracy would prove the closet New England Federalists wrong, and the actions of Jackson and the memories of Jefferson and the Battle of New Orleans would provide the inspiration and the guiding principles for that victory.[27]

Despite the attention many Democratic writers directed toward the supposed former Federalists of New England, there were many around the country uncomfortable with the use of the Battle of New Orleans in political campaigning. In Louisiana, of all places, the state legislature found itself struggling with the efforts of the Jackson supporters to co-opt what had become a popular annual holiday. As the state prepared for the 1828 commemoration of the victory at New Orleans, some legislators suggested that Jackson receive an invitation to the event since the old general had not yet attended one of the celebrations. On its face, the suggestion did not seem surprising, but once Jackson accepted the invitation, the political machine of the future Democratic Party began promoting the event for presidential campaign purposes. The state legislature, which contained a significant number of Adams supporters, issued a clarifying statement that Jackson's attendance only commemorated the national holiday. If Jackson and his supporters wished to use the event for political reasons, the general would have to pay his own travel expenses.[28]

Desirous to have the general attend the Battle of New Orleans ceremonies since the memory of the event was the center of their political campaign, Jackson supporters across the New Orleans area raised funds for the general's visit. Unfortunately for the future Democrats, the $6 per plate price of the subscription dinner they held to raise money for the general's visit proved too pricy, and they had to lower the entrance fee to $3. Though Jackson may have had to travel with less pomp and circumstance than his followers liked, roughly 35,000 people met the old general on the wharf at New Orleans. Despite the efforts of the Adams supporters in the state legislature, Jackson once again proved triumphant at New Orleans and solidified the connection between his military victory and political aspirations at the site of the original battle.[29]

Members of the Louisiana state legislature were not the only Southerners to find the blatant attempts to co-opt the memory of the Battle of New Orleans into a presidential campaign distasteful. Some battle veterans even decided in later years to excuse themselves from the annual commemorations because of their conviction that the events had become too politicized and Jackson too idolized. Beverly Chew, a member of the socially prestigious Beale's Rifle Company, had fought throughout the New Orleans campaign. By the late 1820s and early 1830s, he found himself so disgusted with how his neighbors commemorated the battle that he refused to participate in the annual gathering of veterans in New Orleans. Eventually these sorts of simple personal exemptions from commemoration became full-blown attacks on the memory of the battle, as anti-Jackson political sentiment grew during his presidential campaign and time in office.[30]

During the course of anti-Jackson groups' efforts to contend with the Democrats' promotion of the battle, two prominent criticisms of the Battle of New Orleans surfaced. The first focused on the assertion that the armies fought the battle after diplomats in Ghent, Belgium, had signed the peace treaty. Though neither government had yet ratified the document, Jackson's critics contended that the Battle of New Orleans held little actual importance to the war since the conflict had ended. In their eyes, the battle had been nothing more than "a mere mistake." They assured Americans that they did not intend to "disparage the Battle of New Orleans," but who would not feel "a pang at the thought that such a battle, with all its woe and carnage, was fought by two nations who were at that moment on terms of amity."[31] These individuals sought to dampen the overt nationalistic fervor of Jackson's victory by portraying the battle as a meaningless affair that should stand more as a lamentation of slow communication and the folly of war than as a resounding victory over a longtime foe.

Some New England Democrats continued arguing for the importance of the battle even in the face of these accusations. They asserted whenever they could that England frequently and famously broke treaties when it suited her national interest. They also maintained that control of New Orleans would have allowed Great Britain to control trade in the entire southern half of the United States and dictate the nation's westward expansion. Surely England would not pass up an opportunity such as that just because of a piece of paper signed in Belgium.[32]

The other flaw in the memory of the Battle of New Orleans which emerged in the years surrounding Jackson's prominent period in American politics revolved around him being held in contempt of court following the battle. Anti-Jacksonians pointed to the incident as an example of his behavior as an autocratic military chieftain. They argued that by celebrating the battle, Americans also embraced the events surrounding the campaign, including Jackson's tyrannical behavior while holding New Orleans under martial law.[33]

Criticisms of the battle and hesitancy to celebrate the victory because of its association with the political campaign of Andrew Jackson greatly altered the memory of the Battle of New Orleans for many Americans. Commemorations of the event transitioned from being a popular nationalistic celebration of an American victory to being political fodder for the Democratic Party. Opponents of the Democratic Party felt increasing concern about celebrating the battle because of its associations with their political opponents and feared what would happen if those opponents got or retained power. The politicization of the battle meant that many Americans chose to either ignore passively the memory of the Battle of New Orleans, at best, or actively degrade it, at worst. Despite their efforts, Democrats failed in their attempts to imply that those who did not commemorate the battle were being unpatriotic. Unlike the Federalists before them, Jacksonian detractors successfully argued for the separation of battle memorialization from political usage. They asserted that they would still celebrate the victory on an annual basis, just as they had before. Despite those assurances, the Democrats' continued use of the battle's memory caused Battle of New Orleans memorialization in the most anti-Jackson and anti-Democrat regions of the country to diminish over time. By the end of the 1830s, large-scale public commemorations of the Battle of New Orleans became the exception rather than the rule in New England.[34]

In the rest of the country, the Democrats' efforts to promote their party through the Battle of New Orleans proved highly successful until the eve of the Civil War. Even Andrew Jackson's departure from office did not slow the ability of party boosters to make the connection. Henry Gilpin, a Democratic Party member campaigning in Philadelphia, found the Battle of New Orleans still a popular way to generate interest in his political candidates during the 1836 election. He explained to the Northerners gathered to hear his January 8th speech that "the blow [the troops at New Orleans] struck was for the safety and welfare of the North, as much as for the protection and glory of the South." If the fate had reversed the situations and Pennsylvania had defended the Delaware as Louisiana defended the Mississippi, Pennsylvanians would want Louisianans to remember what they did. Because of that, Americans could "never cease gratefully to cherish, and, as the anniversary returns, cheerfully to commemorate [the battle's] sacrifices and triumphs." Gilpin reminded his audience that while in Europe the majority of soldiers were paid "mercenaries" of the government, that had not yet been the case of US troops, and "such is the triumph we are assembled to celebrate." The soldiers at New Orleans represented "sons of the forest and the plain, hastily summoned from their daily and necessary toil. They left their homes and their families; they deserted their fields from which they gained sustenance . . . they sacrificed their comforts and risked their lives with no possible prospect of profit." All that the troops who fought at New Orleans wanted in return was "a consciousness of deserving gratitude of their country." With the crowd now in a patriotic furor, Gilpin then abruptly changed tack and began a long tirade about the rise of the Whigs and why Martin Van Buren should be the next president of the United States.[35]

The post-Jackson Democratic Party furthered its association with the old general and his victory by linking its policies to the anniversary of the battle. Specifically, Democrats made sure that the day on which the Democratic Party attempted to pay off the national debt coincided with the anniversary of the battle. They argued that it allowed the nation to celebrate Jackson's two most important victories with greater ease, but it also meant that the party's domestic political efforts would always evoke memories of the great and important national memory of the Battle of New Orleans. Soon, chapters of the Democratic Party began to hold annual "Jackson Day" celebrations on January 8 to memorialize the founder of their party, his actions in office, and the battle that rocketed him into the national consciousness.[36]

The celebrations became annual coming-out balls for the prospective leadership of the Democratic Party and an opportunity for emerging politicians to network with the Old Guard of the organization. Throughout the antebellum period, the grandest and most influential of these gatherings occurred regularly in the nation's capital. There, assembled in their finest clothes, the who's who of the Democratic Party gathered and commemorated the Battle of New Orleans and the man it made. The party printed pamphlets of the proceedings and distributed them to state chapters of the organization around the country. The evening traditionally began with a recitation of the popularly remembered rendition of the events of January 8, 1815. Traditionally, speakers placed particular emphasis on the irregular nature of the military forces arrayed to oppose the British. No less a figure than John Breckinridge brought the crowd to cheers when he recalled how "that act of Jackson and his raw militia [would], in any future war be worth an army to the United States of America."[37]

The annual Democratic Party balls assured that the memory of the Battle of New Orleans remained fresh in the consciousness of many Americans during the mid-nineteenth century. Unfortunately for the battle's memory, that image did not remain as positive as it had been in the early 1820s. The political rise of Andrew Jackson, the architect of American victory at New Orleans, left a lasting imprint on how many Americans thought about the January 1815 battle. Some thought that the nation should celebrate the great victory on par with Saratoga and Yorktown. The Battle of New Orleans represented a testament to the moral and physical strength of the young nation. It secured the opportunity for westward expansion, saved the United States from division and conquest, and provided an inspiration for a fledgling nation. For others, though, bullied by the politics of the Democratic Party, the Battle of New Orleans came to symbolize how easy the uneducated masses could be swayed. The battle became an example of blind unthinking patriotism and how individuals with a lust for power could manipulate the voting public. For these Americans, not only did they refuse to celebrate the Battle of New Orleans, but they also began to mock their neighbors for commemorating the annual event.[38]

This attitude pervaded no region of the country more than the New England states. Despite Democratic efforts to follow the old models of James Madison and James Monroe in using the Battle of New Orleans to lure votes from the Northeast, their efforts failed. Whether it was because Democrats pushed too hard or because the memory of the Hartford Convention was too old, northeasterners proved more willing to confront the efforts of their political opponents

Jackson Memorial, Lafayette Park (Square), Washington, DC. Dedicated on January 8, 1853, the statue of Andrew Jackson in Lafayette Square, across from the White House, was built to commemorate both the "Hero of New Orleans" and the founder of the Democratic Party. Detroit Publishing Co.

in the 1830s than they had been in the early 1820s. Large-scale commemoration of the battle died out in New England as a result of the Democratic Party's campaign tactics.

Despite losing the Northeast, proponents for celebrating the Battle of New Orleans still commemorated it in the rest of the country every January 8th, aided by the efforts of the Democratic Party. Only the most fervent Whigs in the South and the West excused themselves from celebrating a battle that many believed had kept their region in the United States. In major East Coast cities like New York, the Democratic Party's efforts to celebrate their organization kept the memory of the Battle of New Orleans alive and commemorated even into the Civil War.

The specter of slavery and fratricidal conflict haunted the United States throughout the 1850s, altering many aspects of American society, and the memory of the Battle of New Orleans proved no exception. In 1852, only a year before he would give the speech at the unveiling of Clark Mills's equestrian statue of Andrew Jackson, Stephen Douglas spoke at the annual January 8th celebration in Washington, DC. Douglas asked the assembled Democrats drawn from across the country, "How can such a union [as the United States] ever be dissolved?" After waiting for the "tremendous applause" to end, Douglas continued: "The North and South may quarrel and wrangle about a great question which should never enter the halls of Congress; but the Great West will say to the South, you must not leave us; and to the North, you must faithfully observe the Constitution." At a forum meant to promote nationalism through the memory of the Battle of New Orleans, Douglas pleaded with the crowd to find a way to work though the sectional differences of the country. To Douglas, the Battle of New Orleans represented a national victory, one that Americans could look to as an example of the things the nation could achieve if they worked together. Some Americans might disagree over domestic politics, but surely, Douglas asserted, an event like the Battle of New Orleans could inspire them to stick together in difficult times. The events of the next few years proved Stephen A. Douglas wrong.[39]

CHAPTER FOUR

"The Union Must and Shall be Preserved"

The Battle of New Orleans and the American Civil War

The citizens of New Orleans had always been proud of the statue. They placed it in the very center of their city. They renamed the 145–year-old square in honor of the statue's figure. It had become a central meeting place for visitors and locals alike and a focal point of community activities. Now the statue appeared different, and many New Orleanians could not decide how that made them feel. There, on the pedestal of the statue to Andrew Jackson, were the words "THE UNION MUST AND SHALL BE PRESERVED." This inscription had been the work of "the Beast," General Benjamin Butler, during the Union occupation of New Orleans in 1863. In front of the statue, Union soldiers paraded on January 8 in "celebration" of Jackson's victory.[1]

The anniversary of the Battle of New Orleans had always been a national holiday, but it had especially been a New Orleans holiday. The battle represented what Americans could do but also provided an especially poignant example of what Southerners could do. In an evolving American national culture that depicted Southerners as strange or different because of their practice of slavery, or unpatriotic because of their strident claims for states' rights, the Battle of New Orleans served as an example of Southern patriotism and genius.[2]

The use of the battle as a source of Southern martial pride and honor evolved as the nineteenth century progressed. That pride came to an awkward halt during the winter of 1862–63. New Orleans had fallen to an enemy that once again invaded up the river. Just like the British in 1815, the Union military had superior numbers, more supplies, and greater professional training than the troops defending the city. Unlike in 1815, though, the invader swiftly blew past the fortifications at the mouth of the Mississippi River and captured the city itself without firing a shot. To make matters worse, and more bizarre, the enemy this time celebrated the same holidays, knew the same history, and had been a friend only a few years before. Union general Benjamin Butler, the federally appointed military governor of the captured city, held membership in the same political party as the secessionist residents of the city and also worshiped the figure of Andrew Jackson as fervently as they did.[3]

The secession crisis, Civil War, and Reconstruction had profound impacts on how American society celebrated the Battle of New Orleans. The process started

Jackson Square and St. Louis Cathedral, New Orleans, LA. Erected in 1856, the statue of Andrew Jackson in New Orleans copied the original in Washington, DC, except for the inscription "THE UNION MUST AND SHALL BE PRESERVED." The discrepancy was rectified by the Union army during its occupation of New Orleans in the Civil War when it added the quote found on the Washington, DC, version. Detroit Publishing Co.

with Southerners' increasing alienation—voluntary at times and involuntary at others—from the rest of American society. As a distinct Southern regionalism transformed into a regional nationalism, the memory of events like the Battle of New Orleans became subtly altered and new meanings developed. By the 1850s, the Battle of New Orleans had become a Southern victory rather than an American victory won in the South. Southerners noted that their ancestors had fought the battle while the ancestors of Northerners had shown cowardice and little martial prowess during the "second war of independence." The South, not the North, shouldered the spirit of Washington, Jefferson, and Madison—all of whom, as antebellum Southerners recalled, were Southern. Jackson and his victory at New Orleans became cornerstones of Southern martial pride and militarist thought during the antebellum era.[4]

Additionally, the Democratic Party used the Battle of New Orleans as a way to try to hold the party and, by extension, the country together. Jackson Day celebrations had always been central to the operation of the Democratic Party, and they took on increased importance on the eve of the Civil War. The Jackson Day celebrations became an opportunity to reflect on a time when the regions of the country had gotten along reasonably well together and when expansionism and slavery had not yet become the divisive partisan issues they were in the 1850s. For Northern Democrats January 8th was a time to focus on national unity and patriotism, a chance to remind all parties involved that their hero, Andrew Jackson, had been a Southerner and a unionist.[5]

For some Southerners, though, January 8th celebrations became a reminder of how much times had changed, which fueled their desire for war. The celebrations also reminded them that the South had defeated a larger, more industrialized enemy before and offered the fallacious hope that they could do it again. Popular memory's omissions of the numerous artillery batteries, professionally designed earthworks, and the minimal effect of aimed rifle fire during the famous battle lulled the South into thinking that a fight against the North would be far easier than it really would be.

After the South lost the Civil War, the region found itself occupied by an army that also celebrated January 8th and, at times, took considerable pride in celebrating the event in a way that further insulted the South. Actions like Benjamin Butler's inscription of Jackson's unionist sentiments on a monument to the hero of the Battle of New Orleans confused the South's memory of the battle. Southern commemoration of the battle dimmed in the aftermath of the Civil War.

The Democratic Party attempted once again to use the battle as an example of national unity, as it had in the 1830s and 1840s, but with people like Butler involved in the party at the national level, those efforts largely failed. Outside the political arena, during the years following Reconstruction, celebrations of the Battle of New Orleans diminished in both size and scope. Only in the namesake city itself did the battle's memory carry on to any significant degree, and even there occasional lulls happened, causing local newspapers to note that it seemed as if no one was celebrating. In the wake of the Civil War, as the "Lost Cause" became fully entrenched into the Southern psyche, many Southerners grew disenchanted with the idea of celebrating any American holiday. From the 1850s to the 1880s, the memory of the Battle of New Orleans became a contested battleground in which various groups tried to shape the memory of the event to their own political aspirations.[6]

As the antebellum period began, Democrats found it increasingly hard to keep the sectional halves of their party together. As Southern fears of Northern intrusion on the economy and society of the Deep South grew, Democrats below the Mason–Dixon line came to think of themselves increasingly as a unique cultural construction. That new self-identification had a profound impact on the memory of the Battle of New Orleans and the way Southerners came to think of themselves in relation to the engagement.[7]

Traditionally, the focus of who fought on the American side at New Orleans had always been the western frontiersman. This individual had blazed a trail through the Cumberland Gap, fought off the hostile Native Americans in the region, and preserved the Louisiana Purchase from the crafty designs of the Spanish and the British. Technically, though, the idea that the "western" states and territories provided the bulk of Jackson's manpower was not entirely accurate. Some people argued for a further distinction. After all, Ohio and Indiana units did not serve on Jackson's line, nor did Michiganders or Illinoisans take part in the decisive battle. Rather, Jackson's "western" heroes hailed from Kentucky, Tennessee, Mississippi, Louisiana, and what became Alabama and Arkansas. States and territories west of the Appalachians could take pride knowing they performed better than troops drawn from the East. The states and territories that allowed slavery could also argue for the lion's share of the distinction from the Battle of New Orleans, the most famous battle of the war.[8]

Southerners had used this boast numerous times since the January 1815 battle. Indeed, even as early as the 1820s some writers felt compelled to argue for a more nuanced understanding of which portion of the country should get the most credit for the battle. In the "Era of Good Feelings," though, most Jeffersonian Democrats found it far more politically expedient to use the memory of the Battle of New Orleans for unifying purposes than to fuel sectional distinction. The Jeffersonians and later the Jacksonians did not intend the promotion of the westerner to encourage the region per se, but rather to support the regions' stereotyped lifestyle and political leanings. For some Southerners on the eve of the Civil War, those preexisting publicities transformed into arguments that secession was possible, despite the logistical and numerical advantages the North had.[9]

Interestingly, the secession crisis was not the first time Southerners used the Battle of New Orleans to promote military activity or argue for Southern military prowess. As early as 1836, Southerners moving into northern Mexico or Tejas argued that to defeat a larger, better-trained army, as General Jackson had done, one need only follow his model. Numerous Anglo-speaking Texans, in their war for independence, looked to Jackson's victory as inspiration and motivation for defeating the large European-style army of Antonio López de Santa Anna. For these men, having fought at the Battle of New Orleans was the ultimate boast of one's martial distinction. The success of the rebels in the Texas Revolution and the subsequent mythology that arose in its aftermath fueled the already-potent desire of some Southerners seeking sources of martial pride and distinction from the North.[10]

Some Southerners felt that they could generate support from their audience if they portrayed the South as a victim. The troops at New Orleans, all Southerners, had saved the country from impending threat, and in return all they received was criticism and looks of disdain from the rest of the country in the 1850s. There had been a time when, as Andrew Ewing reminded his January 8, 1859, audience, "the war-cries of slavery and anti-slavery, union and dis-union, abolition and anti-abolition were . . . unknown." He proclaimed that only a few years earlier "the religious associations were still harmonious, and brethren everywhere recognizing each other as members of the same church. The Northern schoolmaster was warmly welcomed in the South, and the Southern orator heard with delight throughout New England." In those "halcyon days" of the past, "Southern troops . . . were proudly estimated throughout the Union, and the names of Jackson, Carroll, and others were fondly cherished on the banks of the Ohio, the Kennebec, the Hudson, and the Delaware. According to Ewing, though, Jackson's mere name had now "become a watchword of contest from the Aroostook to the placid waters of the Pacific."[11]

Despite what Ewing may have thought, many Northern Democrats, and even some Southern Democrats, longed for a political figure like Jackson to emerge. For the sake of their party's preservation as a national organization, Democrats felt they needed a leader who would transcend sectional differences and hold the Union together. After all, during the 1830s, Jackson had stopped South Carolina's talk of nullification and secession. As Alexander Everett had said to his January 8th crowd some twenty-three years before Ewing's speech, "the Disunion which, under the specious and seductive shape of State Sovereignty will attempt to undermine the foundations of our national greatness shall sink dismayed into silence at your rebuke." If Americans wanted to preserve the great republican experiment that multiple generations of Americans had already fought for, they would have to focus on union over state sovereignty.[12]

Just at it had in 1832, the idea of secession again reared its head in the days before the Compromise of 1850. During the summer of that year, delegates from nine Southern states met in Nashville to discuss the possibility of secession from the Union if the United States Congress could not reach an acceptable decision on issues involved with the western expansion of the United States and slave states' representation in the government. In response to these overtures, native Tennessean and prominent Southern Democrat Robert Armstrong assured the public that he would "unsheathe the sword and rally the people of Tennessee to expel [the Convention], as entertaining treasonable designs." Significantly, Armstrong was not talking about just any sword. Rather, it was the sword that Andrew Jackson had carried at the Battle of New Orleans and that he had given to Armstrong for loyal service during the British invasion. The mention of the sword, the general, and the battle at a moment of crisis like the 1850 Nashville

Convention served as a pointed reminder to those contemplating secession that individuals had broached the idea before. Jackson handled the secessionists in 1832 just as he handled the British in 1814–15. If 1850s secessionists tried anything, those still loyal to the Union, to Jackson, and to the memory of the battle would stop them.[13]

To accomplish that union, Americans would have to learn from their past and preserve the memory of events like the Battle of New Orleans. On the eve of the Civil War, few states were more perplexed by the idea of union and secession than Missouri. Perhaps sensing the tumultuousness of the times, Rev. W. M. Leftwich could not help but editorialize while addressing the Missouri General Assembly on January 8, 1859. His lecture on the Battle of New Orleans began in a standard fashion by focusing on how Jackson, with "only two regiments of regular troops, and a single regiment of Tennessee volunteers . . . advanced to the field of conflict." To his credit, he even mentioned that Old Hickory "called upon the free colored of Louisiana to defend their native soil from invasion by a foreign foe, and invoked the very *pirates* who infested the neighboring coasts to the rescue." Leftwich then began a colorful and dramatic rendition of the final battle and seemed poised to close by informing the assembled politicians that "the 8th of January is observed by the nation as a great commemorative festival, *only* subordinate to the 4th of July." The reverend, though, had still more to say. Leftwich boomed, "When the American people cease to commemorate, with appropriate ceremonies, the events and names associated with these days, it will be a national calamity which 'good men and true' will deeply deplore." He assured them that "when the strife of party, the warring of hostile sections, the jarring of contending factions, the wild spirit of fanaticism, the trickery of office-hunters, the love of money, applause and power, shall obliterate these festivals from the temples and altars of our country, then will our national gratitude degenerate—then will our patriotic fires smolder to ashes, and our country's alters crumble to decay."[14]

Reverend Leftwich reminded them that because of the Battle of New Orleans, "democratic liberty found a home between the seas and amid mountains." During the years following the Revolution, the country had faced numerous troubles and vast resources lay untapped, but because of the battle, "a constellation hung over the 'Chambers of the South,' agriculture, industry, and trade all increased out west." The event "inspired a national confidence—raised higher the national standard, and threw a blaze of glory upon the prowess of American arms." All of this success came because of God's will, Leftwich claimed; He had blessed the United States with this success, and no human had the right to interfere with that.[15]

For organizations like Tammany Hall in New York, perhaps the country's largest and most organized seat of Democratic power, January 8th became all the more important in celebrating the actions and successes of the Democratic Party. As the political crisis in the country became increasingly difficult throughout the 1850s, January 8th represented a day on which Democrats could pat themselves on the back and declare that they held the country together. "Against corrupt combinations of the Pulpit and the Press," Democrats toiled to operate as a national party that bridged sectional division, just as the illustrious Andrew Jackson had done. To many of them, the movement against slavery represented just as great a threat to the security of the Union as the British had in 1815. Therefore, for these Democrats, their celebrations in Tammany Hall, "decorated for the occasion by a full length portrait of our excellent chief magistrate, flags, tri-colors and union jacks, and suitable mottoes," became a tangible measure of their commitment to the Union. Though they may not have said so in the same terms as Reverend Leftwich, for the Democrats at Tammany Hall, actively remembering the Battle of New Orleans became a source of patriotic pride which encouraged their commitment to hold the Union together. The problem for these Democrats, however, was that the memory of the battle lacked a monolithic nature. Just as Southerners developed their own interpretation of the battle before the Civil War, events during and after the sectional conflict drastically impacted the memory of the Battle of New Orleans and its usefulness as a source of both unity and division.[16]

The height of the secession crisis occurred forty-six years after the decisive battle, creating mixed feelings about how to celebrate the day. In New York City, the celebration of the battle became a celebration of "union-loving citizens to demonstrate their attachment to the confederation of States forming the great republic." Across the North, other communities joined the spirit of the occasion and celebrated their attachment to the Union through the only major patriotic celebration to occur during the secession crisis. In Oswego, New York, "a national salute was fired . . . in honor of General Jackson's firmness in resisting nullification in 1832." Out west, in Marshall, Michigan, "one hundred guns" were "fired here today for the Union." Just a hundred miles away in Detroit, "the Union men . . . irrespective of party, are now firing one hundred guns in honor of the memory of Jackson, the hero of New Orleans." In all, the *Milwaukee Daily Sentinel* reported more than eighteen celebrations held in major cities within states that had not seceded. Reports of these events attempted to link General Andrew Jackson and Major Robert Anderson, garrison commander at the besieged Fort Sumter. For these Americans, the January 8th celebrations provided an opportunity to reaffirm their attachment to the Union through the memory of the Battle of New Orleans.[17]

In the South, the situation became much more complicated, perhaps nowhere more than in the city associated with the 1815 battle. For a city the size of New Orleans, and one so closely connected to both the North and the South

Raising the Flag May 1861 (from the original picture by Winner), engraved by L. N. Rosenthal. Both unionists and Confederates laid claim to the 1815 victory at New Orleans during the beginning of the Civil War. For unionists, the battle was an example of American solidarity; for Confederates, it was an example of Southern martial pride.

economically, the Civil War became an especially ideologically divisive event. Throughout the war, both sides attempted to win the allegiance of factions among the city's large and diverse population. The issue became even more complicated after New Orleans fell to Union forces in April 1862. From that moment until 1877 New Orleans found itself under military occupation, which altered greatly the city's perception of the battle.[18]

One of the first incidents occurred just as Union forces took possession of the city. From the moment Louisiana seceded, members of the city's population of free men of color petitioned for service in defense of their home state. Veterans of the original Battle of New Orleans led the formation of these units. These men served in the two battalions of free men of color which were formed immediately before the British invasion and had been staples of the city's commemoration of the battle throughout the Jacksonian and antebellum periods. Citizens of New Orleans held the veterans in high regard, and when they volunteered for service during the secession crisis, many Louisianans supported them. The governor of the state accepted the unit into state service and dispatched communications to Confederate president Jefferson Davis, offering the Louisiana Native Guard Regiment to the Confederate Army for active use in the field.[19]

The Confederate government failed to reply to the overtures from Louisiana, and it quickly became apparent to the members of the Native Guard that their new government did not want their services at the national level. Despite this racial snub, the men volunteered for militia service in the city until its capture by Union forces. After the fleet of Admiral David Farragut arrived on the Mississippi River opposite the French Quarter, the men offered their services to the Union army, again hoping to provide some useful and patriotic duty. Union general Benjamin Butler enjoyed the idea of allowing the unit to serve because he needed troops and wanted to promote unionist sentiment in the city.[20]

Butler's subsequent efforts to encourage unionism in the city raised considerable ire from his superiors, the public, and even foreign nationals. The longest lasting of all of Butler's activities directly challenged some Southerners' memories of the Battle of New Orleans and the understanding of it many of them had grown to accept by the eve of the Civil War. At the heart of the French Quarter lay the old Place d'Armes. During the 1850s, the city leaders rechristened the old parade ground "Jackson Square," with a nearly exact replica of Clark Mills's equestrian statue of Jackson located at the center. Upon viewing the statue, Butler decided to make an improvement. Specifically, he chose a feature planned for the original statue in Washington but that Clark Mills had not actually implemented. In July of 1862, during a string of patriotic celebrations, speeches, and American flag raisings around the city, Butler ordered the words "THE UNION MUST AND SHALL BE PRESERVED" inscribed in the granite of the statue's pedestal. For Confederates who had come to think of the Battle of New Orleans as a call to Southern martial pride, Butler's desecration of the statue served as a hurtful reminder that the man they adored had been not only a Southerner and a slave owner but also a fervent unionist. The Union army's January 8th celebrations that occurred thereafter, during the military occupation of New Orleans, only further limited the enjoyment Confederate-leaning Southerners could gain from the memory of the Battle of New Orleans.[21]

The Union war effort found other ways to make the memory of the Battle of New Orleans useful besides trying to convince secessionists of their erroneousness. Democrats decried many of President Abraham Lincoln's actions during the war, especially his suspension of habeas corpus. In a witty riposte to his critics, Lincoln issued a long and stinging rebuttal that used one of the Democratic

Party's favorite events against it. After the final battle on January 8, Jackson continued to hold New Orleans under martial law until convinced that the British no longer posed a viable threat. Many of the city's residents objected to what they considered Jackson's extraordinary measures and began to protest, at which point Jackson arrested one of the most prominent of them. When ordered by the local federal court judge to release the arrested man, Jackson then had the judge arrested.[22]

For decades after the incident, political opponents on both sides of the aisle continued to debate the events of early 1815. Democrats insisted for almost fifty years that Jackson was right in his decision to hold New Orleans under martial law while the British held it under threat of imminent danger. How, Lincoln argued, did this differ from the situation he faced? In fact, the threat to the United States seemed considerably greater in 1863 than it had been in the winter of 1815 because the enemy was closer, had more resources, and had greater numbers than the British could have ever martialed during their invasion.[23]

Despite some limited uses by Republicans, commemoration of the Battle of New Orleans remained largely a Democratic Party event. In fact, as the war ended, the Democratic Party once again took up the Battle of New Orleans as a unifying force between the North and the South. Because of the gains made by the Republican Party during the war and the known intentions of many Radical Republicans with regard to Reconstruction, Northern and Southern Democrats needed each other.[24]

Though rebuilding trust would take time, the memory of the Battle of New Orleans could provide the Democratic Party a logical place to begin. The battle had "become so interwoven with the political history of the American people, that it [was] by no means probable that it [would] ever be expunged from the national calendar." It had "mingled too deeply with the vital interests of our people ever to be forgotten."[25] Though the war represented a traumatic experience for everyone, Northern Democrats wagered that Southerners still remembered that they had made worthy political allies at one point and hoped that the Battle of New Orleans might help close the rift between them. Yet Northern Democrats failed to appreciate how disaffected some Southerners were toward the members of their own party who had been major players in the Union war effort. After all, Benjamin Butler was a Democrat.

Throughout the postwar period, newspapers around the country printed announcements of the annual January 8th celebrations. Southerners could hardly take pride in these events when the most prominent members of the national gatherings were Northern generals such as George Meade, Winfield Scott Hancock, and William Tecumseh Sherman. These men had systematically destroyed the Confederate States of America and bested Southern military prowess. They had proved false Southern martial boasts; how could the Democratic Party expect Southerners to cavort with these men at an event to celebrate a victory that the South had increasingly tried to claim as its own?[26]

While some Southerners tried to uphold the Southern nature of the battle, for the most part interest in the event waned. No longer did numerous notices of annual Jackson Day picnics and militia parades appear in the newspapers of American cities, either South or North. Perhaps Americans knew the realities of war too well to "celebrate" a battle with a feast. The South also found it awkward to commemorate a victory won by an army that occupied its cities until 1877. Whatever the reasons, except for large Democratic Party gatherings, celebrations of the Battle of New Orleans diminished in both number and scale from the mid-1860s to the mid-1880s.[27]

The sectional dispute of the mid-nineteenth century had a profound impact on the memory of the Battle of New Orleans. Though the period began with many Southerners trying to frame the battle as a regional victory that represented their martial prowess, Democrats at the national level strove to utilize the battle as a source of national unity which overcame regional differences. The problem for these Democrats was that so much of the memory of the battle focused on the role of the rifle-armed Kentucky and Tennessee militiamen. Kentucky and Tennessee were border states with significant amounts of unionist sentiment, but by 1860, the descendants of Jackson's militiamen had populated Alabama, Mississippi, Louisiana, and Texas.[28]

The legend of the western frontiersman promoted the idea of martial virility among descendants of Jackson's soldiers and those who lived near them. Success in later conflicts only catalyzed the already-boisterous attitude of Southerners, as men like David Crockett and Sam Houston led fellow veterans of the 1812 war in new military campaigns farther west. Throughout this period in the Old Southwest, one of the greatest marks of distinction a man could have in his obituary was that he had served with Jackson at New Orleans. The Battle of New Orleans became the standard by which Southerners measured military prowess.

That success in battle came to a violent halt during the 1860s, as Southerners lost the Civil War. The Union attacked New Orleans with superior numbers and equipment just as the British had, but this time western and Southern ingenuity had failed. To make matters worse, Union forces celebrated the January 8th holiday almost the same way as Southerners. The main distinction was the reminder that Jackson himself had been a unionist and threatened to lead personally the effort to squash nullification and secession during his presidency. The commanding officer of the New Orleans occupation force also affixed permanently a reminder of that unionist sentiment on the city's monument to its great hero.

After the war, the Democratic Party tried to use the battle as a source of sectional healing. With former Union generals maintaining prominent roles in the party, reconciliatory overtures went largely unheeded. While Democrats around

Illustration and lyrics for "The Re-union of the Home of the Brave and Free!," by Samuel Canty. The Democratic Party attempted to use the Battle of New Orleans as a source of reconciliation during Re-construction, but those efforts fell flat.

the country still celebrated January 8th, the day became far more about the party and less about the battle with each passing anniversary. In addition, because the celebrations usually included gatherings of prominent social figures highly placed within the party, these efforts at commemoration failed to connect to the average American.

For Americans trying to process the experiences they had just undergone in the Civil War, their minds turned more to the conflicts in which they themselves had fought rather than the battles of their ancestors. Soldiers who had faced the slaughter of Pickett's Charge or Fredericksburg probably felt a kinship for the British soldiers whom Jackson's troops had cut down on the sugarcane fields of the Chalmette plantation. At the same time, Southern soldiers faced the confusion of how they could have lost the war. Events like the Battle of New Orleans had shown them that their bloodline possessed martial prowess. As the various strands of the Lost Cause mentality began to come together, many Southern men increasingly viewed the memorialization of the Battle of New Orleans through the lens of their own wartime experience.[29]

Less than six miles downriver from the "defaced" statue of Andrew Jackson stood another statue forgotten by many. The partially completed obelisk, covered in weeds, stood only yards away from the dilapidated remains of the rampart from behind which Jackson's soldiers fired on the British. The monument's construction began in 1855 as part of the same efforts to construct the much-venerated equestrian statue of Jackson at the heart of the French Quarter. Though the battlefield monument would be a memorial to both the general and his army, it received far less attention than the more prominently located equestrian statue.[30]

By 1859, money for the monument's construction had run out, and because of the outbreak of the Civil War and the resulting period of Reconstruction, no more money appeared for some time. Civil War soldier Elisha Stockwell of the Fourteenth Wisconsin Volunteer Infantry noted that "the monument wasn't finished, and there were a lot of bricks around there. Some boys in another company got some of them and built a Dutch oven of them, using mud for mortar." Twenty years later, the top of the monument was "covered with warped boards, and some of the top stones [had] fallen." The visitor sadly noted that "a general air of decay prevail[ed] about the structure."[31]

The seeds of renewed interest in the site began to take hold by 1890. In a long letter to the editor of the *New Orleans Times-Democrat*, an "Admirer of Andrew Jackson" wrote that they had recently visited the site and could not "refrain from an expression of disgust as a result of the trip. The approach from the river is through a narrow lane, so grown up in weeds and underbrush that even the narrow footpath is almost impassible for ladies by reason of this growth, reaching to eight or ten feet in height." Further, "the entire inclosure [*sic*] surrounding the monument was filled with weeds and rank vegetation eight or ten feet high, and without even footpaths by which the structure can be approached." The individual wondered whether "in the name of common decency invoked by the innate patriotism of every American, [the public should] inaugurate some reform in existing conditions" or " wage such a war upon the negligent authorities who permit so flagrant an outrage as will result in a public sentiment sufficiently strong to force them to their duty to the country and this community." The activism of this admirer would combine with the growing efforts of Progressivism and women's patriotic societies to inspire a revival of the memory of the Battle of New Orleans and help begin healing the sectional wounds of the nation.[32]

CHAPTER FIVE

"True Daughters of the War"

The Battle of New Orleans at One Hundred

The monument made for an impressive sight: a tower of marble one hundred feet tall which shined brightly in the crisp winter air. Only a decade before, the Chalmette Monument sat half-finished and nearly forgotten in a cow pasture. Now in January 1915, it stood overlooking the fifteen thousand spectators gathered around its base. These admirers had come from around the United States to be on the spot where, exactly one hundred years earlier, Andrew Jackson and his army had defeated the invading forces of Great Britain.

Five "true daughters" of the original battle's participants sat in the shadow of the monument as the United States Daughters of 1812 organization dedicated the obelisk "to the memory of the American soldiers who fell in the Battle of New Orleans." Suddenly, American and British flags rose up the shaft of the monument, celebrating the one hundred years of peace between the United States and Great Britain which followed the battle.[1]

Considering the apathy toward the battle's commemoration during the turn of the twentieth century, the event had been a remarkable success. From the 1890s to the 1910s, the public memory of the Battle of New Orleans received bursts of attention and enthusiasm, thanks to women's patriotic organizations around the country. These groups played an important role in battlefield and historic site preservation across the United States. In the South, groups like the Daughters of 1812 were especially important because they provided opportunities for white Southerners still upset over the Civil War to reengage in American patriotic events.

In the early 1890s, numerous women's patriotic organizations formed across the country, such as the Colonial Dames, the Daughters of the American Revolution (DAR), and the United Daughters of the Confederacy (UDC). The UDC in particular played a prominent role in shaping American historical memory, especially in the South. The UDC formed in 1894 through the national consolidation of numerous state organizations. These hereditary patriotic organizations originally organized with the intention of caring for Confederate veterans, widows, and orphans. Yet they quickly became vehicles for airing Southern grievances and coordinating resistance to federal government interference in Southern society. The US government considered these organized

Chalmette Monument, New Orleans, LA. Started prior to the Civil War, the monument to the American victory was only completed in time for the centennial celebration. Detroit Publishing Co.

women's groups less threatening than gatherings of men, who might take up arms, and paid little attention to their meetings. Groups like the UDC played a critical role in shaping the memory of the Civil War and in developing the Lost Cause in the South.[2]

The United States Daughters of 1812 also wrote its official charter in Washington, DC, around the time that the UDC formed. The Daughters of 1812 slightly predated the UDC and formed with the purpose of promoting US rather than Confederate patriotism. The 1812 organization even chose blue and gray for its official colors, ostensibly for the blue worn by the navy and the gray worn by the army during the war. This color scheme also represented a less-than-subtle suggestion of the group's true intentions. The organization strove to emphasize an era before the Civil War, when, as they saw it, regional division did not threaten to tear the country apart. By the early 1900s, the popular memory of the War of 1812 depicted a second American Revolution when the various states of the Union fought as one in a common cause. That memory appealed to some Southerners who grew tired of the Lost Cause and the constant emphasis on a lost war. The successes of the War of 1812 in the west appealed to people during the 1890s and 1900s for the same reasons historians have identified for the advances of the Daughters of the Republic of Texas in the same period. In New Orleans especially, home to the South's greatest non–Civil War military success, the Daughters of 1812 grew dramatically in membership.[3]

The New Orleans–area Daughters of 1812 had assistance in their chapter's formation because they possessed a tangible goal with which to rally support: the completion of the Chalmette Monument. Only one year after the chapter's formation in 1893, the Daughters successfully petitioned the state of Louisiana to hand over administration of the land surrounding the monument to the organization. The state also granted the Daughters a paltry $2,000, which basic care and maintenance of the grounds quickly exhausted. Undeterred, the Daughters commissioned an engineering report, focusing on the necessary steps to finish the memorial to Jackson and his army. Armed with this report, the Daughters traveled to Washington, DC, to meet with President Theodore Roosevelt and a House of Representatives committee. Through their efforts, they persuaded the federal government to contribute $25,000 for the completion of the monument. Despite this, the appropriation made it clear that the Daughters would fund all future care and maintenance. The state of Louisiana also transferred ownership of the land to the US War Department in 1907.[4]

Upon the completion of the monument in 1908, the New Orleans–area Daughters of 1812 assumed official stewardship of the battlefield and monument. Unlike the LHA in Nashville and the Mount Vernon Ladies Association in Virginia, the Daughters had limited opportunities for fund-raising at the Chalmette battlefield. While the historic homes of Nashville and Mount Vernon required constant renovation and upkeep, they also acted as showpieces to help generate fund-raising. Tourists could day-trip from Washington or Nashville to visit the homes of Jackson and Washington and escape the rigors of the urban scene, but Chalmette offered few comforts. The rural pastureland surrounding the battlefield began to change even as the Daughters took over the battlefield's stewardship.[5]

The Chalmette battlefield sits on valuable waterfront property along the Mississippi River. In 1905, the New Orleans Terminal Company announced plans to build a docking slip a few hundred yards from the monument. Construction crews completed the slip two years later, and by the time they had finished, the

Chalmette oaks and monument, New Orleans, LA. For many years, the memorial park consisted only of this narrow strip of land from the Mississippi River to the cypress swamp. It only included the Chalmette Monument and Jackson's rampart. Detroit Publishing Co.

location of Jackson's headquarters lay underwater. The development of the shipping slip also cut motor access to the battlefield, which had traditionally come from a road along the Mississippi River. In addition, the river itself, long the primary method of travel, became increasingly less frequented as the twentieth century progressed.

The Terminal Company also purchased land between the Chalmette Monument and the US military cemetery built during the Civil War—land over which British and American forces had fought throughout the New Orleans campaign. However, the company could not develop the property because an African American neighborhood known as Fazendeville sat in the center of the parcel and its residents refused to sell. Industrial development continued farther downriver, in a location where the British headquarters had been and where the December 23 night battle had occurred. The Daughters, who relied on the sale of pecans from the battlefield's trees, raised funds through membership dues and renting the land north of the monument for pasture. They still had trouble competing with the industrialization transformation surrounding their site. Luckily for the Daughters and the community of Fazendeville, the slip's construction affected access to the military cemetery. The War Department persuaded the terminal company to provide land for a right-of-way over nearby train tracks and the Parish of St. Bernard to extend a nearby highway so that visitors could have access to the cemetery. By extension, this right-of-way also preserved road access for the battlefield and the community of Fazendeville.[6]

The New Orleans Daughters constantly battled industrialization, lack of funds, and even Mother Nature. After lightning struck the monument, the Daughters asked the War Department to help defray the expense of the repairs. Legally, though, the federal government could do little without going through the time and trouble of getting Congress to amend the law that banned the US government from providing money for the site's maintenance. Further, powerful commercial interests worked against the Daughters. Unlike Mount Vernon and the Hermitage, which existed in rural areas, the battlefield rested on property that a 1921 report found to be worth $500,000 on the open market.[7]

Despite what must have been a frustrating decade of lobbying and petitioning, the Daughters of 1812 had a great deal to celebrate. Through their efforts, they raised awareness concerning the plight of the Chalmette Monument, organized a campaign to complete the structure, and renewed efforts to memorialize the Battle of New Orleans. They did so in the face of pervasive industrialization in Chalmette and a resilient Lost Cause sentiment in the city of New Orleans itself which offered vast sums of money for Confederate memorialization. Also, despite the construction around it and the difficulty of getting to it, the most important sixteen acres of the battlefield remained intact. With the centennial of the battle just a few years away, the group could feel optimistic.[8]

Though the Daughters of 1812 made many positive gains in New Orleans and played a major role in advocating for a restored Chalmette battlefield, they made no such headway in Tennessee. This lack of enthusiasm may seem surprising in light of the Volunteer State's prominent role in the War of 1812 and at the Battle of New Orleans. Even so, the Tennessee Daughters of 1812 counted only twenty members statewide in the 1910s. Instead, the LHA took the lead in Tennessee War of 1812 memorialization.[9]

After the Civil War, the state used Andrew Jackson's home, Hermitage, as a respite for aging Southern veterans. In 1856, the state of Tennessee paid $48,000 to needy descendants of Old Hickory who could no longer take care of the five-hundred-acre property. By 1889, the newly chartered LHA took possession of the twenty-five acres that included Jackson's mansion and tomb, holding the state land in trust for the specific purpose of promoting patriotism and tourism to the Nashville area.[10]

The LHA soon decided that the best way to promote interest in the site, and by extension Jackson and patriotism, would be to restore the house to its former glory. Restoration took money, but the founding ladies of the LHA moved in Nashville's most elite social circles. The women quickly recruited new members and planned an event that would make their organization the talk of the Cumberland Valley. "Jackson Day balls" began in 1892 and remained one of Nashville's more prestigious social events into the twenty-first century.[11]

Other events also offered creative opportunities to raise money for the Hermitage's restoration and for the promotion of knowledge about the general and the Battle of New Orleans. A "Jackson Day Sale" occurred across Nashville when the LHA persuaded local businesses to donate 5 percent of their profits to the organization. In addition, the Hermitage's distance from the hustle and bustle of Nashville provided the LHA with opportunities to rent the site for barbeques. During the early 1900s, a day traveler from Nashville could travel by riverboat up the Cumberland to tour the general's former property for a nominal fee.[12]

The LHA was not the only high-profile commemorative group to operate in the Nashville area at the turn of the century. With an eye toward the centennial, area businessmen formed the Andrew Jackson Memorial Association in 1914. The group decried what its members viewed as a lack of enthusiasm toward the upcoming Battle of New Orleans centennial. They also did not like that the replica of Clark Mills's equestrian statue remained the only memorial to Jackson in the Tennessee state capital. Unaware of the statue's historical or technical significance, the organization blustered that the monument was "not of very great artistic merit."[13]

The businessmen of the Memorial Association felt that the general's memory deserved a grand "Jackson Boulevard" to serve as "a second Champs-Elysees." As envisioned, the road would proceed from the steps of the state capital to the doors of the Hermitage—a distance of some twelve miles. To pay for the estimated $1 million of construction, the group proposed to solicit funds from local, state, and federal governments. By 1915, the monetary plan for the boulevard called for $250,000 each from the city, county, and state, in addition to $500,000 from Congress and $50,000–$100,000 that the Association would obtain from private donors. As spectacular as the finished result might have been, the organization never garnered serious momentum toward the project's completion as a result of the cost.[14]

Unlike the short-lived Andrew Jackson Memorial Association, the LHA had no such qualms about the Clark Mills statue. In fact, it greatly distressed the organization to learn in 1914 that Congress questioned the placement of the Jackson statue in Lafayette Square near the White House.

In 1824, the federal government named the square after famed French-noble-turned-American-patriot Gilbert de Lafayette during the former general's visit. In the corners of the square stood monuments to Lafayette, Friedrich von Steuben, Thaddeus Kosciuszko, and Jean de Rochambeau, all prominent foreign-born generals of the American cause during the Revolutionary War. In the center of the square, conspicuously out of place, rested a bronze image of Jackson on his horse. For the sake of theme, Congress wanted to move Jackson's statue to another location. The Ladies protested and quickly sprang into action. They solicited the assistance of Tennessee congressman Joseph W. Byrnes, and Congress's plan soon faltered.[15]

The Ladies also used gendered social norms to their advantage whenever doing so helped promote Jackson and the Battle of New Orleans. Education policy reform and criticism stood as one of the few areas in which women in early twentieth-century America could affect public policy. To that end, the LHA regularly monitored the publication of schoolbooks to make sure that children learned the "real" history of the Battle of New Orleans. The LHA even published in 1935 *Battle of New Orleans, Its Real Meaning: Exposure of Untruth Being Taught Young America Concerning the Second Most Important Military Event in the Life of the Republic.* The book is an impassioned response to those who would argue that the battle lacked significance because of the Treaty of Ghent. It also squarely places the success of Jackson's army in the hands of the Southern frontiersman and his trusty squirrel rifle.[16]

With regard to education, the LHA did not limit their attention merely to textbooks. The children of Tennessee had to prove that they had learned the lessons by way of essay contests held around "Jackson Day." Third-grader Christine Tarwater informed all of Nashville that "Gen. Andrew Jackson made breastworks of mud and cotton bales" after he "formed a small army of Tennessee riflemen." A classmate of Tarwater's, Everett Carlton, further elaborated: "When the British came up the bank at New Orleans they laughed" because "Andrew Jackson's men were just squirrel shooters." The Tennesseans soon halted the British laughter even though Jackson only "had one cannon." The backwoodsmen put the field piece to effective use, firing "scraps of iron and spikes." Despite the dramatics, Carlton summed up the moral of the story nicely, proclaiming, "From that day on the British never fought with the Americans."[17]

Everett Carlton probably never realized it, but in third grade he succinctly explained the driving theme of Battle of New Orleans commemorations around the United States in 1915—one hundred years of peace between Great Britain and the United States. Rather than focus on a war marked by domestic unpopularity and fought between nations whose international relations had greatly improved, the United States, Great Britain, and Canada chose to highlight the Treaty of Ghent. In the United States, the development of the Perry's Victory and International Peace Memorial on Lake Erie exemplified these efforts. In Great Britain, the government sponsored the promotion of a grand Anglo-American exposition. The festival, as planned, would last six months and act as a celebration of peace, prosperity, and the advancement of the arts and sciences which became possible when nations did not go to war.[18]

In a tragic twist of fate, Anglo-American plans to celebrate peace experienced a dramatic change as Great Britain entered World War I. Logistically, the United Kingdom could no longer honor its commitment to hold the grand exposition it had planned. Further, it became increasingly dangerous for Americans and Britons to traverse the Atlantic Ocean because of German naval activities. As a result, the American Peace Centenary Committee, along with its sister agencies in Great Britain and Canada, decided to modify the events planned for 1915. The American group called for the "postponement of all public rejoicing until the war in Europe is ended." The only exceptions would be "churches, schools and colleges in the program of peace celebrations already arranged." Negotiation between Canada and the United States resulted in a limited future schedule of official events. President Woodrow Wilson still spoke at the unveiling of a monument to the Treaty of Ghent in Washington, DC, and held a national address on December 24 to mark the day the peace commissioners had signed the treaty. Finally, New Orleans would host a three-day event for the centennial of the war's last major battle. The century "of peace between English-speaking peoples which followed that battle" should be the focus of the occasion.[19]

As politic as an emphasis on peace would be, it did not always sit well with some Americans. Until war actually began in Europe, some women involved in memorialization efforts, such as those in the Daughters of 1812 and the LHA, rejected the emphasis on peace rather than the battle that brought it. Writing to the *Nashville Tennessean*, one woman expressed concern that she had only heard plans to commemorate the Treaty of Ghent and peace. She remarked that the *New York Times* had recently published drawings of "a costly bridge across the Niagara River and huge memorial monuments at Detroit." She was at a loss, however, to explain how any commemoration of the peace treaty could occur without "some very large hint of Gen. Andrew Jackson and his victory over the British forces at the world-famous Battle of New Orleans." Without Jackson and his men, the "unparalleled prodigious success, which demolished British forces, driving them from [American] shores by land and sea," would have left the Treaty of Ghent a "rope of sand."[20]

Mary C. Dorris shared similar sentiments. She penned a historical treatment summarizing the War of 1812 and the Treaty of Ghent for the *Nashville Tennessean*, which ran her story under the large bold headline "Treaty of Ghent—Last Stand against American Liberty." The editors also assured their readers that the long piece contained "an absorbing narrative of how Americans, forced to fight the British a second time on account of injustices and outrages on the high sea, carried the War of 1812 to a victorious climax with the signing of the Treaty of Ghent." They also explained that "the figure of Andrew Jackson looms high above any other American in this war, and the writer has vividly visualized the stalwart American General." Despite the efforts of peace centennial committees in Great Britain, the United States, and Canada to temper the celebratory aspect of the 1915 commemoration, Tennesseans had their own plans.

Mary Dorris took her case directly to the LHA later that year. She suggested that a commemoration of the battle and not the Treaty of Ghent "ought now to bend our energies and attention." And not surprisingly, the LHA leant a sympathetic ear. After all, whatever was good for the memory of the Battle of New Orleans bolstered the memory of Andrew Jackson, which in turn benefited the preservation efforts of the LHA. Just like the Mount Vernon Ladies Association in Virginia and the Daughters of the Republic of Texas, the LHA faced the political and ethical realities of their commemoration efforts. These groups had a vested interest in defending the historical understanding that most profited the promotion of their respective topic regardless of current politics or even the most recent scholarship. The US government's preference for a change in the commemorative efforts to focus on peace rather than martial success threatened the LHA's carefully sculpted narrative of the battle. For the Ladies, the greatest son of the Volunteer State led an army of backwoods frontier Tennessee rifleman in a desperate gamble that saved the Louisiana Purchase for the United States. If that story did not occur, then why would anyone donate money to preserve Jackson's mansion and promote the history? The centennial festival arranged by the LHA in Nashville existed to promote the Ladies' interpretation of the battle, not to preserve the diplomatic relations of the United States.[21]

The LHA mustered all of its available clout in the Nashville-area business and political communities. The group successfully petitioned local railroad operators to offer tickets to and from the city at a reduced rate on the day of the centennial. They also encouraged local businesses to give their employees a day off on the holiday. The festivities opened with a two-mile-long parade that included numerous area organizations. Marching bands saluted the crowd with airs of both "The Star Spangled Banner" and "Dixie" as the column moved toward the state capitol building. Behind the bands formed units of local police, Confederate veterans, and Tennessee National Guard soldiers, adding a martial element to the proceedings.[22]

Once the procession arrived at the capitol building, the grand Nashville Battle of New Orleans centennial celebration commenced. For weeks, newspapers teased their readers with promises of a sham battle meant to recreate Jackson's famous victory. Event organizers built a replica of the "fort" the Tennesseans hid behind one hundred years earlier. The structure consisted of cotton bales placed near the steps of the state capitol building. The rather elaborate structure stretched for the length of a number of city blocks and stood shoulder high to the men placed behind it.[23]

Confederate veterans had the honor of portraying the Tennessee soldiers who served under Andrew Jackson. Dressed in confederate uniforms and wielding Civil War–era muskets and campaign equipment, the men valiantly fired blank rounds at the troops of the Tennessee National Guard. Smoke filled downtown Nashville as the khaki-uniformed National Guardsmen fell before the withering fire of the Confederate veterans. Eventually, with the "British" assault decimated, the attackers slowly retreated, leaving the cheering Confederates in command of the state capitol. One Confederate veteran interviewed after the event proudly noted that "the boys in grey [were] the victors." Another newspaper remarked that "the old guard were there," and that "it was an inspiring site to watch these veterans in battle lines again and to hear the 'crack, crack' of their rifles in the battle on the boulevard."[24]

Other events only obfuscated further which war the events sought to commemorate. At the Hermitage, Mary Dorris—the same woman who wanted to make sure that the battle's memory took precedence over that of the peace treaty —laid a wreath on Jackson's tomb. A gift of the Thomas Hart Benton Chapter of the Daughters of 1812, the wreath consisted of tree branches from the Civil War– era Battle of Franklin site. Presumably, the Daughters chapter chose Franklin because of its nearby location and its association as a famous Tennessee military event. Yet Franklin represented an ironic selection because Confederate forces fought the battle in a useless attempt to take a heavily entrenched Union position. In fact, the Battle of Franklin stands as one of the Civil War's most needless engagements and as a testament to the foolishness of charging a heavily fortified enemy. Dorris had fought tirelessly both to highlight the importance of the New Orleans battle, despite its late date during the War of 1812, and to promote the idea of American (and Southern) superiority by emphasizing British arrogance in charging Jackson's line in 1815. "Lost Cause" ideals dominated white Southern culture in the twentieth century, however. It is not clear whether anyone in attendance realized the paradox of placing a wreath gathered from the location of a Confederate military disaster on the tomb of a man who had once uttered the words "our federal union; it must be preserved."[25]

Untroubled by these inconsistencies, the Nashville celebrations proceeded as planned. The LHA arranged for the culminating event of the festivities to be a grand banquet at the Maxwell House and the annual Jackson Day Ball at the Hermitage Hotel. At the banquet the city elite sat among local politicians, judges, the governor of Tennessee, and the chancellor of Vanderbilt University. The main topic of the banquet's speeches centered on the need for a new and grander memorial to Jackson, commensurate with the importance of the Battle of New Orleans and its general. If the state did not provide for the monument, then "Tennessee has degenerated," according to one figure. Apparently still unaware of the commemoration's many ironies, another informed this crowd of wealthy supporters that "Jackson was a student of the common people" and a man "who restored this government to the plain people."[26]

After the banquet, the three hundred attendees left for the ball. To commemorate the centennial, the LHA planned a special occasion for the 1915 rendition of their annual event. At the beginning of the ball, "eighteen of Nashville's most popular girls," wearing "gowns of white, sashes of red, and badges of blue," would enter the ballroom. Every girl wore on a badge the name of one of the eighteen states in the Union at the time of the battle. Around the room, the LHA hung banners proclaiming the names of Jackson's military victories during the conflict and also hung laurels of Spanish moss and cotton boles. After all, cotton reportedly played an important part in Jackson's victory.[27]

The LHA's plans for centennial celebrations in Nashville occurred just as advertisements for the events said they would. By all accounts, the festivities had been a resounding success, if not quite what the peace centennial commissions in Washington and London had in mind. The ceremonies in Nashville had been nothing if not triumphant, and the recorded speeches rarely spoke of the importance of peace and understanding between English-speaking peoples.[28]

Though a celebration of the War of 1812 and the Battle of New Orleans, the Nashville centennial ceremonies could not escape the shadow of the Civil War and Reconstruction. The events became an opportunity to highlight Southern military prowess in the wake of the South's greatest defeat. The commemoration efforts in Nashville typified a South still struggling with the memory of its past and trying to find a way to rewrite the history of the Civil War. At the same time, the ceremonies in Nashville marked a distinct success for the idea behind groups like the Daughters of 1812. Promotion of the battle encouraged patriotism in Southerners again. It might be a patriotism that skewed the historical facts when convenient, but its centennial ceremonies in Nashville had managed to convince Confederate veterans literally to march again to the beat of the "Star Spangled Banner."

In New Orleans, the centennial celebrations shared many similarities with the Nashville ceremonies. Because events in the Crescent City carried the official sanction of the peace centennial commission, organizers paid more attention to British sensitivities. According to the official program, at 8:20 a.m. on Friday, January 8, 1915, the Louisiana National Guard began a twenty-one-gun artillery salute timed so "that the last shot will be fired exactly one hundred years after the last cannon was discharged from the American lines." The careful timing continued until 10:15 a.m., as public school children from around the city departed a train station en route to the battlefield. Less than an hour later, the adults boarded a fleet of small watercraft in a "river parade" descending the Mississippi.[29]

At the battlefield, the celebrants cheered as a Congreve rocket arced above the crowd and the drum of Jordan Noble sounded "The Long Role," marking noon and the opening of the ceremonies. A series of speeches occurred, followed by a wreath-laying ceremony at the Chalmette Monument organized by the LHA. Made from evergreens growing on General Jackson's old property, the LHA's choice of wreath appeared more apropos than the one selected for Jackson's tomb in Tennessee. After the wreath-laying ceremony, the festivities continued with the flag raising detailed earlier. The ceremonies in Chalmette concluded with a close-order drill demonstration by the Seventh United States Infantry Regiment—the unit that guarded the extreme right of Jackson's line one hundred years earlier.[30]

Elsewhere in New Orleans, other events celebrated various aspects of the New Orleans campaign. The YMCA sponsored a six-and-a-half-mile race from Lake Pontchartrain to the French Quarter. The run commemorated the Orleans Battalion of Volunteers' forced march from Fort St. John to join Jackson's column descending the river on the night of the British landing. The Ursuline nuns hosted a benediction, *te deum*, and hymn to Our Lady of Prompt Succor, to whom the nuns had prayed the night before the final battle. Mrs. W. C. C. Claiborne, president of the Ursuline Academy Alumni Association and direct descendent to the governor of Louisiana at the time of the battle, gave the opening address.[31]

The festivities lasted well into the first night. Military bands played in Lafayette and Jackson Squares at the same time as the Louisiana National Guard and the Louisiana Naval Battalion hosted a military ball for visiting US Army and Navy units. At the Athenaeum, the Women's Section of the Centennial Commission oversaw an event featuring historic tableaux by students. Depicted were scenes of women sewing clothes for the soldiers, a campfire scene of American troops guarding the Rodriguez Canal, and a street scene of the troops' triumphant return. Period dances conducted in historic costume closed out the opening day.[32]

While the second day of festivities largely centered on the activities of the Louisiana Historical Society and the unveiling of what eventually became the Louisiana State Museum, the third day opened in spectacular fashion. The event organizers arranged for a reenactment of the elaborate ceremony the city conducted on Jackson's return after the battle. Twenty women, adorned in white "Greek robes," stood in Jackson Square. Eighteen of them wore sashes with the name of one of the eighteen states of the Union in 1815, and two wore sashes with the words "justice" and "liberty." The girls paraded in two lines from the gated entrance of Jackson Square to the doors of the St. Louis Cathedral, forming a corridor. A Mr. Charles C. Hard, playing the role of Andrew Jackson, entered the line of girls and received the "palm of victory" from the woman representing Louisiana. The "general" and his staff made their way to the steps of the cathedral, where the Right Reverend J. M. Laval greeted them. Laval played the part of Abbe Dubourg, the highest-ranking priest in New Orleans at the time of the battle. Laval gave the exact speech Dubourg spoke a century earlier and then placed a laurel wreath crown on "the general's" head. Hard then turned to the crowd and, addressing "Abbe Dubourg," also gave Jackson's speech as onlookers had recorded it one hundred years before. With that, the assembly proceeded inside the cathedral.[33]

After a High Mass, a parade marched from Jackson Square to Jackson Avenue three miles away. The procession included mounted police, state officials, and school children, followed by fraternal organizations like the Knights of Columbus, the Woodmen of the World, Elks, and Druids. Unlike in Nashville, no Civil War patriotic organization appeared anywhere in the official program of the centennial ceremonies in New Orleans. Granted, members of the Daughters of 1812 could also be members of the UDC, but the UDC apparently did not act in any official capacity during the ceremonies.[34]

Unlike in Nashville, the specter of the Civil War did not hang over the centennial ceremonies in New Orleans; rather, World War I affected the mood of the ceremonies and altered certain plans. When organizers originally planned the events, they envisioned a reenactment of the battle occurring on the location of the original event. To add to the novelty, descendants of the battle's original participants would defend what remained of the ramparts. By the time of final preparations, though, the reality of World War I trench warfare began to unfold. Suddenly, the idea of showing "British soldiers" charging an entrenched position seemed extremely insensitive and politically incorrect.[35]

Instead, events and commentators focused on the marked contrast of how the centennial events compared to the horrors of Europe. They emphasized the century of peace between Great Britain and the United States, suggesting that if other nations could get along as well as the two Anglo-speaking countries did, there would be less violence in the world. Many of the speakers made overt efforts to avoid any sense of triumphalism.[36]

The description of Samuel Wilson's speech is representative. He "dwelt at length on the Battle of New Orleans and the events that led up to it. He was lavish in his praise for everyone connected with the victory; but brought out the fact that the greatest result was not the victory itself but in the century of peace that followed it."[37]

One of the few exceptions to this trend occurred during the International Peace Banquet on the second night of events. After a round of toasts at the Hotel Grunwald, Major General Franklin Bell of the US Army rose to speak. He assured the crowd that "the army of the United States stood for peace" and had "always stood for peace." A nation that prepared to defend itself did not automatically deserve the accusation of militarism. Clearly responding to the antiwar movement in the United States and the pacifism expressed numerous times at the centennial's events, Bell suggested that "the soldier does not protest that you teach your children it is disgraceful to fight for his rights." He also added, "The soldier has the right to protest, and does protest, against turning the other cheek whether right or wrong. Every human right that has been won . . . has been won at the point of the sword." At that point a disgusted spectator shouted "no" in response to the general, but the cheers of "yes" from the crowd drowned out the attempted rabble-rouser.[38]

The Peace Centennial Commission's efforts to avoid offending Great Britain and Canada during the commemorations of the Battle of New Orleans went well, and probably better than most had hoped. Not only had the forum provided an opportunity to focus on the friendship between the Anglo-speaking nations, but it had also offered an opportunity for encouraging the United States to side with Britain should America enter the war.

For the Daughters of 1812 in New Orleans, the event had also been a great success. Despite the meager and sometimes superficial commemoration of the battle which had occurred at the beginning of the century, by 1915 the Daughters helped to reinvigorate interest in Jackson's victory. Given the attention again paid to the event, the likelihood that the monument and what remained of the ramparts would succumb to Chalmette's growing industrialization dramatically lowered. Could the Daughters translate the new public interest into the financial or political clout necessary to expand the battlefield?

Prior to the centennial, the Daughters paid for the construction of an on-site five-room cottage in which a caretaker could live. Marcel Serpas became the caretaker in June 1915 and moved into the cottage with his family; the Serpases remained the caretakers of the Chalmette battlefield for seventeen years and even named one of their children Andrew Jackson Serpas, at the persuasion of the Daughters of 1812. The Serpas children gave tours of the site and also gathered the pecans the Daughters sold, eventually receiving a portion of the proceeds as their salary. Marcel also kept the money from the ten-cent deposit charged to visitors for borrowing the key to the monument if they wanted to climb to the observation deck on top. Despite the hopes of the Daughters, visitation remained low following the centennial commemoration, averaging only one group per day. Despite the advances in transportation, Chalmette simply remained too far off the path of most tourists, and the site had little to offer besides the monument. By 1929, the Daughters informed the War Department that their organization could not serve as the financial stewards of the site anymore. If the US government wanted to preserve the site of Jackson's famous victory, it would need to manage the site as well.[39]

The federal government doubted that it could do a better job. While to maintain the current property only cost $1,200 annually, expanding it would take significantly more money. The War Department felt, given the rampant industrialization surrounding the site, that not expanding the park's footprint would only lead to even lower attendance as businesses constructed factories only a hundred yards from the monument. Congress balked at spending the necessary money as the War Department contended against influential industrial interests desirous of the same land. Despite the monetary concerns, the government realized that if it could barely plan on winning the battle to preserve the site, it certainly could not ask the Daughters of 1812 to do so. The Daughters had done as much work as they could, and Secretary of War Patrick Hurley informed Congress that if it wished to preserve the site "in a manner commensurate with the importance of a great national victory," the federal government had to come to the Daughters' and the battlefield's assistance.[40]

Though the New Orleans chapter of the Daughters of 1812 had not been as successful as the LHA in fund-raising for their historic site, they played an important role in preserving and shaping the memory of the Battle of New Orleans. By the closing years of the nineteenth century, the commemoration of the battle had faded considerably. The nation still struggled with the events of the Civil War, and the efforts of groups like the UDC only further intensified the mythologies and popular attention of the Lost Cause. The western South had always been the epicenter of Battle of New Orleans celebrations, but by the 1880s, fewer and fewer Southerners commemorated Jackson's victory. Women's organizations like the LHA and the Daughters of 1812 used the UDC's methods to reinvigorate public attention about the War of 1812 and the Battle of New Orleans. White Southerners in Nashville and New Orleans quickly bought into the renewed interest. It gave them an opportunity to focus on a portion of their past which highlighted the success of their ancestors rather than the failure of the Confederacy.

These successes did not occur without controversy. In Nashville, the UDC held enough power to insert itself into the Battle of New Orleans commemorations, and the reenactment of the battle embodied a Lost Cause sentiment. Further, the Nashville commemorations highlighted the power of the Civil War's memory. Southerners blended the Battle of Franklin, an overwhelming Confederate defeat, into a ceremony meant to commemorate one of Tennessee's greatest military victories. The pain of losing the Civil War altered Tennessee's historical memory.

The Louisiana ceremonies, while a dramatic celebration of Anglophone people's friendship, paid almost no attention to the role of nonwhite English speakers. The use of Jordan Noble's drum at the Chalmette ceremonies represented one of the only references to any African American participation in the battle. In a showcase of white pride meant to symbolize Anglo-American unity, many New Orleanians also conveniently forgot that many of their ancestors who fought in the New Orleans campaign had spoken French. The proud Creoles of New

Orleans had often used every trick at their disposal to preserve the Gallic nature of the city in the face of what they perceived as a torrent of Anglo-American immigration. The political needs of the present, though, dictated a focus on Anglo-American unity.

Great Britain and the United States needed that unity as the two nations prepared for possible joint military action. Accordingly, the federal government exerted its influence to halt Anglophobia or triumphalism from entering into the official commemoration. One cannot help but wonder how an ardent Anglophobe like Jackson would have felt about such sentiments.

CHAPTER SIX

"Not Pirate . . . Privateer"

The Battle of New Orleans and Mid-Twentieth-Century Popular Culture

On April 2, 1917, 102 years after the War of 1812 concluded, President Woodrow Wilson stood before Congress. "I have called the Congress into extraordinary session because there are serious, very serious, choices of policy to be made," he contended. Continuing, the president explained, "American ships have been sunk, American lives taken, in ways which it has stirred us very deeply to learn of." Wilson had hoped "it would suffice to assert our neutral rights with arms, our right to use the seas against unlawful interference, our right to keep our people safe against unlawful violence." Nonetheless, "neutrality [was] no longer feasible or desirable. . . . We have seen the last of neutrality in such circumstances."[1]

While James Madison might have completely approved of Wilson's message, it would have surprised him to learn which nation was preying on neutral shipping and shocked to discover on which country's behalf the United States would soon enter the war. The United States would again engage in a war involving Great Britain and the issue of "Free Trade and Sailors Rights," but this time she would join with England in the conflict.[2]

American hostility toward England had diminished by the 1910s. That process only continued as the two nations became allies in not one but two active wars and peacetime allies in the North Atlantic Treaty Organization. Undeterred by the niceties of international politics, though, American popular culture found new ways to interpret the Battle of New Orleans. Ultimately, popular culture iterations such as *The Buccaneer* films and the song "The Battle of New Orleans" became some of the most widespread and longest-lasting versions yet.[3]

These new versions of the battle resulted from changes in both the United States' domestic situation and its international policies. With the United States becoming an increasingly prominent actor on the world stage, the bellicose Anglophobic celebrations of the Battle of New Orleans which characterized much of the nineteenth-century festivities surrounding the event created political concerns. In addition, as the United States grew into a world power, American culture shifted away from an incessant obsession with comparing itself to European nations in an adolescent-like need to justify its own existence. Accordingly, the celebrations surrounding the Battle of New Orleans took an increasingly less antagonistic tone toward the United States' former colonial master. The Battle of New Orleans became a celebration of what many considered the redeeming qualities of American culture rather than a measuring stick of domestic progress. New opportunities for interpretation also opened the door for fuller and more inclusive renditions of the battle. By acknowledging the accomplishments of the many participants on the American side, an even broader constituency could embrace the battle's history.[4]

This development proved especially important as the Battle of New Orleans lost its traditional support by the Democratic Party. In 1941, Democrats abandoned the January 8 date for the celebration of Jackson Day. Like the moment when Wilson gave his speech to Congress in 1917, in 1940 the United States once again prepared to enter a war on the side of Great Britain. Increasingly close friends with both the prime minister and the king of England, President Franklin Roosevelt, nominal head of the Democratic Party, quietly moved Jackson Day to March. Publicly, he claimed to have done so because the new date gave the party time to recover after the 1940 election. In reality, having the most important political day of Roosevelt's party be a celebration of the stunning defeat of his nation's newest and closest ally created political complications. The date never retuned to January, and eventually the event became Jefferson–Jackson Day, occurring near the two men's birthdays. This change in the commemoration was but one incident in a colorful half century of American history during which a number of dramatic external events shaped how the United States viewed the Battle of New Orleans.[5]

The years following the battle's centennial set the stage for a dramatic new rendition of the Battle of New Orleans in American popular culture. Previously, the focus of the battle had regularly centered on more traditional sources of American pride: martial conduct, glorious generals, and celebration of the frontier and westward expansion. Thanks to a new wave of popular attention, by the late 1930s and early 1940s a new group became the center of attention: the outlaw, specifically the privateer Jean Laffite and his Baratarians.

Certainly scholars and artists who examined the Battle of New Orleans had dealt with Laffite and the Baratarians before. These studies, while not overtly negative in their treatment of the skilled artillerists, celebrated the civilizing of the sailors by joining Jackson's force and reveled in their rejection of British overtures. In the traditional narrative of the nineteenth century, Laffite and his men had been criminals and pirates who gave up their ill-gotten gains in a burst of national enthusiasm to smite an invading hoard.[6]

This narrative dovetailed nicely with the American depiction of the British as quick to use morally questionable groups for their nefarious purposes. After all, pirates rampaged across the waters of the world. They raped and pillaged for centuries around the Caribbean basin, and the Anglo-speaking world regularly depicted them as barbarous beasts that the Royal Navy itself had standing orders to execute if captured. How despicable then was it for the British to attempt to coerce pirates to join their force in the assault on New Orleans? Of course, the British also burned Washington, sacked Havre de Graces, and regularly employed Native Americans and former African slaves to attack white Americans. To many Americans growing up within this traditional interpretation of events, the British attempts to employ pirates, while despicable, hardly seemed surprising. The astonishment in the conventional narrative resulted from the pirates' rejection of the British; even pirates did not want to associate themselves with the British. Most importantly for the purposes of the battle's memory, the Baratarians did not play a central role in the story. They added to the grandeur of Jackson's benevolence, to the polyglot nature of the American army, or to the moral right of American victory. They never took center stage, and they were almost always *pirates* and always *criminals*.[7]

In point of fact, the United States did not pardon Laffite and his gang for "piracy." Prior to the New Orleans campaign, the Baratarians' smuggling operations had been the only maritime activity federal officials had charged the group with. The group operated with a letter of marque from the fledgling Republic of Cartagena against the Kingdom of Spain. While most Europeans decried the validity of the Cartagena rebel government, the United States certainly had trouble suggesting that American colonies did not have a right to rebel and create sovereign nations. The issue came when Laffite and his men tried to sell goods captured from Spanish vessels to the citizens of Louisiana. The Baratarians failed to pay taxes on the goods and, because of that, provoked the ire of the state of Louisiana.[8]

Even in contemporary times, the public had mixed attitudes toward the Baratarians. The US government's frequent restrictions on trade in the years leading up to the War of 1812 resulted in many Americans ignoring mercantile restrictions for years. Especially for citizens in New Orleans, on the far edge of the American domestic commercial system, Laffite and his men represented the only way Louisianans could acquire many luxury goods, and even some non-luxury items. Furthermore, it was public knowledge that numerous members of the New Orleans and Louisiana government did business with Laffite and his men. While officials like William C. C. Claiborne decried the Baratarians for their flagrant violations of the law, they did not view Laffite and his men as serious threats to public safety. Though Claiborne and others might have used the word "pirate," they did not harbor fears that Laffite and his men would descend on the banks of the Mississippi and hold New Orleans for ransom like Blackbeard had done to Charleston during the early sixteenth century.[9]

Artists and writers during the nineteenth century rarely used the Baratarians as part of the celebrated narrative of the Battle of New Orleans. Some books and works of fiction did commemorate or promote Laffite and his men; indeed, *The Corsair* by the famed poet Lord Byron supposedly even celebrated the famed rogues of the Gulf Coast, but those incidents had little impact on the larger memory of the battle. Not until the early twentieth century would Laffite and his men fully enter the dialogue on the Battle of New Orleans or join the pantheon of heroes associated with it.[10]

The early twentieth century witnessed a rash of swashbuckling swordsman protagonists, which helped Jean Laffite's image. First performed in 1903, Emma Orczy's *The Scarlet Pimpernel* was a hugely successful British play featuring the exploits of Sir Percy Blakeney, an English aristocrat turned masked swordsman fighting against a corrupt system to help the persecuted. The American Johnston McCulley adapted the character to a North American audience with his creation of the character Zorro in 1919. However, Zorro, the pseudonym of Mexican nobleman Don Diego de la Vega, was not a citizen of the United States; he fought against the corrupt pre-US government of California. McCulley's book was so successful that it led to a film adaptation a year later and a sequel in 1925. In this same time, the Scarlet Pimpernel starred in no less than four movies. These novels and films were wildly popular in the United States but lacked an American lead character for the country's young men to emulate.[11]

The problem with having an American lead was that it required an American to fight against the US government, which—obviously—was not corrupt. Prohibition, however, criminalized many Americans for doing what had been entirely legally acceptable only a few years before. Suddenly, average American citizens could picture themselves standing up to a law they did not agree with, even if their protestations did not involve swashbuckling sword fights. The stage was set for a historical figure like Jean Laffite to receive newfound empathy from American popular culture. After all, the crime most Americans knew that Laffite had been charged with was smuggling, something many Americans in the Prohibition era were guilty of encouraging. The author of Laffite's rebranding was Lyle Saxon.[12]

Born in 1891 of distinguished New Orleans and Baton Rouge families, Saxon became one of the most influential writers of New Orleans and Louisiana history. His works, many of which are still in print today because of their literary flare and scholarship, focused on the romantic history of New Orleans and the eccentricities of the region, which made it stand out from the rest of the Untied States. Because of this interest, Saxon eventually decided to direct his energies toward Laffite. Written with novelistic verve and published in 1930, *Laffite the Pirate* detailed the famed Baratarian during his time in New Orleans.[13]

Saxon's work painted an image of a Laffite who had traversed the Atlantic world for many years and seen many adventures. Yes, he had robbed and stolen at times, but he always did so with a sense of honor and a fluid moral code that justified his unlawful behavior. Throughout the beginning of the book, we read of Laffite's boyish charm and his comical interactions with the bungling Governor William C. C. Claiborne, who consistently tries and fails to halt Laffite's illicit trade. When the serious issue of British invasion rears its head, Laffite rises to the defense of his country. Of course, Laffite defended his country; he is only a criminal, not a traitor![14]

While *Laffite the Pirate* remains in print today and continues to be popular in the New Orleans area, neither the book nor Saxon's interpretation of Laffite would have spread so far if its message had been delivered through print alone. By the 1930s, Americans had grown quite fond of movies involving epic battles and sword fights, and famed Hollywood director Cecil B. DeMille looked for the inspiration behind his next blockbuster. *Laffite the Pirate* had everything DeMille could want: a famous battle, a swashbuckling hero, and a historical epic. Production of *The Buccaneer* began in 1937. Shot on location in southern Louisiana, with technical assistance from the Louisiana State Museum, *The Buccaneer* actually paid surprisingly close attention to historical detail (to the extent possible during the 1930s). The production company even cast people from the Baratarian swamp southwest of New Orleans as extras in the movie to play the role of their supposed ancestors. Criticized by some around the country for exaggerating the narrative of New Orleans, DeMille countered by asserting that his version would actually represent the battle in a more comprehensive way than any had done before.[15]

From the beginning, *The Buccaneer* rehabilitated the image of Jean Laffite in the eyes of the American public. The opening credits explain to all that even the famed Lord Byron felt a warm place in his heart for the Gulf Coast corsair, and Fredric March plays Jean Laffite perfectly for a movie based on Lyle Saxon's interpretation (little surprise since Saxon was on set). The movie opens with scenes depicting the playful nature of Laffite's supposed personality and offering sympathetic explanations of his criminal behavior. The script quickly informs the viewer that Laffite is a man of honor and orders his ships never to attack a vessel flying the American flag. The movie depicts these actions as pseudopatriotic in nature rather than the practical realties of not wanting to antagonize the American government too much while operating a base within US territorial waters.[16]

Laffite and his men lived as a band of misfits, cast out from every decent country in the world. Laffite is a pirate (or privateer) king who has all the power, riches, and fineries a man could want, but he lacks what he most desires: the hand of a beautiful woman. Laffite's love interest is part of New Orleans high society, and she explains to the roguish hero that they cannot be together until Laffite is a respectable man able to walk the streets of New Orleans without a price on his head. When the British approach Laffite with overtures to join them and offers of respectability in British society, the movie's protagonist ultimately rejects a commission in the Royal Navy. He explains his reasoning to his men by

stating that, like the Baratarians, the United States is the underdog in the conflict against Great Britain. America is a land of immigrants who have, for various
reasons, been kicked out by other nations. By siding with the United States, the
Baratarians can finally have a country to call their own, and one that ultimately
reminds the pirates of the upstart, reject nature of their own existence.[17]

Even when the American government orders an attack on Barataria, thanks
to the perfidious actions of a British spy who happens to be in the Louisiana
legislature, Laffite and his men stay true to the United States. Their loyalty rests
on Laffite's and his men's faith in the man who will lead the defense of New
Orleans, Andrew Jackson. While Old Hickory, played by Hugh Sothern, does
not get as much screen time in a movie about the Battle of New Orleans as one
might expect, the meaning behind Jackson's character is critical to the thesis of
DeMille's movie. Like Laffite, Jackson is not a part of "the system." Jackson (in-
variably followed by his buckskin-clad, coonskin-hat-wearing aide Mr. Peavy),
while adored by New Orleans polite society, is not part of it. Jackson is a rough-
and-tumble frontier brawler who only cares about winning and has the ability to
see the inner good in people despite what the larger society normally censures.
The Buccaneer's Andrew Jackson is a myth and memory that would bring a tear
to the mid-nineteenth-century Democratic Party's eyes, but he also is not the
main character of the story. Laffite is the real savior of New Orleans, providing
manpower, material, and inspiration just when the city needs it the most. *The
Buccaneer* paved the way for Laffite, the Baratarians, and their artillery to rise to
the ranks of Jackson, the Tennesseans, and their hunting rifles.[18]

The Buccaneer never became the box office success that DeMille expected,
nor did it receive the attention from film critics that the famous director's other
works did. It did, however, have a lasting impact on the memory of the Battle
of New Orleans and, apparently, on DeMille himself. While the first part of
that assertion is harder to prove tangibly, the latter helped further the memory
of the battle. During the 1950s, after the development of Technicolor and other
methods of making color films, DeMille began working in the new medium.
He decided that he wanted to remake some of his old black-and-white movies
into color and take advantage of the latest cinema technology to make their
stories even grander than before. Of DeMille's entire venerated filmography, he
selected only two movies for this treatment: *The Ten Commandments* and *The
Buccaneer*. In the shadow of his life, DeMille chose movies celebrating his interpretations of God and the United States. Unfortunately for DeMille, by 1957,
when production started on the remake of *The Buccaneer*, his advanced age and
deteriorating health prevented him from being on set during filming. Instead,
he sent his son-in-law, Anthony Quinn, to direct the film for him, and DeMille
put his mark on the product in the postproduction editing.[19]

While the 1958 edition of *The Buccaneer* shares an almost identical plotline and many of the same one-liners as its 1938 predecessor, it is very much its own work of art. The 1958 version has a more serious tone than its predecessor, and the newer movie portrays the danger to the United States as much more imminent and grave. In the 1958 version, Laffite's love interest, this time the fictitious daughter of Governor Claiborne, tries a much more forceful method of obtaining the wayward pirate's allegiance to the United States. As Laffite wistfully pines for her attention in the same manner as he does in the 1938 rendition, his paramour does not leave it to him to figure out a path to respectability; she insults him as she explains how the United States needs all the help it can get. To earn this woman's respect, it is time for Laffite to stop living out the boy's fantasy of playing pirate and being the pretend king of a sandy spit of Gulf Coast property. The implication is that it takes a greater man to be willing to stand up for an ideal and fight for one's country than to revel in personal liberties and individual freedoms carried to excess.[20]

The movie continues this theme when Laffite shows up at the New Orleans jail to free his men. Rather than deliver a bombastic and inspirational speech, the 1958 Laffite has a quiet conversation with his second-in-command, Dominique You. In an earlier scene, a drunk You lambasted Laffite for being willing to fight for a nation and its ideals. After all, Laffite had been the one to convince You to leave France and become a pirate in the first place. Later in the jail, Laffite explains that he had been wrong in his youth. It was easy to fight for nothing and live as an outlaw; real courage meant being willing to stand up for a belief.[21]

That the 1958 version of the *Buccaneer* should take a more sober view of national service is, in many ways, hardly surprising. DeMille, an outspoken critic of the communist Soviet Union, regularly assisted the US military and anti-communist organizations. Indeed, DeMille had used his skills at showmanship both to consult for the National Committee for a Free Europe and to design the uniforms at the US Air Force Academy. While DeMille's medical condition limited his involvement in the day-to-day operations of *The Buccaneer*, he took every opportunity to leave his mark when he could. In fact, he is the first person the audience saw when the film opened. Standing in front of a map showing the Louisiana Purchase, DeMille personally explains the strategic implications of the New Orleans campaign in a professorial style, creating the impression that he is a historian. DeMille explained that in 1815, the United States faced an existential threat of annihilation. One can only imagine how that depiction resonated with an audience regularly practicing nuclear fallout drills.[22]

The nationalistic tones of the 1958 version of *The Buccaneer*, however, should not give the impression that the movie is excessively right leaning in all of its content. Indeed, either DeMille or Quinn made a number of changes dealing with the issue of race. The 1938 version portrays few African Americans in any but servant roles, and all those with speaking roles have the notorious accents of a minstrel show performer. The 1958 *Buccaneer* features a much broader range of African American characters (comparatively speaking) and shows them fighting alongside whites in the final battle against the British. Further, some of the African Americans, presumably middle-class New Orleans Creoles by their dress, speak better English than any of the white soldiers from Tennessee or Kentucky. Further, the casting of Yul Brynner as Laffite reveals an intent to make the character racially ambiguous. Brynner received numerous roles throughout his career when a studio wanted someone "ethnic" looking. Brynner had recently worked with DeMille in *The Ten Commandments*, portraying Egyptian king Ramses II, and had previously played the king of Siam in *The King and I*.[23]

The 1958 *Buccaneer* makes other attempts at expanding the racial diversity of its protagonists. After the capture of the *Corinthian*, an American merchant vessel attacked by a rogue Baratarian ship's captain in both films, the 1958 version features an African American pirate rescuing a young boy and his dog off the sinking ship. In 1938, the pirate was a scraggly looking white male saving a beautiful woman, with the implication that he desired some sort of sexual reward. The 1958 depiction is more selfless and builds on the film's idea that it takes more courage to stand by convictions.[24]

Later, during the final battle on January 8, Laffite rushes forward with a Choctaw warrior to signal the location of the British Army. The "brave," as Laffite and Jackson call him, is rather stereotypically dressed and is, of course, armed with a bow and arrow. The Tennesseans and Kentuckians are similar caricatures of their historical equivalents. More importantly, the 1958 version of *The Buccaneer* exhibited a conscious production effort to portray the multiracial nature of Jackson's army, fighting in unison for a set of ideals. That depiction is best articulated in a scene where a South Asian man reads the preamble of the Declaration of Independence to Laffite's Baratarians. That scene reached millions of American viewers in 1958 and tens of millions more during the fifty years of the film's broadcast on television and subsequent theater screenings.[25]

Those viewers also witnessed a different Andrew Jackson than the 1938 version. Portrayed by Charlton Heston, the 1958 Jackson is a far more forceful and explosive Old Hickory than Hugh Sothern some twenty years earlier. Heston presents Jackson at his prime—fiery, decisive, and borderline crazy. While 1958 Jackson does not receive much more screen time than the 1938 character, he is much more central to the storyline and is actually one of the first characters to appear in the movie.[26]

Both movies present Jackson's army that travels to New Orleans as the traditional band of Tennessee and Kentuckian backwoodsman who can "shoot the eye of a squirrel at 300 yards." They are coarse, they are vulgar, and they are hard fighters. Both versions of *The Buccaneer* depict the final January 8th battle in a manner that makes the historian cringe. Taking cover behind hastily prepared ramparts, both versions of the movie show the Americans still rolling cotton bales into position when Laffite arrives, just as the British begin their assault. The British also suffer the indignity of almost 150 years of historical misrepresentation, as, in both versions, kilt-wearing highlanders slowly march into the maw of lead and iron which dirty-shirted Americans have prepared for them.[27]

The Buccaneer was not the only prominent rendition of the Battle of New Orleans which Americans observed in the late 1950s. In 1959, a year after the release of DeMille's remake, musician Johnny Horton released "The Battle of New Orleans" on the Columbia Records label. The song was an instant success and skyrocketed to the top of the Billboard Hot 100 list. In fact, during the first fifty years of Billboard's influential listing, "The Battle of New Orleans" ranked twenty-eighth overall—the number one country song to appear on the chart.[28]

The success of "The Battle of New Orleans" stemmed in large part from Columbia Records' skillful marketing of the song. The original writer of the lyrics, Jimmy Driftwood, had the thick accent of a native Arkansan. While Driftwood garnered lots of attention in the South, for a national release, Columbia went with the cleaner-accented and younger Horton. The plan worked, and to this day the Horton version of the song is the one most Americans are familiar with; however, in folk music circles, Driftwood's original authorship is well understood.[29]

Born Neil Morris in 1907, Jimmy Driftwood learned to play American folk music at a young age, including the popular bluegrass tune *The Eighth of January*. The exact source of the original fiddle tune is unknown, but according to oral tradition in the Tennessee mountain country and interviews conducted by the Works Progress Administration, its origins lie deep in the nineteenth century. The song was originally without lyrics, but in 1936 Driftwood, while a high school history teacher in Arkansas, wrote words to accompany the tune to help teach the Battle of New Orleans to his students.[30]

In 1957, Nashville record producers learned of Driftwood and signed him to a contract, whereupon he recorded many of his original songs, including "The Battle of New Orleans." By the end of the 1950s and into the 1960s, both Driftwood and Horton toured the United States and Europe performing "The Battle of New Orleans" for a wide variety of audiences. Driftwood achieved significant success in Europe because of his Southern accent and because of his racier lyrics. In the name of politeness, though, Driftwood did ensure that he had alternate wording for performances in England so as not to offend his audience.[31]

Driftwood's original lyrics did not conform to the United States' federal radio standards of the day because of his use of the words "hell" and "damn"— words that, as Driftwood pointed out, people heard regularly in church. Federal standards aside, Driftwood's song opens as the bold and boisterous tale of American frontiersmen journeying south "along with Colonel Jackson down the mighty Missisip . . . to [meet] the bloody British in the town of New Orleans." Driftwood continues,

> I seed Mars Jackson come a-walkin' down the street
> And a-talkin' to a pirate by the name of Jean Lafitte
> He gave Jean a drink that he brung from Tennessee
> And the pirate said he'd help us drive the British to the sea.

French-speaking Creoles

> told Andrew, "You had better run
> For Packenham's a comin' with a bullet in his gun."
> Old Hickory said he didn't give a damn
> He's a-gonna whup the britches off of Colonel Packenham.

The British then appeared, but the Americans, unimpressed with the proper soldiers' high-step marching, hid behind their cotton bales with their hunting rifles. Finally, with their small arms ammunition exhausted and the cannons overheated, the backwoodsmen

> grabbed an alligator and we fought another round
> We filled his head with minie balls and powdered his behind
> And when we touched the powder off, the 'gator lost his mind.

The defeated British

> ran through the briars and they ran through the brambles
> And they ran through the bushes where a rabbit couldn't go
> They ran so fast the hounds couldn't catch em
> Down the Mississippi to the Gulf of Mexico.[32]

While the section about Laffite and concerns over the loyalty of Francophone New Orleanians never made it into Horton's edited radio version, the thesis of the song and its patriotic nature remain intact. The piece is a folky celebration of America which mocks Great Britain for challenging the virility of the American frontiersman. Similar to *The Buccaneer*, though, the song is not inherently anti-British as much as it is pro-American. Driftwood finds it silly that any force would challenge the western rifleman on his home soil in his native element. Like his contemporary DeMille, Driftwood celebrated in his art what he perceived as intrinsic values of American culture, which should be highlighted and commemorated as part of the stand made by Jackson's forces. He did this without resorting to the demonization of British soldiers and culture which occurred in much of the nineteenth century's popular works that focused on the battle.[33]

The 1930s and 1950s witnessed a revival of the Battle of New Orleans in American popular culture. Artists such as Johnny Horton, Jimmy Driftwood, and Cecil B. DeMille harnessed the burgeoning American postwar patriotism and confidence to market their work and celebrate their image of the United States. The rekindled enthusiasm for the military victory at New Orleans differed from the nineteenth-century interpretation, however.[34]

During the 1800s, the Battle of New Orleans had been an important victory over Great Britain, one of the world's superpowers. By the mid-twentieth century, the United States stood as one of the world's two superpowers (along with the Soviet Union), and Great Britain (while an important and close ally) had clearly lost a step in the international arena. While both versions of *The Buccaneer* and "The Battle of New Orleans" in no way attempted to hide that Great Britain had been the enemy in the War of 1812, the films and song lacked an overtly anti-British character. More pro-American than anything, they used British stereotypes of military pomp and ordered ranks slowly marching forward into aimed rifle fire as straw men to lionize the typecasts of the American soldiers.

By the 1950s, the United States no longer needed to "prove" itself to the world. It had, according to many Americans still today, bailed Great Britain out of losing two world wars and, at the height of the Cold War, "made the world safe for Democracy." Great Britain and the United States were now partners, with the old colonial power clearly the junior member of the alliance. Thus, commemorations of the Battle of New Orleans like *The Buccaneer* and "The Battle of New Orleans" could focus on what their creators believed made America great without relying on a demonization of the British. Indeed, except for the issue of historical accuracy, one gets the feeling when watching *The Buccaneer* or listening to "The Battle of New Orleans" that Nazi Germany or Communist Russia could have just as easily been Jackson's enemy. It would not matter; Jackson, Laffite, and their men could take on anyone as long as the United States remained dedicated to the ideals that captured the hearts of DeMille's Baratarians and kept hold of the frontier craftiness of Driftwood's artillerymen.[35]

This rekindled focus on the Battle of New Orleans also opened the door for more diverse interpretations of the battle's story. While historians and writers had paid attention to the Baratarians before, this culturally heterogeneous group received newfound popularity in the first half of the twentieth century. At the same time, the inclusion of African American participation in the battle depicted in the 1958 version of *The Buccaneer* exposed many Americans to a side of the engagement rarely presented before. These steps, while small, paved the way for the reaction against a narrative of the battle which had gotten rather whitewashed over time. That reaction would not be without its opponents, but with hundreds of millions of people around the country having watched *The Buccaneer* and listened to "The Battle of New Orleans," these renditions of Jackson's victory became some of the most lasting and influential interpretations.[36]

CHAPTER SEVEN

"Tourism Whetted by the Celebration"

The Battle of New Orleans in the Twentieth Century

Their vapory clouds of breath appeared and disappeared with vibrant frequency in the crisp January air. They were tired, so very tired. They had pushed themselves hard on the route from Fort St. John to the Vieux Carré. Thankfully, though, the end of their journey lay within sight. There, standing before them, the blue-coated officer waved them on and encouraged them, his shock of white hair clearly visible beneath the bicorn hat resting on his head. Andrew Jackson did not cheer these young participants on; rather, Hugh Sothern did. The runners were not Plauche's battalion in 1815, but, instead, New Orleans–area joggers in 1938.[1]

In recognition of the world premiere of *The Buccaneer*, New Orleans hosted a grand spectacle around the city. At this particular event, the winner of the "Brave Creoles Run" would receive the "Cecil B. DeMille" trophy. Elsewhere in New Orleans, city boosters carefully crafted an image of their region which mirrored the fantasy and myth depicted in DeMille's screen version of New Orleans. Indeed, during a radio interview between Lyle Saxon and Cecil B. DeMille, the famous director opined, "More than a hundred years have passed since Jean Laffite held the future of America in the palm of his hand, yet here in New Orleans, steeped in tradition and romance, it almost seems as if he were still alive."[2]

New Orleans in the mid-twentieth century was a city struggling to find an identity. Trying to cash in on the growing industry of cultural tourism, many in the New Orleans area lobbied for an aura that highlighted the romanticized past of the city. Others, looking at the success of Southern cities such as Dallas and Atlanta, felt that New Orleans must modernize at all costs to survive. This debate had dramatic implications for elements of the city's past such as the Battle of New Orleans commemoration and the event's historical memory.[3]

The most tangible evidence for New Orleans's tri-cornered conflict between modernization, preservation, and cultural tourism lay six miles downriver from the French Quarter at the Chalmette Monument. The Daughters of 1812 had fought a valiant delaying action against the encroachment of industry on the Chalmette battlefield, but by the end of the 1920s, they needed help. The efforts of the federal government in general and the NPS specifically during the next thirty years provided an intriguing story that highlights the dynamic struggles of historic preservation efforts. Whereas many of the nation's most famous battlefield parks (Gettysburg, Antietam, Saratoga) reside in largely rural areas, the Chalmette battlefield contended with a host of urban planning issues. As a result, the NPS faced considerable difficulty in its preservation efforts, and the outcome of those efforts had a lasting impact on citizens' memories of the Battle of New Orleans.[4]

Despite their efforts, the Daughters of 1812 had struggled to muster the monetary resources and political clout necessary to combat the growing industrialization near the battlefield. On June 2, 1930, President Herbert Hoover signed legislation giving the federal government control over the Chalmette Monument and the grounds surrounding it. Thereafter, the US government took charge of efforts to preserve and care for the battlefield. Initial federal appropriations to the site, though, totaled only $1,200 annually—not really enough to persuade local business interests that Washington seriously intended to make preservation efforts a priority.[5]

Despite the paltry $1,200, federal assistance made an immediate impact on the monument property. The superintendent of the national cemetery just a few hundred yards downriver conducted an initial survey of the memorial grounds and provided it to his superiors. He recommended that the site needed immediate help, including repairs to the maintenance garage, outhouse, cistern, and chicken coop. His recommendations highlighted the rural and neglected nature of the memorial. Even as late as the 1930s, when National Military Parks like Gettysburg, Shiloh, and Vicksburg already had numerous wayside exhibits and extensive plans for museum buildings, the Chalmette battlefield remained a rural backwater only six miles from one of the largest cities in the South. The fences were an especially important item of needed repair because they confined the cattle that ate the grass. Without the cattle, the park would have to pay someone to mow the grounds. The War Department eventually decided to let the cattle go, and maintenance personnel from the cemetery began caring for the monument grounds.[6]

While the NPS administered the original "Big 5" Civil War sites (Shiloh, Gettysburg, Vicksburg, Chickamauga, Antietam), there was no clear indication that the organization would remain in the business of battlefield preservation. During the same period, the War Department had assumed control of a number of sites, including Chalmette. To clarify the department's mission regarding these sites, the secretary of war put the US Army War College in charge of developing a plan for the Chalmette battlefield. Well versed in the study of military history, the War College launched a sweeping assessment of battlefields across the country. As that study concluded, to accurately place historical markers depicting important battle events or indicating battle lines, the government needed to purchase 136 acres of land at a cost of $540,000. The annual cost of maintaining this expanded footprint would be some $10,000, considerably more than the $1,200 annual budget Congress had appropriated. As such, the War Department awaited directions for the next course of action.[7]

Publicity of the federal government's investigation into the battlefield's plight sparked new local interest in assisting with the preservation. The Louisiana Landmark Society, the Louisiana Historical Association, and the New Orleans Association of Commerce also championed an expanded historic site. The Association of Commerce's newfound interest in history came from the growing business of cultural tourism. The War Department's efforts to build up the Chalmette site coincided with a growing interest from the business community in New Orleans to shape the image of the Crescent City and emphasize what made the city unique. These organizations thirsted for anything that might convince a potential tourist to visit the area and to open his or her wallet. "The establishment of this park can mean much to New Orleans," the Association of Commerce wrote, "as a drawing card to tourists, aside from the historic and sentimental value." Even if their efforts remained less than benevolent, the chamber of commerce could be a valuable ally in convincing the New Orleans Terminal Company to sell its property to the federal government. Luckily for the War Department, though, the future of the Chalmette battlefield became the problem of the NPS when, in 1933, the War Department turned over control of its battlefield sites.[8]

The problem of how to expand the site into a viable park still remained, despite the Chalmette Monument resting under the auspices of the NPS. The New Orleans Association of Business and local history groups continued their efforts to convince the federal government to purchase the necessary land. In 1935, Congressman Joachim O. Fernández presented a bill before Congress to acquire the land. Despite its passage in both the Senate and the House, President Franklin Roosevelt vetoed the bill. In the middle of the Great Depression, the president could not justify spending half a million dollars to buy land for the purpose of creating a park that would potentially limit industrial development and job creation.[9]

Unable to convince the federal government to purchase the land, park boosters shifted tactics, trying to convince the state of Louisiana to buy the property and then donate the land to the federal government. The park's advocates received assistance from an unlikely source—Hollywood. In 1937, Cecil B. DeMille traveled to New Orleans to begin production on the film *The Buccaneer*. To raise public awareness about its efforts to purchase the land required for a park, the Louisiana Historical Society held a grand celebration during the film's premier in 1938.[10]

The historical society worked with Paramount Studios to promote the film during the months before its release. In January, DeMille's film had its world premiere at the New Orleans Saenger Theatre in front of a packed house of Hollywood elite. To encourage national attendance for a premiere so far from Los Angeles, Paramount hosted a semiannual meeting of its distribution executives from around the country.[11]

With national attention once again focused on the Battle of New Orleans, events moved quickly. In July of 1938, Governor Richard Leche signed a bill authorizing the state to purchase $300,000 worth of land for the establishment of a battlefield park. With state action finally under way, the federal government did its part and passed legislation officially establishing the Chalmette National Historical Park on August 10, 1939. With that action, Chalmette became only the third "national historical park" in the country.[12]

Despite these successes, the future viability of the Chalmette battlefield became mired in a morass of Louisiana politics. Leche resigned the governorship shortly after the federal government indicted him on corruption charges. The monetary appropriation for the battlefield turned into a political football exploited by the various candidates for the governor's office during the following election.[13]

The question centered on the source of the money for the battlefield. Tax revenue from mineral extraction within Louisiana normally contributed to nature conservation and education. While education might seem a fitting justification for the purchase of the Chalmette battlefield land, public school teachers in Louisiana disagreed. They argued that the $300,000 cited in the bill could supplement teacher salaries and improve classroom conditions around the state; instead, the government had tagged that money for the purchase of an empty field. Democratic gubernatorial candidates such as Sam Houston Jones argued in favor of the teachers in an effort to win their support at the polls. After winning the election, Jones quickly rescinded the state's pledge to purchase the land and left the NPS baffled about how to proceed. By 1939, the NPS managed a park that only consisted of a narrow thirty-three-acre strip commanded by a big marble obelisk; the agency lacked any congressional authority to purchase land.[14]

With no immediate prospect of gaining additional property, the NPS delayed major improvements to the site. Nonetheless, work proceeded to make the monument grounds more comfortable to visitors and increase attendance. In fact, the Works Progress Administration assisted in these efforts, but still lack of funding hindered progress.[15]

One instance of these abandoned improvement plans highlights the struggles the NPS faced in telling the story of the battle in the context of the Jim Crow–era South. While designing bathrooms for the site, NPS officials realized they had forgotten to provide for the "colored" facilities necessary to comply with

Louisiana state law. Though Andrew Jackson himself had called for racial unity in New Orleans during the British invasion, 120 years later the NPS faced the prospect of endorsing racial segregation. Though a lack of funding prevented the NPS from building the new restroom facilities, the attempted segregation of African Americans at the site did not occur only when they required a restroom. Segregation from battle commemorations affected the memory of the battle for most African Americans because few realized that more than five hundred free men of color fought in the campaign on the American side.[16]

Louisiana's fiscal decisions, combined with World War II, hindered all Americans' ability to tour the Chalmette battlefield and memorialize the Battle of New Orleans. Even so, the NPS planned for the day when it would have the desired land. The agency also lobbied the New Orleans Terminal Company to make the donation. The NPS especially desired the portion of the land that included the Rodriguez Canal's remnants and the Malus-Beauregard House. Jackson's army used the canal as the basis for their famed rampart, and it was the only surviving physical indication that two armies had fought over the otherwise-flat field. The Malus-Beauregard plantation house postdated the Battle of New Orleans, but park officials felt that it would make a useful teaching tool and a good building for a museum. Fortunately, both of these sat on the near (western) edge of the land the park wanted to purchase. Even if the park could not get the whole piece of property, at least the most historically relevant portions were the closest.[17]

To acquire this land, the park and its boosters launched a lobbying campaign in Baton Rouge. They sent one thousand brochures to legislators and influential persons in the state. These brochures highlighted the familiar tropes of the New Orleans campaign: rustic frontiersmen, a brave general, and slow-moving toy soldier–like British soldiers. Ultimately, these efforts succeeded in convincing the state to agree once again to purchase land for the park and donate it to the federal government. This time, the state of Louisiana appropriated only $100,000 for the endeavor, yet the decreased sum could be enough to get the land that included the Rodriguez Canal and Malus-Beauregard House.[18]

The Louisiana State Parks Commission began negotiations with the New Orleans Terminal Company in an effort to acquire as much land as possible. The state hoped to purchase all of the land that lay between the Chalmette Monument tract and the national cemetery. The state appealed to the corporation on philanthropic grounds and pointed to the tax benefits of such a large donation. The terminal company insisted, however, that the $2,000 per acre that the state offered was not enough for the property. The company could not accept anything less than $3,000 per acre. Eventually, the state and the terminal company settled on $2,750 per acre, and Louisiana turned over to the NPS some thirty-six acres. The terminal company also offered the state and federal government a one-year guarantee on the negotiated price if they could raise the

Mural of Andrew Jackson at the Battle of New Orleans, January 8, 1814, by Ethel Magafan, at the Recorder of Deeds Building (built in 1943), 515 D Street NW, Washington, DC. The legend of the cotton bales being an integral part of the New Orleans defenses persisted well into the twentieth century. Also note that the only African Americans are depicted in the role of shoeless servants.

additional money to buy the remaining land. That would give the park access to all of the land between the monument and the Fazendeville neighborhood.[19]

Knowing that the federal government desired the land and had raised almost $500,000 for its purchase at one point, the New Orleans Terminal Company had little reason to lower its asking price. Any threat to build on the land only raised public outcry for its preservation and raised the amount of money the state or federal government might be willing to pay. Once the state and federal governments saw that the company would guarantee the initial price of $2,750 per acre for up to one year, officials immediately petitioned the state legislature and Congress for the additional funds. After it became clear that the terminal company had as much money as it could get from the state of Louisiana, it sold the remaining portion of the battlefield to the Kaiser Aluminum Corporation for only $1,000 per acre.[20]

Kaiser purchased the land in 1951, and as part of the defense industry, the new corporation became an even trickier opponent. The federal government had bankrolled the development of the Kaiser Corporation in an effort to increase aluminum production during the Cold War. Fully aware of the history that took place on the site of the new facility, Kaiser's public relations department invoked the memory of Jackson's victory, declaring that its factory was engaged in a "second Battle of New Orleans." The company announced that "a threat of foreign domination was removed by the American victory of the past. Today, some of the silvery aluminum now being made on the same ground is being used for national defense to safeguard this country from aggression once again."[21]

Many local residents quickly adopted the opinion that a battlefield park may not be the best idea. After all, national defense was important, and the one thousand jobs that the aluminum factory brought to the small community did not hurt either. Further, before the new facility opened, Kaiser announced that it intended to double production capacity and, presumably, expand onto the battlefield land. Preservation groups fought an uphill battle, since a doubled production capacity could mean doubled employment numbers. The guarantee of jobs and income from the industrial site offered far more tempting prospects than the possibility of income from tourism to a hypothetical battlefield park. Business groups had always arrayed themselves against park proponents because of their hope that wealthy investors might use the land. With Kaiser Aluminum in their backyard, the local chambers of commerce fought even harder against government and preservationists' efforts to set aside Chalmette.[22]

Park activists became even more concerned when rumors surfaced of Kaiser's building plans: a mammoth rolling mill for the production of aluminum sheeting. NPS officials repeatedly appealed to Kaiser officials to work out some sort of deal for the donation of the land, but many locals now squarely sat in the Kaiser camp and advocated increased production capacity and more jobs. Local government officials also rallied against the NPS and preservationists. New Orleans mayor deLesseps Morrison even recommended that Kaiser build something on the property as soon as possible in order to drive any remaining support away from the conservationists. "It would be a good idea to announce plans soon," Morrison opined, "because of the possibility of a controversy raised by groups which want to see the site set aside as a national monument commemorating the Battle of New Orleans."[23]

The Parish of St. Bernard, long an advocate for a battlefield park, also publicly thwarted conservation efforts. The federal government had repeatedly warned the parish, which had dumped raw sewage into the Mississippi River, to update its public works. To avoid the impending fines, the parish begrudgingly constructed a new sewage treatment plant. Though the plant's placement could have occurred in a variety of spots near the river, the parish decided to build it next to the Fazendeville neighborhood on the route taken in 1815 by the British column assaulting along the river road. Despite Kaiser's repeated insistences to the NPS that it needed all of the available land, the company swiftly sold the 1.5 acres required for the sewage treatment plant to the parish. The construction of the odorous plant would, in the hopes of Kaiser and St. Bernard Parish officials, encourage the African American residents of Fazendeville to move and discourage preservationists in their efforts. After all, Jackson's battlefield could only look so scenic with a sewage treatment plant on it.[24]

The sewage facility's construction did not deter park proponents, but rather drove them further into action. Fortuitously for their cause, they received help from one new source and one old ally. The first came in the form of the office of the president of the United States. Apparently, the secretary of the interior managed to use his cabinet position to gain the attention of President Dwight Eisenhower, whose subordinates made known Ike's desire for some sort of compromise to occur.[25]

The second fortuitous ally came, once again, from Hollywood in the form of Cecil B. DeMille. In 1957, DeMille began production on a Technicolor remake of his 1938 *The Buccaneer*. As in 1938, New Orleans again hosted the world premiere of the film. This time, in addition to the expected festivities in New Orleans proper, several hundred Boy Scouts reenacted the Battle of New Orleans on the Chalmette battlefield for the entertainment of onlookers. This activity had already become an annual event held in connection with the anniversary, but the local scout troops provided a special performance just for the film's release.[26]

Several people involved with the film, including some of the principal actors, toured the battlefield and learned of its struggles. They and preservationists began an all-out effort to bring Kaiser to the table. With public attention fixed on the Battle of New Orleans because of the movie's release and advocates with more clout backing the idea of a park, Kaiser agreed to negotiate.[27]

Negotiations with Kaiser centered on its ability to find a suitable tract of land with which the company could replace its portion of the battlefield. Eventually, Kaiser officials and park proponents worked out a land swap between Kaiser, the NPS, and a third party that owned land on the east side of the Kaiser faculties. Kaiser agreed to give a portion of the requested land to the park, but only in installments, so that it could generate the greatest tax deductions from the donations. Once the donations were complete, the NPS would be in possession of all the former Kaiser Aluminum land between the national cemetery and the park's current eastern boundary.[28]

NPS officials ecstatic with the rapid pace of progress during the previous two years soon faced a number of new concerns and issues. Given the difficulty in acquiring the land, officials decided to abandon efforts for an even further expanded park. The NPS focused all future planning strictly on the property it would soon possess. The second issue stemmed from the staggered nature of the Kaiser donation. The primary interpretive item the NPS wanted to construct was an automotive tour road that visitors could use to quickly traverse the battlefield's main features. Even though construction on the loop could not begin until the park possessed all of the land, officials made the necessary preparations so that efforts could begin as soon as possible. With the 150th anniversary of the battle only a few years away, the park wanted to make sure it had the site completed for the big event. The park now faced the last issue for completing its footprint—land negotiations with the residents of the Fazendeville community.

The NPS had delayed negotiations with the Fazendeville residents, because if the agency could not acquire the industrial land on either side of the neighborhood, the residents' property would be useless to the park anyway. Though individual negotiations with roughly thirty-five property owners would take time, the government officials did not feel that the acquisition of the property would be overly challenging. Most of the properties lacked running water and electricity, meaning that without that infrastructure the NPS could acquire the plots for relatively little money. Also, as a government agency, the NPS could invoke eminent domain, if necessary, and order the residents off the land, as long as the residents' removal was for the general welfare of the public and as long as the government paid a fair market value.[29]

Accordingly, in 1962, Congress passed legislation that allowed officials to begin negotiations for the Fazendeville land and authorized $165,000 for the expenses. The park requested "disinterested, experienced, and reputable appraisers" to estimate the value of the land so that negotiations could begin. Whatever good intentions the park may have had, though, it had to operate within the realities of the 1960s Deep South.[30]

Just a few decades before, when the park first moved to NPS control, the editors of the *St. Bernard Voice* wrote an editorial about the realities the Fazendeville community faced. "The situation which the inhabitants of Fazendeville must eventually face is apparent to the more intelligent colored folks," the editors wrote. "They must bear segregation in mind—that is to say, the new village must be on a site that will meet with the approval of adjoining property holders." The writer continued, "The question of price is an important element and may be a deciding factor in the consideration of a new colored village. Then, again, the lump sums received by the negro property holders for their homes may so charm them that they will go to renting in New Orleans instead of building, and in a short time 'the coin of the realm' shall have vanished." The article ended with the closing observation that "the more intelligent and thrifty would like to found a new village, but whether they will succeed remains to be seen."[31]

Though the editorial appeared in 1939, for African Americans in St. Bernard Parish, the situation had actually gotten worse in some ways. By 1965, St. Bernard's white population had steadily risen as white families fled to the suburbs. White flight from New Orleans proper raised property values in St. Bernard and decreased the chances that the Fazendeville residents could move as a group and remain within their home parish. Further, since Fazendeville was one of the few concentrated African American groups in St. Bernard, many whites in the parish welcomed the opportunity to encourage black residents to move out of the area.[32]

Consequently, the residents of Fazendeville, many of whose families had owned their property since just after the Civil War, moved into the Ninth Ward of lower New Orleans and began renting homes. For families that had never possessed a substantial income, the necessity of monthly rent quickly drained the lump sum of money the NPS provided them for their original properties. With little education, few job opportunities, and a desperate economic reality, the removal of the Fazendeville community crippled those families for many years. Many New Orleans–area African Americans became aware of the Fazendeville residents' plight. Consequently, the NPS's actions also soured many African Americans to the park and negatively affected their attitudes toward the Battle of New Orleans in general.[33]

Business and government played a significant role in the development of the memory of the Battle of New Orleans during the mid-twentieth century, but no event makes that connection clearer than the planning and execution of the sesquicentennial celebration in 1965. One hundred and fifty years after the battle, and with Great Britain now an important ally, the US government had little trouble suggesting that the event should not focus on British military defeat. In fact, during initial planning, one member of the organizing committee repeatedly lobbied for events to focus on peace in general and not glorify war. With the United States already sending troops into Vietnam, many saw the glorification of armed conflict as distasteful. Instead, the organizing committee decided to make the sesquicentennial an enormous ad campaign for the city of New Orleans and the surrounding area. Considering that the committee consisted of representatives from Avondale Shipyards, American Sugar, Sears, Maison Blaunche, AT&T, Mississippi Shipping, Coca Cola, and Louisiana Power and Lighting, the focus on business was hardly surprising.[34]

Noticeably absent from the initial committee was a trained historian of the battle, or indeed anyone prominently representing education. The presidents of Dillard University, Grambling College, and Southern University, the most prominent historically black universities in the state, did eventually gain seats on the committee, but only after the NAACP threatened trouble. The committee, as originally organized, lacked any African American representation, but the groups hoped that the inclusion of the university presidents would "prevent trouble that would cause bad publicity for New Orleans." Clearly focused on image and business rather than history, the planning committee began its work.[35]

In an effort to top the centennial celebrations, the sesquicentennial events lasted a week. Most events bore little connection to the Battle of New Orleans, but they did promote New Orleans tourism. A Saturday afternoon tour of the French Quarter featured numerous houses that did not exist in 1815 and that event organizers had selected for architectural reasons or only because of who had resided in the property. On Monday, visitors could travel on a special tour up the Mississippi River, visiting post–War of 1812 plantation homes, and then stop at the governor's mansion in Baton Rouge. On Wednesday, tourists departed for a bus excursion to St. Bernard Parish from 1:00 to 5:00 p.m., yet organizers limited time at the battlefield to only one hour.[36]

Unlike the centennial anniversary, the sesquicentennial featured a significantly diminished American military presence. In 1915, the Seventh Infantry Regiment and other US military units presented a grand spectacle and paraded in large numbers through the streets of New Orleans. Fifty years later, the Royal Highland Regiment of Canada provided the largest contingent of troops. The sailors of the USS *Newport News* and the Keesler Air Force Base marching band represented the only federal troops attending the commemoration. In the military parade, the Canadians received the honor of leading the procession even though their nation did not participate in the Battle of New Orleans and Crown forces had lost the engagement. Event organizers wanted to be good hosts.

Other events also highlighted the target audience of the sesquicentennial committee. The Roosevelt Hotel, one of the city's most prominent hotels, served as the central registration area and the official host hotel of the 150th anniversary. Numerous restaurants around the city hosted special Battle of New Orleans–themed menus, featuring such items as "Filet Mignon a la Pakenham, Crevettes Baratarienne, Demi Tasse au General Coffee, and Baked Alaska Flambe Jackson." The city's most elite restaurants offered this select fare, intentionally given a Francophone name to make the dishes seem more exotic. This naming convention facilitated the New Orleans business interests' carefully crafted public relations campaign for city tourism.[37]

Many of the official events the sesquicentennial commission planned also required significant amounts of money to attend. The banquet, for example, required $12.50 per person or $25 per couple, a substantial amount of money at a time when more than half of Americans made less than $500 a month. Further, the tours up and down the Mississippi and around the French Quarter catered mostly to moneyed tourists rather than educating locals or preserving the memory of the battle. The official pamphlet for activities at the Chalmette battlefield on January 8, 1965, reinforced the connection between business and commemoration: "The rewards of our investment will come back to us for years to come . . . in terms of tourism whetted by the celebration . . . of Anglo-American military spectacle . . . of industry reminded pleasantly of our areas resources (the richest of which, and the least noted of which, is its historic heritage)."[38]

Even before the invention of the automobile, culture tourism generated significant sums of money in the United States. With the invention of the automobile, though, tourism became a major part of urban areas' commercial health. During the early 1910s, in recognition of that trend, New Orleans embarked on a careful and thoughtful campaign to develop what made New Orleans unique. To accomplish this goal, city fathers placed particular emphasis on the city's jazz and antebellum qualities.

The possibility of using the memory of the Battle of New Orleans to make huge profits also provided dividends. Cecil B. DeMille and Johnny Horton had proven that the battle itself still retained some significance in American historical memory. Further, the success of rural parks like Gettysburg, Saratoga, and Shiloh suggested that Chalmette, much closer to an existing tourist destination than many other famous battlefields, could make a profit. Unfortunately for park boosters, a competing financial interest and industrialization threatened the viability of a Chalmette battlefield park.

Parks like Gettysburg thrived precisely because of their rural nature. With little development near them, these battlefield parks became important facets of the local economy and spurred preservation efforts. Chalmette, resting on half a million dollars' worth of riverfront property, represented a potential hindrance to the local economy as a preserved battlefield site. Though a park might make money, little chance existed that it would generate the tax revenue or employ the number of people a full-scale factory complex could. Thus, the development of the Chalmette National Historical Park differed from how many of the nation's other prominent battlefield parks came into existence.[39]

The influence of business and tourism on the site's development affected not only whether the largest tangible piece of the battle's memory continued to exist but also the memory of the Battle of New Orleans itself. The most prominent groups to advocate for a preserved battlefield consisted of upper-middle-class and upper-class white Americans. To them, the economic realities of the Fazendeville community remained subordinate to the imperative of the battlefield's preservation. In the best of circumstances, this belief represented a naive understanding of the situation. Fazendeville residents, extremely undereducated and desperately poor, had little understanding of how park advocates intended to use their land. Many, upon returning in later years, did not understand why they had to move just so that their homes could become empty plots of mowed grass. Parks had slides. Parks had ball fields. Parks served a tangible purpose for communities. Why had the government forced them into even worse economic circumstances just so that a tour road could traverse their old neighborhood?[40]

The Fazendeville residents' lack of understanding stemmed from the "separate but equal" education denied them and from the consistent whitewashing of the memory of the Battle of New Orleans. If they had learned of the African American participation, Southern society most likely presented them with an interpretation that depicted happy and compliant blacks gratefully upholding the status quo in the face of British suggestions of freeing slaves that rebelled against their US masters. Indeed, as late as 1965, a locally produced television documentary on the battle presented just such a version of history, even noting that the famed African American "drummer boy of the Battle of New Orleans," Jordan Noble, had later raised a black unit in defense of the Confederacy. It failed to note that Noble also later helped raise a regiment for the Union after it captured New Orleans in 1862.[41]

The 1965 sesquicentennial consisted of a massive public relations campaign for the city of New Orleans and the surrounding area. Compared to the centennial anniversary, the sesquicentennial celebrations, though twice as many days, had only half the number of events that directly related to the Battle of New Orleans. In the face of domestic racial unrest and international military conflict, city boosters wanted to promote New Orleans as a relaxing and vibrant place to get away from the troubles of the world. For many members of the planning committee, the Battle of New Orleans and its memory represented a source of potential profit.

Not all of the park's promoters were as economically driven, and their alliance with the business interests in the city and surrounding area ultimately helped preserve the Chalmette battlefield. Guaranteeing the preservation of the site had been a long and arduous process, but in the years that followed, the Chalmette National Historical Park became the epicenter of the memory of the Battle of New Orleans.

CHAPTER EIGHT

A "Rustic and Factual" Appearance

The Battle of New Orleans at Two Hundred

The staccato ripple of musket fire surprised them. Leaping from their campfire, the red-coated soldiers reached for their own weapons to defend themselves. Officers darted about, trying to get the troops into line. Suddenly a haggardly looking Tennessean took aim at one of the British officers and fired. After his body convulsed, the British soldier slowly crumpled to the ground, and the crowd went wild with cheers and applause.[1]

In an effort to increase tourism, St. Bernard Parish began hosting a reenactment of the Battle of New Orleans during the early 2000s. The NPS had conducted "living history" encampments for years, but local officials feared that the events had stalled and the public was losing interest. Parish officials had good reason to think this.[2]

Since the sesquicentennial, public interest in the Battle of New Orleans had waned. A variety of factors resulted in this decreased public commemoration. Traditionally, local advocacy groups had lobbied for the promotion of the battle's memory. With the establishment of the national park, though, these groups trusted the park to be the caretaker of the memory. The bureaucracy of the NPS, combined with its struggle to find a viable message in the modern age, diminished the memory of the Battle of New Orleans in the late twentieth century. As the battle's bicentennial approached, coordination between the various stakeholders diminished, and by 2015, multiple Battle of New Orleans commemorations took place across the country with little coordination between them. Even events less than two miles apart showed little effort to support each other, with the biggest losers being the general public looking for historical information about the battle.

After the centennial celebrations in Nashville, commemorations connected with the Battle of New Orleans declined. Instead, the LHA increasingly focused on Jackson rather than on the battle that made him famous. The most elaborate annual event connected to the Battle of New Orleans continued to be the LHA's Jackson Day Ball. The soiree remained one of the high points of the Nashville social scene for many years and often served the same purpose debutant balls did in other cities around the United States. During the late 1980s, the Ladies began hosting the "Hermitage Gala," which replaced the old Jackson Day Ball and moved the group's biggest event to an April date not connected with the Battle of New Orleans.[3]

The events organized by the LHA remained rooted in historical education, but they began to focus on Jackson's life in general. The interpretive decision resulted from the organization having possession of property that clearly emphasized the man rather than the battle. As the Hermitage's educational programs developed, they endeavored to explore the complicated persona of Andrew Jackson and the nuances of the home and its other residents. Some programming explored Jackson's wife, Rachel, while other exhibits explored Jackson's time as president.[4]

During more modern times, the Hermitage's interpretation has responded to the field of social history by including exhibits the LHA would never have considered in 1915. Museum panels study Jackson's treatment of his slaves and their lives on his plantation. Other exhibits question Jackson's relationship with Native Americans and offer visitors the chance to form an opinion of the general.[5]

The evolution of the Hermitage's interpretative programming represented a critical factor in keeping the site educationally relevant, but it also affected the memory of the Battle of New Orleans. Once a central facet of the Ladies' narrative about the general, the Battle of New Orleans has become just another event in Jackson's life. Whereas in 1915 Nashville and New Orleans had led the nation in Battle of New Orleans commemoration, by 1965 the scale of the LHA's celebrations had diminished significantly. A wreath-laying ceremony at the Nashville and Washington, DC, Jackson equestrian monuments was all that the Ladies arranged.[6] For the bicentennial in 2015, the LHA unveiled a $1.1 million exhibit entitled "Andrew Jackson: Born for a Storm," which Hermitage CEO Howard Kittell described as "all about Jackson." Kittell continued, "We all love stories, and this is the story of Andrew Jackson. You can't make this stuff up. He was over the top." Describing the exhibit design, he commented, "It is very contemporary and very much in your face. It will change your perception of history, and help people better understand the man and how his indomitable spirit changed history."[7]

The LHA's increasing focus on Jackson the man meant that New Orleans stood alone as the last area in the country to commemorate the event in a way that focused on the battle itself. What had been a large-scale national celebration in 1825 had evolved into a regional commemoration by 1915 and a local event by 2015. While most Americans still learned of the battle through their high school textbooks, relatively small decisions in New Orleans came to have a disproportionate effect on the battle's memory and commemoration.

At Chalmette, the NPS looked for ways to increase public interest in the battle. As a federal agency, the NPS strove to include as many people as possible in its interpretive planning efforts. Although the park resided in the segregated

Deep South, park officials tried to generate public interest in the site from across the region's socioeconomic and racial spectrum. The other reason for the park's large target audience resulted from the uncertain future of the site. In the 1940s and 1950s, when the park struggled to attain a viable footprint of land, the park needed especially large amounts of popular support. Consequently, it behooved park officials to generate as much public awareness about the battlefield as they could.

The formation of the "Little Colonels," a volunteer group of teenage girls named after the mascot of the local high school, represented one of these early efforts. These young ladies developed brief interpretive programs about the Battle of New Orleans and took visitors on tours of the battlefield and the Malus-Beauregard House. While working at the park, the girls wore anachronistic antebellum gowns in an effort to "add a quaint charm" to the park.[8]

While well intentioned, the Little Colonels presented a number of challenges to a proper memory of the battle and to efforts at teaching the history of the event to the larger community. The antebellum outfits worn by the volunteers consisted of hoop skirts rather than Empire or Georgian-era dresses appropriate to the era of the battle. At first glance the historically inaccurate dresses might seem like a slight error, but politically and interpretively the dresses presented a serious issue.[9]

The hoop skirt long served as a shining symbol of the "moonlight and magnolias" myth of Southern history. Moreover, the distinctly Civil War–era feel of the organization did not encourage African American participation in the group, despite the fact that the club's charter specifically prohibited race-based admissions standards. In addition, the club's participation in events such as the Confederate Ball in Natchez, Mississippi, further alienated blacks from participating in interpretive efforts.[10]

Despite these shortcomings, the Little Colonels club logged more than three thousand volunteer hours during its first eighteen months of existence. The colorful nature of the girls' dresses and their group generated considerable attention in travelogues across the country and undoubtedly helped promote visitation to the site. By 1964, the club had sixty-four members (all white) and performed a combined 22,000 volunteer hours. One newspaper even reported that "these attractive southern belles" had become "a unique nationally known organization" within the NPS.[11]

Park officials also made efforts to include boys in their Battle of New Orleans interpretive programming. In January 1957, the park inaugurated the first of many annual "reenactments" of the battle featuring scout troops from the New Orleans area. The events quickly grew in size and elaborateness.[12]

At first, the Boy Scouts' costumes were limited to blue or red sweatshirts to represent either Americans or the British, but eventually parents developed more creative options. Within a few years, local scout troops competed with each other to field increasingly "authentic" costumes. Soon British Highlanders took the field wearing plaid schoolgirl skirts. Opposing them, behind the remnants of Jackson's original rampart, stood brave American regulars adorned in cardboard shakos and eye patch–wearing pirates manning homemade cannons. Firecrackers and bottle rockets simulated the thunderous reports of Jackson's artillery, and little boys threw themselves to the ground in the agony of fake death.[13]

While part of a creative effort that generated public attendance to the anniversary celebrations, the reenactments represented shallow efforts at interpretation. These endeavors promoted a fallacious, mythological understanding of the Battle of New Orleans which detracted from the greater job of the park site. Moreover, the Boy Scout reenactments, like the Little Colonels program, suffered from a whitewashing of history.

The park superintendent did try to encourage the participation of African American Boy Scout groups in the reenactments, even offering to assist in the formation of a local chapter for the Fazendeville community. In the 1950s and 1960s, though, few African Americans in the New Orleans area would risk allowing their children to partake in the reenactments. If a black scout group participated, white groups might refuse to join in, opening the chance for whites to blame the black children for the event being canceled that year. African Americans simply did not feel welcome at the Battle of New Orleans anniversaries, a situation that only grew worse after the NPS pressured the Fazendeville residents to sell their land.[14]

Ultimately, as the NPS's interpretive standards matured during the 1970s, the park abandoned the scout reenactments. The scale and scope of the scout reenactments at their height, though, had provided a major source of public reminiscence concerning the Battle of New Orleans. The event also drew large numbers to the battlefield and gave the public a chance to monitor the site's improvements over time. Once the scouting events stopped, the number of attendees for the park's January 8th event diminished significantly. This lack of public interest decreased the local community's sense of ownership in the site and hindered efforts to develop a substantive interpretive program at the park. Though many visitors still came to the park every year, their opportunities to learn the true history of the battle as opposed to the myths or counterfactual information they learned in their youth diminished.[15]

The lack of scholarly attention toward the Battle of New Orleans also hindered the public's understanding of the event. Numerous popular histories of the battle existed, but those works rarely challenged the accepted narrative of events or used new sources. This popular attention also discouraged scholars from pursuing the topic and adding their voice to a repetitive interpretation. Further, any attempt to seriously reexamine the battle would have to ultimately

question the existing understanding, and many Americans enjoyed the traditional history of the battle. The old interpretations had endured for so long that
few scholars felt the need to question them.[16]

Fortunately, during the sesquicentennial a number of young scholars and ama-
teur historians reinterpreted the event. Two of the most influential books to appear included Charles B. Brooks's *The Siege of New Orleans* and Wilbert S. Brown's
The Amphibious Campaign for West Florida and Louisiana. These works peeled
back the veneer of the battle's popular myth and suggested that something more
occurred than just dumb luck or American providential success. Brown's book
especially highlights the logic behind Jackson's disposition of forces and places
more importance on the employment of artillery than other writers.[17]

The NPS's interpretation during the mid-twentieth century failed to keep
pace with these scholarly developments. Institutionally, the NPS's administration of the site faced a number of challenges in this regard. Originally founded
as a nature conservation organization, the NPS attracted many fantastic rangers
with backgrounds in science, but these same rangers often had little training in
history. What interpreters with history degrees the NPS did attract often had
specialties or interest in the Civil War rather than the War of 1812. Only in cities
like New Orleans and Baltimore and regions like northern Ohio and western
New York did substantial interest arise in what historian Don Hickey later called
"The Forgotten Conflict." With few rangers who stayed up to date on the latest
scholarly developments concerning the Battle of New Orleans, interpretive efforts at the park suffered. The rangers who did take the initiative to improve the
park's educational programming had a number of options for where to conduct
that research by the 1960s. Earlier, though, Battle of New Orleans–related documents and artifacts had not been easy to come by for use in historical research.[18]

The popularity of the nineteenth-century event created a huge market for
Battle of New Orleans–related items in private hands. From paintings to snuff
boxes, from plays to sculpture, Americans thirsted for items related to the battle.
The highest-value items had been artifacts that played a part in the great event
or could be directly associated with individuals who participated in the engagement. Consequently, many of the relics related to the Battle of New Orleans
ended up in private hands and remained so for some time.[19]

The Louisiana Historical Society made considerable efforts to collect items
during the late nineteenth and early twentieth centuries. The owners of these
items, members of the society, collected them out of antiquarian interest and
gathered monthly to show their latest finds. With the centennial of the battle
approaching in 1915, the group discussed the idea of putting the most valuable
items on permanent public display. This collection became the foundation of
the Louisiana State Museum, and many of these items can still be seen today at
the Cabildo in Jackson Square.[20]

Aware of the funding difficulties that public institutions faced in collecting documents, native Louisianans Lewis Kemper Williams and his wife Leila Williams embarked on their own collection effort. The president of a lumber company in south central Louisiana, Kemper had access to considerable wealth. Starting in 1938, Kemper used that fortune to acquire documents related to New Orleans history in general and to the Battle of New Orleans specifically, for the express purpose of eventually making them available to the general public. In 1966, the Historic New Orleans Collection opened to the public, and it has continued its collecting efforts to this day.[21]

Even as research materials became more available and increasingly consolidated into centralized repositories, though, the NPS continued to struggle with its interpretation for Chalmette. The first interpretive feature the park wanted to complete was an automotive tour loop around the battlefield. Built two years before the passage of a federal law that required archeological work prior to construction, the tour loop breached the remains of Jackson's lines in two locations. Unfortunately for the memory of the battle, that lack of archeological effort caused the layout of the entire tour road to be wrong.[22]

For decades, students of the Battle of New Orleans believed that the Mississippi River had eroded a significant portion of the ramparts. Indeed, initial NPS estimates relied on the idea that the extreme right of Jackson's line rested as much as 150 yards into the Mississippi River in 1954. Accordingly, when the NPS built the tour road and the interpretive signs that went with it, the organization informed the public that a significant portion of the battlefield had succumbed to erosion.[23]

The lack of archeological work also affected how Americans continued to understand the construction of Jackson's rampart. For more than 150 years Americans believed that the American soldiers threw up crudely fashioned defensive works in front of their position along the Rodriguez Canal. Indeed, the NPS itself perpetuated this myth through a reconstruction of the rampart that it built.[24]

From 1955 to 1957, the NPS constructed a one-hundred-foot section of Line Jackson. By 1958, they had increased the interpretive feature to more than four hundred feet in length. In preparation for the 150th anniversary, some park supporters lobbied for the completion of the entire 1,200 feet available to the park. The NPS's efforts generated considerable attention in the world of wood preservation and historic construction, but, unfortunately, their structure had little historical basis. The interpretive effort depicted a flimsy mud rampart braced by thin vertical strips of wood. Though the park intended for a "rustic and factual" appearance, it only achieved the former. The rampart did not attain a height the primary sources almost universally discuss, nor would the construction, as depicted, have offered any substantive protection from artillery fire.[25]

The park claimed that the variety of source descriptions made an exact reconstruction difficult. Normally, the next step would be to use archeological evidence to aid in verifying the various sources' reliability. As a result of almost 150 years of historical memory, though, park officials fallaciously believed that Jackson's men had constructed the ramparts so crudely that archeological investigation would not turn up any new knowledge. Instead, they proceeded with a construction that fit their preconception about what the rampart must have resembled. Further, through the use of heavy equipment to build the reconstruction, they potentially endangered any archeological evidence that existed underground.[26]

The last, and most controversial, feature of the reconstructed rampart was the infamous cotton bale. The park spent $7,000 on replica cotton bales after considerable debate between park officials and local boosters. NPS officers felt that not enough definitive information existed to warrant the replication of the feature. Park boosters had considerable clout in Washington and, through petitions to both of Louisiana's senators, pushed for the cotton bales' installation.[27]

The use of cotton bales presented a number of issues. First, the cotton bale of popular imagination did not exist in the same form as in 1815. Rather than a neat block of cotton pressed firmly into burlap squares, early nineteenth-century cotton bales consisted of tube-like sacks. Numerous sources indicated that, while the Americans may have initially used the cotton bales, soldiers removed them by the time of the January 8th battle because they caught fire and hindered the soldiers' sight. The only use of cotton bales along Jackson's line by the final battle seems to have been in supporting the artillery pieces from sinking into the soft mud underfoot. The NPS's use of the cotton bales in the rampart's reconstruction only perpetuated a myth that, by the mid-twentieth century, serious historians already knew to be false. Fortunately for the memory of the Battle of New Orleans, in September 1965 Hurricane Betsy destroyed the reproduced cotton bales, and because of the expense, the park did not replace them. Even so, interpretive personnel continued to mention their use along Line Jackson.[28]

The problems associated with the reconstruction of Jackson's line were not the only issues to hinder accurate battlefield interpretation and, by extension, the battle's memory. The biggest concerns resulted from the lack of a purpose-built visitor's center. Whereas even Civil War battlefields of secondary rank such as Stones River National Battlefield obtained visitor's centers, at Chalmette the Malus-Beauregard House served that purpose. This made sense in 1965, when the park had recently assumed control over the entirety of the site, but later efforts to construct a purpose-built interpretive center dragged along for many years. Aside from budgetary reasons, NPS documents provide no clear indication of why efforts to construct a visitor's center at Chalmette lagged. For visitors who had been to other national park sites, the deficiency of a proper visitor's center gave the appearance that the Battle of New Orleans lacked importance. After all, how could they consider the Battle of New Orleans on par with Gettysburg and Saratoga when the federal government did not believe that the commemoration of Jackson's victory deserved the same facilities?[29]

For interpretation at Chalmette, the situation only got worse. This time the Baratarians and their bayou waterways worked against the memory of the Battle of New Orleans. In 1963, residents of that region began petitioning for the establishment of a nature preserve. Their solicitations to the federal government stemmed from forward-thinking attitudes toward wetland conservation. Even during the mid-1960s, residents noticed the erosion of the wetlands and the effect that overactive efforts at land reclamation had on the local environment. Unfortunately, nothing from an environmental standpoint made the Louisiana wetlands in Barataria unique compared to similar spots on the Gulf Coast.[30]

To help, the NPS suggested that the proposed park focus on the culture of the area rather than environmental preservation. By the 1970s, all NPS properties paid close attention to environmental impact and conservation. Consequently, a specific designation as an environmental park would be superfluous for what the residents desired. Rather, the NPS recommended establishing a park to explore the unique cultural milieu of southern Louisiana. The NPS would establish a series of sites across the area, each of which would tell the narrative of a specific ethnic group native to the region. However, having half a dozen or more small parks in such close proximity, each with its own administrative structure, would be organizationally inefficient. As such, an overarching Jean Laffite National Historical Park and Preserve would manage the various locations, including Chalmette. Not only did the Battle of New Orleans not rate a visitor's center, but it did not even rate its own park administration.[31]

By the early 1980s, residents of St. Bernard Parish clamored for the NPS to finally finish constructing a visitor's center. The parish had long hoped that the Battle of New Orleans would be a source of tourism and revenue. Rural locations around the country made millions of dollars annually off of battles and events far less important than Jackson's victory. Chalmette, only six miles from one of the nation's most popular travel destinations, should have had higher attendance than any of these locations. Some residents felt that the lack of NPS attention negatively affected the memory of the battle and consequently their bank accounts.[32]

In 1984, the NPS drew up a number of sketches for possible interpretive centers, but the organization could not decide on one. Eventually, local park officials pressed the issue enough to get a temporary visitor's center built until the park could develop plans for a more permanent structure. In 1986, Marogne Electric Company built the park's first museum. While the company did commendable work structurally, they had never built a museum before, and the facility lacked for educational quality. The *temporary* structure built in 1986 operated as the site's primary interpretive facility until Hurricane Katrina destroyed it in 2005. In twenty-one years, the park was unable to reach a decision on a purpose-built, professionally planned museum for Chalmette.[33]

The construction of the first visitor's center represented part of the reason the park had trouble proceeding with a permanent replacement. By the 1980s federal law mandated that before construction could begin, park officials had to conduct an archeological survey of the site on which the building would rest. While doing the excavations, they discovered a portion of the Rodriguez plantation house a considerable distance from where it should have been. To confirm this finding, archeologists also excavated a section of the rampart. Based on the location of what they believed to be the old plantation home, they expected to find battery 3. Sure enough, almost 150 yards from where people had for decades believed it to be, they unearthed the gun position from which the Baratarians had fought in 1815.[34]

On its face, the revelation might seem to lack significance. The Mississippi River had not eroded as much of the battlefield as many had believed, but the discovery also discouraged park officials from making any future facility construction plans and, consequently, improvements to museum interpretation. The archeological work raised more questions than it answered and highlighted the need for more physical investigation of the battlefield, something that the NPS had not previously done.[35]

Over the next twenty years, the NPS developed a number of plans for improving the Chalmette battlefield. Common themes among all of them were the need for an interpretive center worthy of the topic and calls for more archeological work on the site. Forensic investigation could answer many of the myths surrounding the Battle of New Orleans, but, as was the case regarding a professionally designed visitor's center, the site lacked the budget to fund these projects. Park funding went first to the Jean Laffite Park and then to the Chalmette unit. Physical improvements to the battlefield park simply did not rank that high on the list.[36]

After August of 2009, the NPS had no choice but to improve the old visitor's center. Hurricane Katrina had destroyed the aging facility, prompting the construction of a new one. While from a design standpoint the new visitor's center, completed in 2011, is a great improvement over its predecessor, the new facility perpetuates a number of myths, the most egregious of which is its discussion of cotton bales in the construction of Jackson's rampart. A diorama within the museum features a cross section of the rampart which indicates a base twenty feet thick and five feet tall made entirely of cotton bales, on which an additional fifteen-by-four-foot shield of cotton and mud rests. Archeological surveys conducted by the US Army Corps of Engineers in 2004 clearly indicate that this model is unrepresentative of Jackson's fortifications, and it is unclear why the museum designers chose to ignore a report done on behalf of the NPS.[37]

Other exhibits in the museum are far less troubling and provide excellent examples of the NPS's current interpretive philosophy for Chalmette. The panels around the visitor's center describe the Battle of New Orleans as one of unity in the face of adversity. The exhibits emphasize the multiracial, multiethnic background of Jackson's army as it confronted the British assault. They do not dwell on some overdramatized suggestion that the battle saved the United States, but they do put the visitor in the place of New Orleanians during 1815. Whatever historians may know almost two hundred years later about British intentions, Americans did not know it at the time. The panels explain that in the face of what they thought to be an impending disaster for New Orleans, Americans of various racial and ethnic backgrounds unified in the city's and the nation's defense.[38]

The exhibits also treat the British more gingerly than Andrew Jackson would have probably preferred. Filmmakers shot the video describing the final battle of January 8 almost entirely from the British perspective. A bell slowly tolls as the camera pans across a field of dead British soldiers and a voice actor reads Andrew Jackson's description of the battlefield after the guns fell silent. It does not glorify the victory, nor does it suggest that the battle lacked importance.

If the exhibit provides any sort of suggestion for the importance of the Battle of New Orleans, it places it squarely in the memory of the battle rather than its military effects. "The victory inspired a wave of patriotic nationalism," one panel proclaims. "Americans became more confident in their country's future," at the same time that "foreign governments began to view the United States as a legitimate power capable of defending its own territory." The exhibit concludes with the final statement that "the battle also established Jackson as the 'Hero of New Orleans' paving the way for him to become the seventh president of the United States." By 2013, for the NPS, the lasting impact of the battle had become the memory of the battle.

Interpretation of a historic site does not require purpose-built exhibits, and in the 1960s, many parks and museums began experimenting with living history programs. Indeed, Chalmette became one of the first national park sites in the country to do so, and evidence suggests that the program was quite popular. During the sesquicentennial, the *Times-Picayune* carried an intriguing story of reenactors firing a cannon off the Toulouse Street Warf just outside the French Quarter. When questioned about their activities, the reenactors described themselves as the "Garde Grenadiere d'Orleans." The sound of simulated gunfire had its desired effect and aroused public interest in their activities. The group talked to passersby about their uniforms, the role of the city's militia in the defense of New Orleans, and the artillery drill used by soldiers in Jackson's army 150 years earlier. When reporters of the local newspaper arrived to investigate the impromptu commemoration, the commander of the organization explained that they were not part of the official ceremonies, but "thought that New Orleanians need[ed] something more authentic and colorful. We think we're providing it—and it's free."[39]

Their point about their activities being free and unofficial reveals much. During the 150th anniversary, officials strove to downplay an event that smacked of martial triumphalism. The Sesquicentennial Committee's official report to Congress mentioned the activities of Garde Grenadiere d'Orleans. However, based on the reenactor's interview with the *Times-Picayune*, it appears that the committee only made the cannon firing official after the fact and because of its popularity.[40]

The growing trend of reenacting has also represented an important part of keeping the Battle of New Orleans alive. While groups like the Sons and Daughters of 1812 hold annual wreath-laying ceremonies and commemorative balls in New Orleans, those events are often closed to the general public or are very formal affairs. In contrast, since 1990, the Chalmette battlefield has witnessed great success with its annual living history weekend, featuring reenactors from around the United States and Canada. With multiple school districts in the New Orleans area busing in children and local residents, the event attracts thousands of extra visitors to the battlefield annually.[41]

Museums that rely on reenactors for extensive interpretation are limited to the demographics of the living history volunteers. Across the United States, most reenactors are white middle-aged men. While, interpretively, a middle-aged man playing the role of a soldier in the prime of his life possesses its own issues, for an event like the Battle of New Orleans, the lack of African American representation appeared more troubling. The park for years fought against the notion that it was a "white park" and tried to make inroads into the local African American community.[42]

When Geraldine Smith took over as superintendent in 1998, she wanted to rectify this fallacy. She used $55,000 in NPS funds to outfit Orleans Parish high school Junior ROTC cadets in period garb so that they could portray Lacoste's and Daquin's battalions of free men of color for the annual reenactment. The program won NPS awards for creativity and interpretive spirit. Since the program's founding, the park has also expanded it to include high school students from Choctaw reservations in Mississippi and Oklahoma. These students participate alongside other volunteers from around the country to educate the public about the Battle of New Orleans and keep its memory alive.[43]

As the bicentennial of the Battle of New Orleans approached, planning for how that commemoration should take place got under way. In 2010, the Louisiana state legislature created the Battle of New Orleans Bicentennial Committee.

It was a large and complex board authorized to consist of up to fifteen members appointed by a variety of political officials.[44] As of April 2013, the committee had only eleven of the fifteen possible committee members in place. The state of Louisiana had also failed to provide any funding for the group to conduct operations.[45]

This state of affairs began to worry some people. Watchdog groups feared that the various government entities would make their appointments on political grounds rather than professional reasoning. With the bicentennial expected to be a high-profile event, the committee would most likely invite the president of the United States and the prime minister of Great Britain to the ceremonies. The opportunity for committee members to "rub elbows" with such important figures made a position on the panel a tempting opportunity for those seeking political advancement. The failure to appoint adequate members knowledgeable of history and interpretive event planning could lead to a commemoration that was educationally questionable, as it did during the sesquicentennial.[46]

A number of individuals emerged as prominent figures in the planning for the bicentennial. Tim Pickles was a longtime volunteer at the Chalmette battlefield and part of the impetus behind the site's revival of a living history program in 1990. Because what would occur in 2015 was "still rather up in the air as to what the local communities are interested in supporting," Pickles struggled at first to convince living history volunteers from around the country to make travel plans for the event. He reported, "We have interest from international bodies including historical societies and the British Army but as yet it has not been possible to move forward with [them]." Pickles's proposals for the event ranged from single-day spectaculars to a "month-long series of recreations and historical events . . . including the naval Battle of Lake Borgne" and "a Grand Victory Ball in mid-January." Further, his "idea would be that the site for the recreated battles could remain as a permanent . . . Southern version of Colonial Williamsburg."[47]

The notion of the anniversary as a tourist attraction also had been on the mind of Bill Hyland, the St. Bernard Parish historian. "It is necessary to use this occasion to educate Louisiana and the rest of the United States about the significance of this piece of history," Hyland said; another goal was to guarantee that "the event be presented to ensure repeat cultural tourism." He also stated that "there are people all over the world interested in the efforts intended to take place, and it's difficult to get them excited about it when the commission has not met in over a year." Committee members were convinced that "without those travelers coming in to New Orleans, local business owners would lose out on a possible uptick [in] sales, and the local governments would forgo a sizable amount of sales tax revenue. A major event could provide a generous economic benefit to the city from all the myriad of tourists eager to see the commemoration."[48]

The aspirations of the St. Bernard Parish government, combined with the slow pace of federal planning, led to a partnership between local officials and the reenactment community associated with the battle. The Louisiana Living History Foundation (LLHF), a not-for-profit educational group, formed just prior to the bicentennial to facilitate planning between the local officials and reenactment community. In 2014 they acquired land less than two miles from the NPS site and began to make improvements to the location which would allow the LLHF to hold the largest Battle of New Orleans reenactment ever. For over a year, the group raised funds and solicited volunteers from across North America and Europe.

In terms of both participant reenactors and public attendance, the LLHF's events in 2015 were a resounding success. Roughly 19,000 visitors came to the LLHF site, paying an entry fee, and watched 1,500 reenactors portray various aspects of the New Orleans campaign.[49]

The NPS site recorded roughly 12,000 visitors to the actual Chalmette battlefield throughout the anniversary weekend. While they had fewer visitors than the LLHF's event, it was still more than double the ten-year average of 4,500 visitors. The NPS felt that their partnership with the LLHF was a "win-win situation" because "the more there is to do and see that's Battle of New Orleans–related, the more people will want to learn about it and the more people will want to see where it actually happened." Also, "the off-site reenactments allowed the park to experiment with different programs during the anniversary event too, including the hands-on and public-involving Battle of New Orleans University activities and programs." These programs involved lectures by academic historians and various hands-on displays that explored other, nonmilitary aspects of the British attack on the Louisiana Gulf Coast.[50]

Elsewhere in the New Orleans metropolitan area, numerous other events were held to commemorate the bicentennial. As in 1965, a local television station ran a low-budget documentary, the Historic New Orleans Collection and the Louisiana State Museum each held academic symposiums and lecture series that investigated the Battle of New Orleans and its legacy, and the Sons and Daughters of the War of 1812 each held commemorative ceremonies and dinners. However, unlike in 1965 or especially in 1915, unless someone was at one of these events, they would hardly have known that there had once been a national day of commemoration for the Battle of New Orleans. In a culture of round-the-clock social media updates, in a city that hosted more than 74,000 fans of the University of Alabama Crimson Tide and the Ohio State University Buckeyes for the Sugar Bowl on January 1, 2015, the commemorative events of January 8, 2015, just didn't stand out very much.[51]

Commemoration of the Battle of New Orleans faded considerably during the middle and late twentieth century. The inability to generate more public interest

in the battle stemmed from a number of factors. In Nashville, as the LHA updated its historic site's interpretative programming, it began to devote less space to
Jackson's victory. While the organization continued to hold the annual Jackson
Day Ball, the event evolved into a social gathering rather than a commemorative
effort. It became, in effect, a soiree that happened to be on January 8, rather than
an event held because of January 8. Eventually, the Ladies did away with the
Jackson Day Ball altogether.

In New Orleans, the place where one would expect the battle to receive the
most attention, interest in celebrating the battle also waned. When the NPS
established the Chalmette battlefield, many locals believed that the site would
generate the kinds of cultural tourism that made other battlefields around the
country such desirable destinations. Unfortunately for those boosters, the small
size of the park, as well as its eventual inclusion as a subunit of a larger park,
hindered the NPS's efforts. Lack of substantial interpretive facilities and a limited budget impeded the park's impact in the local community and its draw as
a tourist attraction. While many Americans make pilgrimages to the nation's
battlefields every year, the Chalmette site is rarely one of them. The job of the
NPS is to make informed decisions for its parks' maintenance based on need
and visitation. Because Chalmette did not generate high visitation, it did not
get more money. Since the site did not get enough money to enhance facilities,
it did not receive more visitors.

Further, local political boundaries also hinder development and coordination of events outside the federal park grounds. The Chalmette battlefield rests
within the borders of St. Bernard Parish, while most tourism occurs in Orleans
Parish, which includes the city of New Orleans. Similarly, commemoration of
the battle in the French Quarter often requires the coordination of the Louisiana
State Museum, the city of New Orleans, the Historic New Orleans Collection,
and the NPS. The bureaucracy involved in this coordination has traditionally
stalled efforts for large-scale events and encouraged the various institutions to
hold their own, smaller commemorations. These, in turn, attract fewer crowds
because they are less noteworthy.[52]

Traditionally, groups such as the Daughters of 1812 played an important role
in battle memorialization in the New Orleans area. Since the Daughters gave
up control of the battlefield, though, their commemorations, as well as similar events by the Sons of 1812, have consisted largely of social gatherings and
wreath-laying ceremonies. These events are sometimes closed to nonmembers
or are small affairs that do not generate public interest.[53]

The history of segregation in the New Orleans area also had a lasting affect
on commemoration efforts and the memory of the battle. The exclusion of
African Americans from the celebrations and the oftentimes-bigoted interpretation of African American participation during the battle diminished interest in

commemoration for that segment of the population. In the field of museum studies and public history, scholars pay considerable attention to the notion of "buy-in," the extent to which the community cares about its history and its cultural resources. Almost two hundred years of segregation has resulted in the African American community having almost no buy-in to the memory of the Battle of New Orleans.[54]

The NPS sought to rectify this by inviting African American high school students to participate in the anniversary celebrations through its living history program. With these invitations, along with the program's expansion to include Choctaw children, NPS officials feel that they are succeeding in efforts to bolster buy-in.[55]

The final factor that has decreased interest in the Battle of New Orleans in the late twentieth century is the question of just how important the battle had been. Even in the 1910s and 1930s the LHA disagreed with those who contended that the battle lacked meaning because it occurred after the signing of the peace treaty. The Ladies felt that that interpretation would diminish public interest in the event. Ultimately, they may have been right. Panels in the NPS's official museum exhibit close with the opinion that the memory of the battle came to be more important than the battle itself. That interpretation hardly generated significant interest in comparison with popular battles such as those at Gettysburg and Yorktown, battles that remained grander in the American public's imagination than the Battle of New Orleans does currently.

"What Is Past Is Prologue"

The memory of the Battle of New Orleans has always been affected by and a product of the generation of Americans retelling the event. Through an examination of these iterations, later generations can gain insights into the preceding cultures and societies that created each reimagining of the British invasion of southern Louisiana.

In the immediate aftermath of the battle, Republicans used the event as a way to distract the American public from the party's failings during the War of 1812. The United States struggled considerably during the war. Republican reliance on state militias, lack of a substantive financial system, and a poor national logistical structure all had hindered American success in the conflict. For many years, the Republican Party had championed each of these items in the face of their political opponents' criticisms. The War of 1812 highlighted the correctness of many Federalist Party policy goals.[1]

As the guns fell silent at New Orleans, Republicans had a victory that showcased many of their political ideals. Jackson's army, largely composed of militia, defeated a stronger and better-equipped force of professional soldiers. They did it in defense of hearth and home and against long odds. Further, the scale of the British defeat only fueled public interest and generated curiosity about discovering how the Americans had won the unlikely victory. Republicans across the United States informed the country that Jackson's army won precisely because of the political ideals that Republicans espoused.[2]

During the spring of 1815, the Federalist Party had to contend with the embarrassing situation of holding the Hartford Convention and considering secession only months before the peace agreement. Republicans used the Battle of New Orleans and the Hartford Convention to rally centralist voters into the Republican camp. This political firestorm hindered the effectiveness of the Federalist Party and doomed the organization's future. The lack of any tangible opposition to the Republican Party's narrative of the battle also allowed many of the myths surrounding the event to grow into fact.[3]

By the 1820s, the anniversary of the Battle of New Orleans became a national holiday celebrated on par with the Fourth of July and Washington's Birthday. Westerners especially took pride in the January anniversary because they had manned Jackson's ramparts in the greatest numbers. The legend of the battle also aided a shift toward the West in the United States' political center of gravity. The Republican Party's version of the battle and its corresponding political message highlighted the frontier farmer, a rugged individualistic man with a by-the-bootstraps mentality. That political message, meant to court and retain western voters, bolstered the political ascension of the victory's architect, Andrew Jackson.[4]

Jackson's boosters, masters of the new electoral campaigning, harnessed the preexisting popular culture surrounding the Battle of New Orleans to further their champion's run for the White House. Correspondingly, Jackson's opponents grew to detest the anniversary as commemorating the victory became too much like celebrating the man. The hagiography of Jackson created the first substantive weakening in the memory of the battle as the memorialization turned into a Democrat versus Whig issue.[5]

The 1840s and 1850s also witnessed the rise of a new sectional component to Battle of New Orleans commemoration. Political and cultural divisions between North and South over the issue of slavery began to dominate American society. Southerners refined the memory of the battle to exclude the North. Westerners in general did not stop the British forces in 1815, these sectional firebrands contended. Rather, residents of what became the states of Louisiana, Mississippi, Alabama, Arkansas, Tennessee, Kentucky, and Texas did. These soon-to-be secessionists asserted that the Battle of New Orleans highlighted the martial prowess of the South. Let the North invade with its better-equipped and larger armies. Southerners trounced the British in 1815, and they would also defeat the North should political debate turn to war.[6]

This politically motivated interpretation, like the Jacksonian Democrats's version before it, alienated many people who had vociferously commemorated January 8th and kept the memory of the battle alive. Opponents contended that celebration of the Battle of New Orleans only fueled secessionist propaganda, and some communities halted their January 8th celebrations altogether.[7]

The northern portion of the Democratic Party strove throughout this era to combat the Southern interpretation of the Battle of New Orleans with its own political message. Northern Democrats tried to use the battle as a way to showcase the strength of the United States. Jackson had fought to preserve the Union. If Southerners cared about the general and his greatest military victory, they should help keep the nation together.[8]

Those efforts changed after the Civil War. Northern Democrats again attempted to use the battle as a symbol of party unity and to bring their Southern counterparts back into the fold. Actions of individuals such as Union general Benjamin Butler during the war hindered the party's efforts at unity after the peace. During his time as commander of occupied New Orleans, Butler had ordered what Southerners took as the defacing of the city's most prominent memorial to the battle, the general's statue in Jackson Square. Thereafter, many prominent January 8th celebrations featured former Union army generals such as Butler, Philip Sheridan, and Joseph Hooker, discouraging Southern participation in the commemorations.

Eventually, Southerners again memorialized the Battle of New Orleans. The efforts of groups such as the Daughters of 1812 provided a forum for Southern male military celebrations that did not focus on the Lost Cause or the embarrassment of the Civil War. Southerners could again relish in their martial achievements. The same blood of the victors of the Battle of New Orleans flowed through the Civil War veterans' veins. Their ancestors had defeated one of the most powerful military forces in the world at that time. Surely, that triumph of Southern military prowess must be reason to celebrate.[9]

The white-dominated commemorative efforts in the Jim Crow era downplayed the role of African American Southerners in the battle. Commemoration during the first half of the twentieth century paid little attention to the fact that roughly 15 percent of the troops manning Jackson's line had been people of color. When interpretive efforts did mention African American participation, they did so as a presentation of blacks assisting in the maintenance of the status quo against outside intervention.[10]

While American culture downplayed African Americans' participation in the Battle of New Orleans during the early twentieth century, a different group of the battle's participants received a reappraisal and renaissance. Jean Laffite and his pirates became an integral part of the narrative of the Battle of New Orleans through American film and music. Those same mediums reignited interest in the battle and aided the memory of the event through public awareness concerning the original battlefield's plight.[11]

Preserving the Chalmette battlefield came with difficulties the nation's other prominent martial sites did not face. Many of these structures, such as Fort McHenry, stayed under War Department control well into the twentieth century. When the army did release its jurisdiction over these sites, preservationists had an easier time arguing against their demolition. To build over a historic structure required the action of its demolition. Building on a battlefield only required construction. The symbolism of those differences aided forts. Further, most battlefields targeted for preservation have existed away from major urban areas. Rather than a rural landscape, the Chalmette battlefield rested on valuable riverfront property that numerous commercial interests desired. In addition, a long-established minority community resided on the location. Keeping the battlefield safe for future generations required dealing with several urban planning issues the United States had just started developing modern policies for.[12]

Eventually the federal government assumed control of the site, and the NPS began handling the commemorative efforts. Previously, private groups of interested citizens around the country had formed committees and raised funds for the battle's celebratory events. With the NPS in charge, a single organization financed by the federal government directed the most elaborate memorializations of the battle. That singular control meant that the bureaucracy and dynamics of an individual organization thereafter played a much greater factor in affecting the memory of the Battle of New Orleans.

The latest iteration of the battle's narrative has focused on the diversity of the forces arrayed against the British in 1815. The NPS and numerous American history textbooks highlight the nonprofessional, multicultural, multiracial force that stood shoulder to shoulder against a common opponent. There is no way to tell whether this interpretation of the battle's memory will resonate with twenty-first-century generations, but if history is any indication, it will not be the final version of the story.[13]

For two hundred years, the memory of the Battle of New Orleans has inspired generations of Americans. Each of those generations conveniently chose a narrative of the battle which fit the political, social, and cultural needs of the group retelling the story. The decline in memorialization of the Battle of New Orleans over the past two centuries might give the impression that Americans have forgotten the event. This is not the cultural amnesia of a traumatic group experience or an embarrassing fact of the past often pointed to in cases of de-remembrance. Rather, the decline in Battle of New Orleans memorialization resembles a slow fading within the mind of American cultural memory of something that it has no need for anymore. In fact, though, the Battle of New Orleans is an event that only current American politics and culture do not feel a use for. Numerous times throughout the past two hundred years various groups have shaken the dust off of the memory of Jackson's victory and used it to their own ends. Jackson's victory is not as divisive a piece of American historical memory as the Civil War, slavery, or Vietnam. Rather, the memory of the Battle of New Orleans is sufficiently apolitical, yet well enough known, for Americans to continuously recycle and reshape the interpretation as needed. As almost two centuries of commemoration have shown, the memory of Andrew Jackson's victory is not forgotten, but merely awaiting its next reimagining in the public eye.

Preface · ***"A Correct Remembrance of Great Events"***

1. Isaac Hill, Nathan Buckman Felton, Joseph M. Harper, and James B. Thornton, *An address, delivered at Concord, N.H. January 8, 1828, being the thirteenth anniversary of Jackson's victory at New Orleans* (Concord, NH: Manahan, Hoag, 1828).

2. Hill et al., *An address.*

3. This book is by no means the first to embark on such an endeavor. Len Travers's *Celebrating the Fourth* and David Blight's *Race and Reunion* played fundamental roles in inspiring the methodology behind this work's investigative strategy. Like many other projects in the growing field of historical memory, Travers and Blight examine how a generation that experienced significant events in history shapes the narrative of their actions. These studies often, but not always, continue to explore how the succeeding generation reacts to earlier interpretation of events. Blight and Travers both insist that often children of the first generation try to live up to their understanding of the initial generation's presumptive ideals. Not only is the original narrative not questioned, but subsequent generations often embellish the story further. Len Travers, *Celebrating the Fourth: Independence Day and the Rites of Nationalism in the Early Republic* (Amherst: University of Massachusetts Press, 1997); David W. Blight, *Race and Reunion: The Civil War in American Memory* (Cambridge, MA: Belknap Press of Harvard University Press, 2001). Memory studies that explore how a society "forgets" have focused on dramatic events that the larger world community views as distasteful, such as massacres. Historians have paid far less attention to the memory of historical incidents that fade slowly or are overshadowed by subsequent events. Deborah E. Lipstadt, *Denying the Holocaust: The Growing Assault on Truth and Memory* (New York: Free Press, 1993); Susanne Buckley-Zistel, *Conflict Transformation and Social Change in Uganda: Remembering after Violence* (Basingstoke: Palgrave Macmillan, 2008); Marita Sturken, *Tangled Memories: The Vietnam War, the AIDS Epidemic, and the Politics of Remembering* (Berkeley: University of California Press, 1997).

4. Stereotypes concerning the nature of Jackson's rampart have existed for over 150 years and regularly focus on Jackson's ramparts as being extremely improvised in nature, especially as concerns the use of cotton bales. To this day, the insignia of the Seventh Infantry Regiment features a cotton bale because of the supposed use of cotton bales as protection during the unit's service at New Orleans; Regular Army Special Designation Listing, United States Army Center for Military History, www.history.army.mil/html/forcestruc/spdes-123 -ra_ar.html. For more on the supposed use of cotton bales and veterans' public assertions that it did not occur, see *Bennington Vermont Gazette*, Jan. 29, 1828; *New Orleans Daily Picayune*, May 29, 1845; *Little Rock Arkansas Whig*, Aug. 28, 1852; *New Orleans Daily Picayune*, Sept. 14, 1877; *New York Times*, Jan. 28, 1894. For real information on the rampart, see Howell Tatum,

Major Howell Tatum's Journal While Acting Topographical Engineer (1814) to General Jackson Commanding the Seventh Military District, ed. John Spencer Bassett (Northampton, MA: Department of History of Smith College, no. 19), 112; Ted Birkedal and John Coverdale, *The Search for the Lost Riverfront: Historical and Archeological Investigations at the Chalmette Battlefield, Jean Lafitte National Historical Park and Preserve* ([New Orleans, LA]: National Park Service, US Department of the Interior, 2005), 485–87, 924.

    5. Arsène Lacarrière Latour, *Historical Memoir of the War in West Florida and Louisiana in 1814–15: With an Atlas*, ed. Gene A. Smith, expanded ed. (Gainesville: University Press of Florida, 1999), 91–92, 104–5,108–9; Frank Lawrence Owsley Jr., *Struggle for the Gulf Borderlands: The Creek War and the Battle of New Orleans, 1812–1815* (Tuscaloosa: University of Alabama Press, 2000), 158–59. The British also felt that the American artillery deserved praise. One officer commented that "on no occasion did they [the Americans] assert their claim to the title of good artillery-men more effectually than on the present. Scarce a ball passed over or fell short of its mark, but all striking full into the midst of our ranks, occasioned terrible havoc." In G. R. Gleig, *The Campaigns of the British Army at Washington and New Orleans, 1814–1815* (1834; repr., San Francisco: Lulu Press, 2012), 281.

    6. Latour, *Historical Memoir of the War*, 295. In fact, Louisiana militia units defended posts on the Gentilly road, the Rigolets and Chef Menteur Passes that allowed access to Lake Pontchartrain and Bayou St. John, and downriver of the main British force on the east bank of the Mississippi. While these troops' effectiveness in a head-on conflict with the British is doubtful, they provided intelligence to Jackson, denied intelligence to the British forces, and limited the ability of the British to find alternate routes around Jackson's main position. For an in-depth study of the origins of the largely non-Anglophone Batalion d'Orleans and its artillerymen, see Jane Lucas De Grummond and Ronald R. Morazan, *The Baratarians and the Battle of New Orleans* (Baton Rouge, LA: Legacy, 1979).

    7. For some views on the role of militia, see Samuel Woodworth, *The Hunters of Kentucky; or, The Battle of New Orleans* (New York: Brown, [1818]); *Boston Patriot and Daily Chronicle*, Feb. 3, 1818.

    8. *New York National Advocate*, Jan. 11, 30, 1819; *City of Washington (DC) Gazette*, Jan. 25, 1819; *American Beacon and Norfolk and Portsmouth Daily Advertiser*, Jan. 20, 1819; *Baltimore Patriot and Mercantile Advertiser*, Jan. 11, 1819; *Springfield (MA) Hampden Patriot*, Jan. 28, 1819; *New York Columbian*, Jan. 11, 1819; *Hartford American Mercury*, Jan. 19, 1819; *Independent Chronicle and Boston Patriot*, Jan. 16, 1819; *Boston Patriot and Daily Chronicle*, Jan. 12, 1819; *New York Commercial Advertiser*, Feb. 8, 1819; *New York Spectator*, Feb. 9, 1819; *Wilmington (DE) American Watchman*, Feb. 13, 1819; *Newport (RI) Mercury*, Feb. 13, 1819; *Alexandria (VA) Gazette*, Feb. 18, 1819; *Camden (SC) Gazette*, Feb. 25, 1819.

    9. *Boston Patriot and Daily Chronicle*, Feb. 10, 1820; *Independent Chronicle and Boston Patriot*, Feb. 16, 1820; *Charlestown (MA) Franklin Monitor and Middlesex (CT) Republican*, Mar. 18, 1820; *Boston Patriot and Daily Chronicle*, Mar. 23, 1820; *Boston Essex Patriot*, Apr. 1, 1820; *Boston Agricultural Intelligencer*, Mar. 24, 1820; *Portland (ME) Eastern Argus*, Mar. 28, 1820; *Haverville (MA) Essex Patriot*, Apr. 1, 1820. For more on the Hartford Convention and its fallout, see David Hackett Fischer, *The Revolution of American Conservatism: The Federalist Party in the Era of Jeffersonian Democracy* (New York: Harper & Row, 1965), xix; Sean Wilentz, *The Rise of American Democracy: Jefferson to Lincoln* (abr. college ed.; New York: W. W. Norton, 2009), 81–82; George Dangerfield, *The Era of Good Feelings* (New York: Harcourt, Brace, 1952), 88, 98; Shaw Livermore Jr., *The Twilight of Federalism: The Disintegration of the Federalist Party,*

1815–1830 (Princeton, NJ: Princeton University Press, 1962), 61; Richard Buel Jr., *America on the Brink: How the Political Struggle over the War of 1812 Almost Destroyed the Young Republic* (New York: Palgrave Macmillan, 2006).

10. Lynn H. Parsons, *The Birth of Modern Politics: Andrew Jackson, John Quincy Adams, and the Election of 1828* (Oxford: Oxford University Press, 2009), 159–64; John William Ward, *Andrew Jackson: Symbol for an Age* (New York: Oxford University Press, 1955), 13–15. For more on the tactics and methods Jackson supporters came up with to get their message out to the voting public, see Andrew W. Robertson, *The Language of Democracy: Political Rhetoric in the United States and Britain* (Charlottesville: University of Virginia Press, 2005), 14, 36–37, 68–81.

11. *Portsmouth (NH) Journal of Literature and Politics*, Jan. 12, 1828; *Keene New Hampshire Sentinel*, Dec. 7, 1828.

12. *Richmond Enquirer*, Jan. 3, 1835; *Pittsfield (MA) Sun*, Jan. 8, 1835; *Concord New Hampshire Patriot and State Gazette*, Jan. 17, 1835.

13. For more on the Texas Revolution and its connections to the War of 1812 in general and the Battle of New Orleans specifically, see Stephen L. Hardin, *Texian Iliad: A Military History of the Texas Revolution, 1835–1836* (Austin: University of Texas Press, 1994); Edward L. Miller, *New Orleans and the Texas Revolution* (College Station: Texas A&M University Press, 2004); William C. Davis, *Lone Star Rising: The Revolutionary Birth of the Texas Republic* (New York: Free Press, 2004); H. W. Brands, *Lone Star Nation: How a Ragged Army of Volunteers Won the Battle for Texas Independence, and Changed America* (New York: Doubleday, 2004).

14. For early uses of the battle as an example of Southern and western states' military prowess, see *Norfolk American Beacon and Commercial Diary*, Dec. 13, 1816; *Baltimore Patriot*, Jan. 8, 1822; *Charlestown (MA) Franklin Monitor*, Mar. 18, 1820; *Boston Patriot and Daily Chronicle*, Feb. 3, 1818.

15. *Concord New Hampshire Patriot and Daily Gazette*, Mar. 7, 1850; *Pittsfield (MA) Sun*, Feb. 28, 1850; William M. Leftwich, *Anniversary Address Delivered by Rev. W. M. Leftwich, in the Capitol of Missouri, on the Eighth Day of January 1859; by Invitation of the General Assembly* (Jefferson City, MO: C. J. Corwin, 1859).

16. *Las Vegas Daily Gazette*, Jan. 9, 1883, Jan. 17, 1884; *Nashville Republican Banner*, Jan. 6, 1867, Jan. 10, 1868.

17. James Parton, *General Butler in New Orleans: Department of the Gulf in the Year 1862: With an Account of the Capture of New Orleans, and a Sketch of the Previous Career of the General, Civil and Military* (New York: Mason Brothers, 1864).

18. *Nashville Banner*, Jan. 8, 1915.

19. Wallace Evan Davies, *Patriotism on Parade: The Story of Veterans' and Hereditary Organizations in America, 1783–1900* (Cambridge, MA: Harvard University Press, 1955). For the Daughters of 1812 specifically, see Frank J. Douglas, Robert Bachman, George Lynn Woodruff, and LeRoy Habenight, *National Society of United States Daughters of 1812, 1892–1989: History* (Metairie, LA: National Society of United States Daughters of 1812, 1989). For more on the formation of the Daughters of the Confederacy and their impact on Southern culture and the Lost Cause, see Karen L. Cox, *Dixie's Daughters: The United Daughters of the Confederacy and the Preservation of Confederate Culture* (Gainesville: University Press of Florida, 2003); John A. Simpson, *Edith D. Pope and Her Nashville Friends: Guardians of the Lost Cause in the Confederate Veteran* (Knoxville: University of Tennessee Press, 2003). For more on battlefield preservation in this time period, see Edward Tabor Linenthal, *Sacred Ground: Americans and*

Their Battlefields (Urbana: University of Illinois Press, 1991); Timothy B. Smith, *The Golden Age of Battlefield Preservation: The Decade of the 1890s and the Establishment of America's First Five Military Parks* (Knoxville: University of Tennessee Press, 2008). For more on battlefield preservation, see Timothy B. Smith, *This Great Battlefield of Shiloh: History, Memory, and the Establishment of a Civil War National Military Park* (Knoxville: University of Tennessee Press, 2004); Timothy B. Smith, *A Chickamauga Memorial: The Establishment of America's First Civil War National Military Park* (Knoxville: University of Tennessee Press, 2009).

20. *Nashville Tennessean*, Apr. 12, 1914; Henry Watterson, *The Perry memorial and centennial celebration under the auspices of the national government and the states of Ohio, Pennsylvania, Michigan, Illinois, Wisconsin, New York, Rhode Island, Kentucky, Minnesota and Indiana* (Cleveland: Interstate Board of the Perry's Victory Centennial Commissioners, 1912); *The Battle of New Orleans, Official Programme* (New Orleans: Louisiana Historical Society, 1915).

21. Mary Devereux, *Lafitte of Louisiana* (Boston: Little, Brown, 1902); Alexander E. Powell, *Gentlemen Rovers* (New York: C. Scribner's Sons, 1913); James Joseph Alcée Fortier and Charles Gayarré, *The story of Jean and Pierre Lafitte, the pirate-patriots, including a note on the indispensable victory at New Orleans, January 8th, 1815; a publication of the Louisiana State Museum, James J. A. Fortier, editor; and a reprint of Historical sketch of Pierre and Jean Lafitte, the famous smugglers of Louisiana, 1809–1814, by Charles Gayarré, from the Magazine of American history, v.10, July–Dec., 1883, Historical publication co., New York, by courtesy of Howard Memorial Library* (New Orleans, [ca. 1880]).

22. *The Buccaneer*, directed by Cecil B. DeMille (Paramount Pictures, 1938); *The Buccaneer*, directed by Anthony Quinn (Paramount Pictures, 1958); Johnny Horton, "The Battle of New Orleans," *The Battle of New Orleans*, 1959 by Columbia Records, 45 rpm; Jimmy Driftwood, "The Battle of New Orleans," *Jimmie Driftwood Sings Newly Discovered Early American Folk Songs*, 1958 by RCA Records, Victor RPM; Lyle Saxon, *Lafitte the Pirate* (Gretna, LA: Pelican, 1989). As the twentieth century progressed, movies and music played an ever-larger role in the memory of historical events. Though music and theater always had a significant impact on the memory of events like the Battle of New Orleans, the commercialism of the twentieth century extended the leverage of these mechanisms to a scale without parallel. Peter Rollins's works *Why We Fought: America's Wars in Film and History* and *Hollywood as Historian: American Film in a Cultural Context* played an invaluable role in shaping how this author approached the sections dealing with Cecil B. DeMille's depiction of the New Orleans campaign. Peter C. Rollins and John E. O'Connor, *Why We Fought: America's Wars in Film and History* (Lexington: University Press of Kentucky, 2008); Peter C. Rollins, *Hollywood as Historian: American Film in a Cultural Context* (Lexington: University Press of Kentucky, 1983). On this topic, see also Lawrence H. Suid, *Guts and Glory: The Making of the American Military Image in Film* (Lexington: University Press of Kentucky, 2002); Gary R. Edgerton and Peter C. Rollins, *Television Histories: Shaping Collective Memory in the Media Age* (Lexington: University Press of Kentucky, 2001).

23. Robert W. Blythe, *Administrative History of Jean Lafitte National Historical Park and Preserve* (Atlanta: Cultural Resources Division, Southeast Regional Office, National Park Service, 2013).

24. Anthony J. Stanonis, *Creating the Big Easy: New Orleans and the Emergence of Modern Tourism, 1918–1945* (Athens: University of Georgia Press, 2006); Jonathan Mark Souther, *New Orleans on Parade: Tourism and the Transformation of the Crescent City* (Baton Rouge: Louisiana State University Press, 2006).

25. Ron Chapman, "Fazendeville," *Louisiana Life*, Winter 2004, www.myneworleans.com/ Louisiana-Life/Winter-2004/Fazendeville/; Allison H. Peña, "Fazendeville: Highlighting Invisible Pasts and Dignifying Present Identities," *Cultural Resources Management* 24, no. 5 (2001): 24–27; Joyce Marie Jackson, "Declaration of Taking Twice: The Fazendeville Community of the Lower Ninth Ward," *American Anthropologist* 108, no. 4 (Dec. 2006): 7665–80. For more on the interplay between commemoration and urban planning, see Richard Moe and Carter Wilkie, *Changing Places: Rebuilding Community in the Age of Sprawl* (New York: Henry Holt, 1997); Max Page and Randall Mason, eds., *Giving Preservation a History: Histories of Historic Preservation in the United States* (New York: Routledge, 2004). For more on the issues surrounding preservation efforts, see Robert E. Stipe, *A Richer Heritage: Historic Preservation in the Twenty-First Century* (Chapel Hill: University of North Carolina Press, 2003); Norman Tyler, *Historic Preservation: An Introduction to Its History, Principles, and Practice* (New York: W. W. Norton, 2000); William J. Murtagh, *Keeping Time: The History and Theory of Preservation in America* (Pittstown, NJ: Main Street Press, 1988).

26. *New Orleans Times-Picayune*, Apr. 7, 2008, Feb. 5, 2009, Jan. 7, 2013, Jan. 10, 2013, Feb. 7, 2013.

27. *New Orleans Times-Picayune*, Jan. 9, 2004, Jan. 16, 2013.

Chapter 1 · *"By the Eternal, They Shall Not Sleep on Our Soil"*

1. Frank Lawrence Owsley, *Struggle for the Gulf Borderlands: The Creek War and the Battle of New Orleans, 1812–1815* (Gainesville: University Press of Florida, 1981), 96–99. Owsley's work is perhaps the most balanced and well-researched account of the New Orleans campaign to date. It weaves the Battle of New Orleans into the broader narrative of conflict in the Old Southwest in the early nineteenth century, especially the influence of the Creek War on the British invasion.

2. For a true military history of the battle, there is no better work than Wilburt Scott Brown's book. A former Marine Corps general as well as a historian, Brown brings a unique perspective to the historiography of the British attack. Wilburt S. Brown, *The Amphibious Campaign for West Florida and Louisiana, 1814–1815: A Critical Review of Strategy and Tactics at New Orleans* (Tuscaloosa: University of Alabama Press, 1969).

3. Fort St. Philip anchored this defense. Twenty miles from the mouth of the river and sixty miles from New Orleans, this fort guarded a commanding bend in the Mississippi. Howell Tatum, *Major Howell Tatum's Journal While Acting Topographical Engineer (1814) to General Jackson, Commanding the Seventh Military District*, ed. John Spencer Bassett (Northampton, MA: Department of History of Smith College, 1922), 98–100; G. R. Gleig, *A Narrative of the Campaigns of the British Army at Washington and New Orleans, Under Generals Ross, Pakenham, and Lambert, in the Years 1814 and 1815: With Some Account of the Countries Visited* (London: J. Murray, 1821), 256–59.

4. Tatum, *Major Howell Tatum's Journal*, 100–101; Gleig, *Narrative of the Campaigns*, 259–60.

5. Arsène Lacarrière Latour, *Historical Memoir of the War in West Florida and Louisiana in 1814–15: With an Atlas*, ed. Gene A. Smith, expanded ed. (Gainesville: University Press of Florida, 1999), 21.

6. Latour, *Historical Memoir*, 33–41.

7. Latour, *Historical Memoir*, 42–45; Tatum, *Major Howell Tatum's Journal*, 72–83.

8. Latour, *Historical Memoir*, 46; Tatum, *Major Howell Tatum's Journal*, 85–89.

9. Latour, *Historical Memoir*, 48; Tatum, *Major Howell Tatum's Journal*, 89.

10. Latour, *Historical Memoir*, 48–49; Tatum, *Major Howell Tatum's Journal*, 96–102.

11. Latour, *Historical Memoir*, 47.

12. Tatum, *Major Howell Tatum's Journal*, 105–6.

13. Latour, *Historical Memoir*, 50–51; Gleig, *Narrative of the Campaigns*, 261–63. Gene Smith's biography of Jones provides an excellent overview of the Lieutenant's naval service in Louisiana and his role in the New Orleans campaign. Gene A. Smith, *Thomas ap Catesby Jones: Commodore of Manifest Destiny* (Annapolis, MD: Naval Institute Press, 2000).

14. Latour, *Historical Memoir*, 51–52, 262–64.

15. Latour, *Historical Memoir*, 53, 54; Tatum, *Major Howell Tatum's Journal*, 102.

16. Latour, *Historical Memoir*, 64–65; Tatum, *Major Howell Tatum's Journal*, 106; Gleig, *Narrative of the Campaigns*, 266–68.

17. Latour, *Historical Memoir*, 65–68; Gleig, *Narrative of the Campaigns*, 272–75.

18. Gleig, *Narrative of the Campaigns*, 276–80.

19. Latour, *Historical Memoir*, 68; Tatum, *Major Howell Tatum's Journal*, 107.

20. Latour, *Historical Memoir*, 68–69. The best history of this unit to date is Jane Lucas De Grummond and Ronald R. Morazan, *The Baratarians and the Battle of New Orleans with Biographical Sketches of the Veterans of the Battalion of Orleans, 1814–1815* (Baton Rouge, LA: Legacy, 1979).

21. Latour, *Historical Memoir*, 69.

22. Latour, *Historical Memoir*, 68; Tatum, *Major Howell Tatum's Journal*, 107.

23. Latour, *Historical Memoir*, 72, Tatum, *Major Howell Tatum's Journal*, 108–10; Gleig, *Narrative of the Campaigns*, 286.

24. Latour, *Historical Memoir*, 68, 74–75, 80–83; Gleig, *Narrative of the Campaigns*, 288–92.

25. Latour, *Historical Memoir*, 75; Tatum, *Major Howell Tatum's Journal*, 110–11; Gleig, *Narrative of the Campaigns*, 297–98.

26. Latour, *Historical Memoir*, 83–84; Tatum, *Major Howell Tatum's Journal*, 111; Gleig, *Narrative of the Campaigns*, 305–6.

27. Ted Birkedal and John Coverdale, *The Search for the Lost Riverfront: Historical and Archeological Investigations at the Chalmette Battlefield, Jean Lafitte National Historical Park and Preserve* ([New Orleans, LA]: National Park Service, US Department of the Interior, 2005), 481–87, 924; Tatum, *Major Howell Tatum's Journal*, 112. Even as early as December 28 Latour reported that the "lines . . . though not completed, were yet proof against musket-shot, and had already five pieces of cannon in battery." Latour, *Historical Memoir*, 88.

28. Latour, *Historical Memoir*, 90; Tatum, *Major Howell Tatum's Journal*, 115–17; Gleig, *Narrative of the Campaigns*, 308, 317.

29. Latour, *Historical Memoir*, 87–90; Tatum, *Major Howell Tatum's Journal*, 116; Gleig, *Narrative of the Campaigns*, 317–21.

30. Latour, *Historical Memoir*, 94–95; Tatum, *Major Howell Tatum's Journal*, 119–20; Gleig, *Narrative of the Campaigns*, 322–24.

31. Latour, *Historical Memoir*, 95–97; Tatum, *Major Howell Tatum's Journal*, 120–22; Gleig, *Narrative of the Campaigns*, 325–26.

32. Latour, *Historical Memoir*, 101–2. An excellent account of the Royal Navy's part in the land campaign is Robert Aitchison, *A British Eyewitness at the Battle of New Orleans: The Memoir of Royal Navy Admiral Robert Aitchison, 1808–1827*, ed. Gene A. Smith (New Orleans, LA: Historic New Orleans Collection, 2004).

33. Latour, *Historical Memoir*, 103.
34. Quotes from Tatum, *Major Howell Tatum's Journal*, 124–25. Artillery information from Latour, *Historical Memoir*, 104.
35. Latour, *Historical Memoir*, 104.
36. Gleig, *Narrative of the Campaigns*, 328–29.
37. Gleig, *Narrative of the Campaigns*, 329–32.
38. Tatum, *Major Howell Tatum's Journal*, 129; Gleig, *Narrative of the Campaigns*, 332–33.
39. Latour, *Historical Memoir*, 108–10; Tatum, *Major Howell Tatum's Journal*, 125; Gleig, *Narrative of the Campaigns*, 333.
40. Latour, *Historical Memoir*, 110; Tatum, *Major Howell Tatum's Journal*, 125; Gleig, *Narrative of the Campaigns*, 333–34.
41. Latour, *Historical Memoir*, 110; Tatum, *Major Howell Tatum's Journal*, 126; Gleig, *Narrative of the Campaigns*, 334.
42. Gleig, *Narrative of the Campaigns*, 334–35.
43. Latour, *Historical Memoir*, 109; Gleig, *Narrative of the Campaigns*, 335–36.
44. Latour, *Historical Memoir*, 118–19; Tatum, *Major Howell Tatum's Journal*, 127–29; Gleig, *Narrative of the Campaigns*, 338.
45. Latour, *Historical Memoir*, 111; Tatum, *Major Howell Tatum's Journal*, 131–32; Gleig, *Narrative of the Campaigns*, 336.
46. Latour, *Historical Memoir*, 122–23, 140–44; Tatum, *Major Howell Tatum's Journal*, 134–35; Gleig, *Narrative of the Campaigns*, 334–35, 349–50.
47. Tatum, *Major Howell Tatum's Journal*, 135–36.

Chapter 2 · *"Half a Horse and Half an Alligator"*

1. *New York National Advocate*, Oct. 8, 1817; quote from *Boston Weekly Messenger*, Oct. 16, 1817.
2. "A national point of view" from *Washington City (DC) Weekly Gazette*, Oct. 18, 1817; remaining quotes from *Albany Argus*, Nov. 18, 1817; *Troy (NY) Farmer's Register*, Nov. 9, 1817; *Boston Patriot and Independent Chronicle*, Nov. 19, 1817; *Norfolk American Beacon and Commercial Diary*, Nov. 20, 1817; *Boston Yankee*, Nov. 21, 1817; *Providence (RI) Patriot and Columbian Phoenix*, Nov. 22, 1817; *Brattleboro (VT) American Yeoman*, Nov. 25, 1817; *Petersburg (VA) American Star*, Nov. 27, 1817; *Stockbridge (MA) Berkshire Star*, Nov. 27, 1817; *Hallowell (ME) American Advocate and Kennebec Advertiser*, Nov. 29, 1817.
3. *Albany Argus*, Nov. 18, 1817. Samples of the snuffboxes can be found in the holdings of the Historic New Orleans Collection, New Orleans, LA.
4. Samuel Woodworth, *The Hunters of Kentucky; or, the Battle of New Orleans* (New York: Brown, [1818]); *New York National Advocate*, Nov. 30, 1818; *Providence (RI) Patriot*, Mar. 10, 1821; *Amherst (NH) Hillsboro Telegraph*, Feb. 9, 1822; *New York Mercantile Advertiser*, Aug. 23, 1919; *Baltimore Patriot and Evening Advertiser*, Dec. 30, 1816; *New York Columbian*, Jan. 8, 1820; *Easton (MD) Republican Star and General Advertiser*, Dec. 24, 1822; Robert V. Wells, *Life Flows On in Endless Songs: Folk Songs and American History* (Urbana: University of Illinois Press, 2009), 60; Simon P. Newman, *Parades and the Politics of the Street* (Philadelphia: University of Pennsylvania Press, 1997), 177–83.
5. For more on the importance some historians argue the battle had in American political culture, see David Hackett Fischer, *The Revolution of American Conservatism: The Federalist Party in the Era of Jeffersonian Democracy* (New York: Harper & Row, 1965), 181; George

Dangerfield, *The Awakening of American Nationalism, 1815–1828* (New York: Harper & Row, 1965), 1–4; George Dangerfield, *The Era of Good Feelings* (New York: Harcourt, Brace, 1952), 89–90; Shaw Livermore Jr., *The Twilight of Federalism: The Disintegration of the Federalist Party, 1815–1830* (Princeton, NJ: Princeton University Press, 1962), 264–65; Sean Wilentz, *The Rise of American Democracy: Jefferson to Lincoln* (abr. college ed.; New York: W. W. Norton, 2009), 87–89; David Waldstreicher, *In the Midst of Perpetual Fetes: The Making of American Nationalism, 1776–1820* (Chapel Hill: University of North Carolina Press, 1997), 290–91.

6. For a history of the communications revolution and the influence newspapers and popular culture had on the early American political process, see Jerry W. Knudson, *Jefferson and the Press: Crucible of Liberty* (Columbia: University of South Carolina Press, 2006); Jeffery L. Pasley, *The Tyranny of Printers: Newspaper Politics in the Early Republic* (Charlottesville: University Press of Virginia, 2001); Newman, *Parades and the Politics of the Street.*

7. C. E. Grice, *The Battle of New Orleans; or, Glory, Love, and Loyalty: An Historical and National Drama* (Baltimore: Commercial Press, 1815); John Blake White, *The Triumph of Liberty; or, Louisiana Preserved: A National Drama* (Charleston, SC: John Hoff, 1819); *New York Columbian*, Mar. 18, 20, 24, 27, 28, 1816; *Washington (DC) Daily Intelligencer*, Feb. 16, 21, 26, 1816; *New York Daily Advertiser*, Apr. 25, 1817; *Salem Gazette*, Oct. 3, 1817; Jeffrey H. Richards, *Drama, Theatre, and Identity in the American New Republic* (Cambridge: Cambridge University Press, 2005); Heather Nathans, *Early American Theater from the Revolution to Thomas Jefferson: Into the Hands of the People* (Cambridge: Cambridge University Press, 2003); Jason Shaffer, *Performing Patriotism: National Identity in the Colonial and Revolutionary American Theater* (Philadelphia: University of Pennsylvania Press, 2007).

8. *New York Columbian*, Feb. 19, 1816; *Bennington Vermont Gazette*, Oct. 22, 1816; *New York Weekly Museum*, Feb. 10, 1816; *Norfolk American Beacon and Commercial Diary*, Dec. 13, 1816; *Boston Patriot and Daily Chronicle*, Mar. 23, 1820; *Boston Essex Patriot*, Apr. 1, 1820; *Boston Agricultural Intelligencer*, Mar. 24, 1820; *Portland (ME) Eastern Argus*, Mar. 28, 1820; *Haverville (MA) Essex Patriot*, Apr. 1, 1820; *Salem Essex Register*, May 30, 1821; *New York Spectator*, May 6, 1821; *Baltimore Patriot*, May 7, 1821; *Richmond Enquirer*, May 18, 1821; *New Bern Carolina Centennial*, June 16, 1821; *Danville (VT) North Star*, June 19, 1821; *St Louis Enquirer*, July 28, 1821; *Nashville Gazette*, June 30, 1821; James Ross, *Victoria Neo-Aurelina: Pax Gandavensis*, trans. Michael Fortune (Philadelphia: Lydia R. Bailey, 1816); Leo M. Kaiser, *Early American Latin Verse, 1625–1825* (Wauconda, IL: Bolchazy-Carducci, 2005), 285.

9. *New York Spectator*, May 6, 1821; *Baltimore Patriot*, May 7, 1821; *Richmond Enquirer*, May 18, 1821; *Salem Essex Register*, May 30, 1821; *New Bern Carolina Centennial*, June 16, 1821; *Danville North Star*, June 19, 1821; *Nashville Gazette*, June 30, 1821; *St. Louis Enquirer*, July 28, 1821.

10. *Albany Argus*, Nov. 18, 1817; *Boston Independent Chronicle*, Nov. 19, 1817; *Norfolk American Beacon and Commercial Diary*, Nov. 20, 1817; *Boston Yankee*, Nov. 21, 1817; *Providence (RI) Patriot and Columbian Phoenix*, Nov. 22, 1817; *Brattleboro (VT) American Yeoman*, Nov. 25, 1817; *Petersburg (VA) American Star*, Nov. 27, 1817; *Stockbridge (MA) Berkshire Star*, Nov. 27, 1817; *Hallowell (ME) American Advocate and Kennebec Advertiser*, Nov. 29, 1817.

11. *New York National Advocate*, Jan. 11, 30, 1819; *City of Washington (DC) Gazette*, Jan. 25, 1819; *American Beacon and Norfolk and Portsmouth Daily Advertiser*, Jan. 20, 1819; *Baltimore Patriot and Mercantile Advertiser*, Jan. 11, 1819; *Springfield (MA) Hampden Patriot*, Jan. 28, 1819; *New York Columbian*, Jan. 11, 1819; *Hartford American Mercury*, Jan. 19, 1819; *Independent Chronicle and Boston Patriot*, Jan. 16, 1819; *Boston Patriot and Daily Chronicle*, Jan. 12, 1819;

New York Commercial Advertiser, Feb. 8, 1819; *New York Spectator*, Feb. 9, 1819; *Wilmington (DE) American Watchman*, Feb. 13, 1819; *Newport (RI) Mercury*, Feb. 13, 1819; *Alexandria (VA) Gazette*, Feb. 18, 1819; *Camden (SC) Gazette*, Feb. 25, 1819.

12. For more on commemorations of the Fourth of July and the American Revolution, see Waldstreicher, *In the Midst of Perpetual Fetes*; Len Travers, *Celebrating the Fourth: Independence Day and the Rites of Nationalism in the Early Republic* (Amherst: University of Massachusetts Press, 1997); Newman, *Parades and the Politics of the Street*, 84–86. For more on the nature of American Revolution battles, see Robert Middlekauf, *The Glorious Cause: The American Revolution, 1763–1789* (Oxford: Oxford University Press, 2005); Michael Stephenson, *Patriot Battles: How the War of Independence Was Fought* (New York: HarperCollins, 2007).

13. "Species of force" from an opinion article written by the Southern Patriot, *Boston Patriot and Daily Chronicle*, Feb. 3, 1818; Woodworth, *Hunters of Kentucky*.

14. *New York Columbian*, Jan. 1, 1818; *Boston Patriot and Daily Chronicle*, Jan. 12, 1818; *Baltimore Patriot and Mercantile Advertiser*, Jan. 14, 1818; *Norfolk American Beacon and Commercial Diary*, Jan. 20, 1818.

15. Joseph Dorris and Jesse Denson, *The Chronicles of Andrew: Containing an Accurate and Brief Account of General Jackson's Victories South, Over the Creeks, Also His Victories Over the British at Orleans with Biographical Sketches of His Life, &c.* (Milledgeville, GA: S&F Grantland, 1815); "half a horse" from Woodworth, *Hunters of Kentucky*.

16. Woodworth, *Hunters of Kentucky*; Dorris and Denson, *Chronicles of Andrew*; "of foreign" from *Norfolk American Beacon and Commercial Diary*, Dec. 13, 1816.

17. Grice, *Battle of New Orleans*.

18. Grice, *Battle of New Orleans*.

19. "Into the heart" from an opinion article written by the Southern Patriot, *Boston Patriot and Daily Chronicle*, Feb. 3, 1818; "the smiles of" from *An Oration Delivered at Mr. Days Hotel on Friday, 16th April 1819 on the Rise and Progress of New Orleans Since The Memorable Battle on the 8th of January, 1815: With Observations of Its Future Prospects* (New Orleans: John McPherson, 1819).

20. Steven Mintz and Susan Kellogg, *Domestic Revolutions: A Social History of American Family Life* (New York: Free Press, 1988), 53; for additional information on the role of women in early America, see also Rosemarie Zagarri, *Revolutionary Backlash: Women and Politics in the Early Republic* (Philadelphia: University of Pennsylvania Press, 2007).

21. William C. C. Claiborne, *Militia General Order*, New Orleans, Jan. 26, 1815; Resolutions of the Louisiana Legislature, in Arsène Lacarrière Latour, *Historical Memoir of the War in West Florida and Louisiana in 1814–1815*, ed. Gene A. Smith, expanded ed. (Gainesville: University Press of Florida, 1999), 296.

22. "The delicate fair" from Dorris and Denson, *Chronicles of Andrew*; Robert V. Remini, *The Battle of New Orleans: Andrew Jackson and America's First Military Victory* (New York: Viking, 1999), 187–88.

23. Grice, *Battle of New Orleans*.

24. Grice, *Battle of New Orleans*.

25. Laura S. Seitz and Elaine D. Baxter, *Before the Throne of Grace: An Evangelical Family in the Early Republic* (Franklin, TN: Providence House, 1999), 5; John R. Dichtl, *Frontiers of Faith: Bringing Catholicism to the West in the Early Republic* (Lexington: University Press of Kentucky, 2008), 1.

26. Nathan Torrey, *Verses on the Signal Victory Obtained over the British Troops at New*

Orleans, January 8th, 1815 by Gen. Andrew Jackson, and the Brave Troops Under his Command (Hindsdale, MA, Mar. 24, 1815).

27. Dorris and Denson, *Chronicles of Andrew*.

28. Claiborne, *Militia General Order*.

29. Gilbert J. Hunt, *The Late War Between the United States and Great Britain, From June 1812 to February 1815, Written in the Ancient Historical Style* (New York: David Longworth, 1816); *Bennington Vermont Gazette*, Oct. 22, 1816.

30. For more on the role of the artillery, see Latour, *Historical Memoir*, 91–92, 104–5, quote from 108–9; Frank Lawrence Owsley Jr., *Struggle for the Gulf Borderlands: The Creek War and the Battle of New Orleans, 1812–1815* (Tuscaloosa: University of Alabama Press, 2000), 158–59; G. R. Gleig, *The Campaigns of the British Army at Washington and New Orleans, 1814–1815* (1834; repr., San Francisco: Lulu Press, 2012), 28. See also Ted Birkedal and John Coverdale, *The Search for the Lost Riverfront: Historical and Archeological Investigations at the Chalmette Battlefield, Jean Lafitte National Historical Park and Preserve* ([New Orleans, LA]: National Park Service, US Department of the Interior, 2005), 462–63, 472, 485–87, 924; Howell Tatum, *Major Howell Tatum's Journal While Acting Topographical Engineer (1814) to General Jackson Commanding the Seventh Military District*, ed. John Spencer Bassett (Northampton, MA: Department of History of Smith College, 1922), 112.

31. For works on the Republican fascination with agrarian culture, see Douglas Hurt, *The Ohio Frontier: Crucible of the Old Northwest, 1720–1830* (Bloomington: Indiana University Press, 1996); Stephen Aron, *How the West Was Lost: The Transformation of Kentucky from Daniel Boone to Henry Clay* (Baltimore: Johns Hopkins University Press, 1996), Andrew R. L. Cayton, *The Frontier Republic: Ideology and Politics in the Ohio Country* (Kent, OH: Kent State University Press, 1986); Peter S. Onuf, *Statehood and Union: A History of the Northwest Ordinance* (Bloomington: Indiana University Press, 1987); Alan Taylor, *William Cooper's Town Power and Persuasion on the Frontier of the Early American Republic* (New York: Norton, 1995).

32. *Salem Essex Register*, Feb. 9, 1815; "Unparalleled Victory," broadside (Boston: Coverly, 1815). For books on the War of 1812 and the US military's less than successful campaigns, see Donald R. Hickey, *The War of 1812: A Forgotten Conflict* (Urbana: University of Illinois Press, 1989); Richard V. Barbuto, *Niagara 1814: America Invades Canada* (Lawrence: University Press of Kansas, 2000); David Curtis Skaggs and Gerard T. Altoff, *A Signal Victory: The Lake Erie Campaign, 1812–1813* (Annapolis, MD: Naval Institute Press, 1997); Alan Taylor, *The Civil War of 1812: American Citizens, British Subjects, Irish Rebels, and Indian Allies* (New York: Vintage, 2011); Charles G. Muller, *The Darkest Day: The Washington–Baltimore Campaign during the War of 1812* (Philadelphia: University of Pennsylvania Press, 2003); George C. Daughan, *1812: The Navy's War* (New York: Basic Books, 2011).

33. Woodworth, *Hunters of Kentucky*; *Boston Patriot and Daily Chronicle*, Feb. 3, 1818.

34. *Norfolk American Beacon and Commercial Diary*, Dec. 13. 1816; *Baltimore Patriot*, Jan. 8, 1822. The NPS interpretive panels at the Chalmette National Battlefield continue to promote the myth of the Kentucky rifleman to thousands of visitors every year.

35. Quote from *Salem Essex Register*, Feb. 9, 1815. For more on the debate concerning a standing army vs. a national militia, see Lawrence Delbert Cress, *Citizens in Arms: The Army and the Militia in American Society to the War of 1812* (Chapel Hill: University of North Carolina Press, 1982); J. C. A. Stagg, *Mr. Madison's War: Politics, Diplomacy, and Warfare in the Early American Republic, 1783–1830* (Princeton, NJ: Princeton University Press, 1983);

Marcus Cunliffe, *Soldiers and Civilians: The Martial Spirit in America, 1775–1865* (Boston: Little, Brown, 1968).

36. Quotes from *Philadelphia Franklin Gazette*, July 13, 1818. Reference to British soldiers reported in *St. Francisville (LA) Time Piece*, Jan. 17, 1815. For more on the Republican advocacy of militia service, see Mary Ellen Rowe, *Bulwark of the Republic: The American Militia in the Antebellum West* (Westport, CT: Praeger, 2003), 13; Harry S. Laver, *Citizens More Than Soldiers: The Kentucky Militia and Society in the Early Republic* (Lincoln: University of Nebraska Press, 2007); Theodore J. Crackel, *Mr. Jefferson's Army: Political and Social Reform of the Military Establishment, 1801–1809* (New York: New York University Press, 1989).

37. Woodworth, *Hunters of Kentucky*; *Norfolk Beacon and Commercial Diary*, Dec. 13, 1816; *Baltimore Patriot*, Jan. 8, 1822; *Boston Patriot and Daily Chronicle*, Mar. 23, 1820. For an examination of what actually occurred on January 8, 1815, see Latour, *Historical Memoir*; Wilburt S. Brown, *The Amphibious Campaign for West Florida and Louisiana, 1814–1815: A Critical Review of Strategy and Tactics at New Orleans* (Tuscaloosa: University of Alabama Press, 1969).

38. *Boston Patriot and Daily Chronicle*, Feb. 2, 1818. For Federalist attempts to encourage a professional national army, see Richard H. Kohn, *Eagle and Sword: The Federalists and the Creation of the American Military Establishment, 1783–1802* (New York: Free Press, 1975); William B. Skelton, *The American Profession of Arms, 1784–1861* (Lawrence: University Press of Kansas, 1992); Allan Peskin, *Winfield Scott and the Profession of Arms* (Kent, OH: Kent State University Press, 2003).

39. *Charlestown (MA) Franklin Monitor*, Mar. 18, 1820. For more on the demise of the Federalist Party, see Fischer, *Revolution of American Conservatism*; Livermore, *Twilight of Federalism*; Dangerfield, *Era of Good Feelings*.

40. *Boston Patriot and Daily Chronicle*, Feb. 10, 1820; *Independent Chronicle and Boston Patriot*, Feb. 16, 1820; *Charlestown (MA) Franklin Monitor and Middlesex (CT) Republican*, Mar. 18, 1820; *Boston Patriot and Daily Chronicle*, Mar. 23, 1820; *Boston Essex Patriot*, Apr. 1, 1820; *Boston Agricultural Intelligencer*, Mar. 24, 1820; *Portland (ME) Eastern Argus*, Mar. 28, 1820; *Haverville (MA) Essex Patriot*, Apr. 1, 1820. For more on the Hartford Convention and its fallout, see Fischer, *Revolution of American Conservatism*, xix; Wilentz, *Rise of American Democracy*, 81–82; Dangerfield, *Era of Good Feelings*, 88, 98; Livermore, *Twilight of Federalism*, 61; Richard Buel Jr., *America on the Brink: How the Political Struggle over the War of 1812 Almost Destroyed the Young Republic* (New York: Palgrave Macmillan, 2006).

41. For more on Monroe's goodwill tours, see Waldstreicher, *In the Midst of Perpetual Fetes*, 298–302; Livermore, *Twilight of Federalism*, 47–55; Dangerfield, *Era of Good Feelings*, 95–96; James Monroe, *The Papers of James Monroe: A Documentary History of the Presidential Tours of James Monroe, 1817, 1818, 1819*, vol. 1, ed. Daniel Preston (Westport, CT: Greenwood, 2003), vxi–xxvii.

42. For more on the 1820 presidential election, see Wilentz, *Rise of American Democracy*, 113; Livermore, *Twilight of Federalism*, 86–87; Dangerfield, *Era of Good Feelings*, 239–41; Dangerfield, *Awakening of American Nationalism*, 141.

43. For more on Jackson's rise to power, see Wilentz, *Rise of American Democracy*; Daniel Walker Howe, *What Hath God Wrought: The Transformation of America, 1815–1848* (Oxford: Oxford University Press, 2007); Robert V. Remini, *Andrew Jackson* (New York: Harper Perennial, 1999).

Chapter 3 · *"Under the Command of a Plain Republican— an American Cincinnatus"*

1. *Amherst (NH) Farmer's Cabinet*, Jan. 13, 1853; *Pittsfield (MA) Sun*, Jan. 13, 1853; *Barre (MA) Patriot*, Jan. 14, 1853; *Amherst (NH) Farmer's Cabinet*, Jan. 20, 1853; *Pittsfield (MA) Sun*, Jan. 20, 1853.

2. For an excellent survey of the period, see Daniel Walker Howe, *What Hath God Wrought: The Transformation of America, 1815–1848* (New York: Oxford University Press, 2007); pages 15–18 are particularly useful in highlighting the contested meaning of the battle.

3. For a summary of Jackson's early years, see Robert V. Remini, *Andrew Jackson and the Course of American Empire, 1767–1821* (New York: Harper & Row, 1977), 1–26. For more on Jackson's initial flirtations with the idea of running for president, see Harry Watson, *Liberty and Power: The Politics of Jacksonian America* (New York: Hill & Wang, 1990), 78–79. For the importance of personal politics and how the Battle of New Orleans helped Jackson appeal to the average American voter, see Lawrence Frederick Kohl, *The Politics of Individualism: Parties and the American Character in the Jacksonian Era* (New York: Oxford University Press, 1989), 33, 39–41. For the relationship between westerners, Jackson, and the future of the Democratic Party, see Homer C. Hockett, *Western Influences on Political Parties to 1825: An Essay in Historical Interpretation* (New York: Da Capo, 1970).

4. The 1824 presidential campaign was far from the first time that political movements had harnessed popular sentiment. As Simon P. Newman points out, "the ideology of impoverished and disenfranchised white men who were absorbed into the Jefferson polity pushed forward to Jacksonian democracy." Simon P. Newman, *Parades and the Politics of the Street: Festive Culture in the Early American Republic* (Philadelphia: University of Pennsylvania Press, 1997).

5. *Salem Essex Register*, Jan. 5, 1824; *Concord New Hampshire Patriot and State Gazette*, Jan. 12, 1824; *Richmond Enquirer*, Jan. 13, 1824; Remini, *Andrew Jackson and the Course of American Empire*, 62.

6. Quoted in M. J. Heale, *The Presidential Quest: Candidates and Images in American Political Culture, 1787–1852* (London: Longman, 1982), 55.

7. For varying interpretations on Jackson as a candidate and the meaning behind the popular support of Jackson, see Howe, *What Hath God Wrought*, 205; Robert V. Remini, *Andrew Jackson and the Course of American Freedom, 1822–1832* (New York: Harper & Row, 1981), 71–75; Charles Sellers, *The Market Revolution* (New York: Oxford University Press, 1991), 174–81.

8. Lynn H. Parsons, *The Birth of Modern Politics: Andrew Jackson, John Quincy Adams, and the Election of 1828* (Oxford: Oxford University Press, 2009), 159–64; John William Ward, *Andrew Jackson: Symbol for an Age* (New York: Oxford University Press, 1955), 13–15. For more on the tactics and methods Jackson supporters came up with to get their message out to the voting public, see Andrew W. Robertson, *The Language of Democracy: Political Rhetoric in the United States and Britain* (Charlottesville: University of Virginia Press, 2005), 14, 36–37, 68–81.

9. In an earlier incident than the one described below, Jackson had to face off against James Monroe himself. Monroe, secretary of war at the time of the battle, believed that he should deserve at least as much credit for the victory as Jackson since it had been Monroe's leadership on the strategic level that had allowed Jackson to succeed at the operational level. Donald B. Cole, *Andrew Jackson: The 1828 Election and the Rise of the Two-Party System* (Lawrence: University Press of Kansas, 2009), 77–81.

10. *Salem Gazette*, Aug. 11, 1826; *Hartford Connecticut Courant*, Aug. 14, 1826; *Cooperstown (NY) Watch-Tower*, Aug. 21, 1826.

11. *Richmond Enquirer*, Sept. 5, 1826.

12. All quotes from *Richmond Enquirer*, Sept. 5, 1826. For more reactions, see *Richmond Enquirer*, Sept. 8, 1826.

13. *Pittsfield (MA) Sun*, Oct. 15, 1826; *Baltimore Patriot and Mercantile Advertiser*, Dec. 2, 1826.

14. *Salem Gazette*, Jan. 4, 1825.

15. *Salem Gazette*, Aug. 3, 1827; *Salem Essex Register*, Aug. 6, 1827; *Portland (ME) Eastern Argus*, Aug. 10, 1827; *Portsmouth (NH) Journal of Literature and Politics*, Aug. 11, 1827; *Pittsfield (MA) Sun*, Aug. 10, 1827; *Cooperstown (NY) Watch-Tower*, Aug. 27, 1827.

16. As Adams and others began to realize that Jackson was a serious contender for the office of the president in 1828, their supporters laid the groundwork for opposition to the former general. January 8th became the natural date to refute their claims and assertions in a public forum meant to celebrate the heroes of New Orleans, Jackson among them. Abner Greenleaf, "Address Delivered at Jefferson-Hall, Portsmouth, N.H., Jan 8, 1828, Being the Thirteenth Anniversary of Jackson's Victory at New Orleans" (Portsmouth, NH, 1828).

17. For example, in 1828 Amos Kendall called on the citizens of Kentucky to form county nominating committees in preparation for a state convention to nominate Jackson as their party's candidate for president. The date he proposed for the convention was January 8. Donald B. Cole, *A Jackson Man: Amos Kendall and the Rise of American Democracy* (Baton Rouge: Louisiana State University Press, 2004).

18. *Keene New Hampshire Sentinel*, Nov. 7, 1827.

19. *Concord New Hampshire Patriot and State Gazette*, Nov. 26, 1827.

20. *Portsmouth (NH) Journal of Literature and Politics*, Jan. 12, 1828; *Keene New Hampshire Sentinel*, Dec. 7, 1828.

21. *Hartford Connecticut Courant*, Jan. 7, 1828. For more on the nature of the Democratic Party's operational methods, see Richard Hofstadter, *The Idea of a Party System: The Rise of Legitimate Opposition in the United States, 1780–1840* (Berkeley: University of California Press, 1969), 242–71; Richard Patrick McCormick, *The Second American Party System: Party Formation in the Jacksonian Era* (Chapel Hill: University of North Carolina Press, 1966), 216–18.

22. "Hearts glow" from *Concord New Hampshire Patriot and State Gazette*, Jan. 28, 1828; "the anniversary of the victory" from *Portsmouth New Hampshire Patriot*, Jan. 28, 1828; "friendly to the election" from *Pittsfield (MA) Sun*, Jan. 24, 1828. See also *Pittsfield (MA) Sun*, Jan. 17, 1828.

23. Isaac Hill, Nathan Buckman Felton, Joseph M. Harper, and James B. Thornton, *An address, delivered at Concord, N.H. January 8, 1828, being the thirteenth anniversary of Jackson's victory at New Orleans* (Concord, NH: Manahan, Hoag, 1828).

24. Hill et al., *An address*.

25. Francis V. Yvonnet, *An Oration Delivered at the Baptist Church in the City of Troy, on the Eighth Day of January, 1828, in Commemoration of the Victory Obtained at New-Orleans, on the Eighth of January, 1815, by Gen. Andrew Jackson, and the forces under his command* (Troy, NY: Francis Adancourt, 1828).

26. For an excellent examination of the intellectual differences between the regions of the country, see Daniel Walker Howe, *The Political Culture of the American Whigs* (Chicago: University of Chicago Press, 1979), 15–22; Yonatan Eyal, *The Young America Movement and*

the Transformation of the Democratic Party (Cambridge: Cambridge University Press, 2007), 18–19.

27. Charles Gordon Atherton, *An Oration, Delivered on the Fourteenth Anniversary of the Battle of New Orleans, at Goffstown, January 8, 1829* (Concord, NH: R. H. Sherburne, 1829).

28. John M. Sacher, *A Perfect War of Politics: Parties, Politicians, and Democracy in Louisiana, 1824–1861* (Baton Rouge: Louisiana State University Press, 2003), 15, 38; Parsons, *Birth of Modern Politics*, 147–50.

29. Sacher, *Perfect War of Politics*, 34–36; Heale, *Presidential Quest*, 72–73.

30. Sacher, *Perfect War of Politics*, 42, 60, 99.

31. *Middlesex (CT) Gazette*, Jan. 16, 1828.

32. Alexander H. Everett, *An Address Delivered at Salem on the Eighth of January, 1836, at the Request of the Democratic Young men of that Place, in Commemoration of the Victory of New Orleans* (Boston: Beals & Greene, 1836).

33. Sacher, *Perfect War of Politics*, 35; Cole, *Jackson Man*, 140–41; Donald B. Cole, *Vindicating Andrew Jackson: The 1828 Election and the Rise of the Two-Party System* (Lawrence: University Press of Kansas, 2000), 157–59; Amos Kendall, "General Jackson's Fine," *United States Magazine and Democratic Review*, Jan. 1843, 58–77; Robert V. Remini, *Andrew Jackson: The Course of American Democracy, 1833–1845* (Baltimore: Johns Hopkins University Press, 2013), 478–79. Jackson's allies, like Amos Kendall, made various efforts to combat the criticisms surrounding his behavior while the city was under martial law. Most notable was the argument that the women of New Orleans actually took up a collection to pay the fine for the general, and that Jackson, in his benevolence, asked that the money instead be donated to charity.

34. Another possible explanation for the ability of the press and popular culture to manipulate New England sentiment in the late 1830s more easily than in the late 1810s is the increased literacy rate in New England and the level of readership and number of publications. As Richard Brown points out, by the 1840s, New Englanders had such a diversity of information from which to choose that it was possible for them to select their sources and insulate themselves from ideas with which they were less enthralled. Richard D. Brown, *Knowledge Is Power: The Diffusion of Information in Early America, 1700–1865* (New York: Oxford University Press, 1989), 243–44.

35. Henry D. Gilpin, *A Speech Delivered at the Union and Harmony Celebration, by the Democratic Citizens of the City and County of Philadelphia, of the Twenty-first Anniversary of the Victory of New Orleans, January 8, 1836* (Boston: Beals & Greene, 1836).

36. *Richmond Enquirer*, Jan. 3, 1835; *Pittsfield (MA) Sun*, Jan. 8, 1835; *Concord New Hampshire Patriot and State Gazette*, Jan. 17, 1835. Jackson Day balls and dinners continued to be held annually on January 8 until the eve of World War II, when a shift began to hold the celebrations on Jackson's birthday rather than on the anniversary of the battle. *The Young Democratic Clubs of the District of Columbia Present the Jackson Day Dinner for the Benefit of the Democratic National Committee: To be Held at the Willard on Wednesday, January the Eighth, Nineteen Hundred and Thirty-six at Seven-thirty O'clock* (Washington, DC: National Capital Press, 1936).

37. Quote from *Jackson Banquet at Washington City, January 8, 1854* (Washington, DC: Jackson Democratic Association, 1854). See also *Proceedings at the Banquet of the Jackson Democratic Association, Washington, Eighth of January, 1852* (Washington, DC: Jackson Democratic Association, 1852); *Proceedings of the Democratic Celebration of the Anniversary of the Glorious Battle of New Orleans, by "the Personal and Political Friends" of George Mifflin Dallas . . . the*

oration . . . by Horn R. Kneas with an Appendix Containing Very Interesting Letters Written by Vice President Dallas in the year 1845 (Philadelphia: Office of *The Daily Keystone,* 1846).

38. *Portsmouth (NH) Journal of Literature and Politics,* May 17, 1834; *Keene New Hampshire Sentinel,* Feb. 4, 1836, Jan. 29, 1840.

39. *Proceedings at the Banquet of the Jackson Democratic Association.*

Chapter 4 · "The Union Must and Shall Be Preserved"

1. James M. Goode, *Four Salutes to the Nation: The Equestrian Statues of General Andrew Jackson* (Washington, DC: White House Historical Association, 2010), 14–15.

2. For more on the growing regional divisions in the United States, see Bruce C. Levine, *Half Slave and Half Free: The Roots of Civil War* (New York: Hill & Wang, 1992); Leonard L. Richards, *The Slave Power: The Free North and Southern Domination, 1780–1860* (Baton Rouge: Louisiana State University Press, 2000).

3. Studies of the Union fleet's capture of New Orleans include Chester G. Hearn, *The Capture of New Orleans, 1862* (Baton Rouge: Louisiana State University Press, 1995); Charles L. Dufour, *The Night the War Was Lost* (Lincoln: University of Nebraska Press, 1994).

4. For some early works on the rise of Southern militarism, see Avery Craven, *The Growth of Southern Nationalism, 1848–1861* (Baton Rouge: Louisiana State University Press, 1953); Charles S. Sydnor, *The Development of Southern Sectionalism, 1819–1848* (Baton Rouge: Louisiana State University Press, 1948); Richard H. Sewell, *A House Divided: Sectionalism and Civil War, 1848–1865* (Baltimore: Johns Hopkins University Press, 1988).

5. For the growing problems faced by the Democratic Party, see Wallace Hettle, *The Peculiar Democracy: Southern Democrats in Peace and Civil War* (Athens: University of Georgia Press, 2001); Susan-Mary Grant, *North over South: Northern Nationalism and American Identity in the Antebellum Era* (Lawrence: University Press of Kansas, 2000).

6. The Lost Cause has generated a substantial historiography. For some especially poignant works, see Gary W. Gallagher and Alan T. Nolan, *The Myth of the Lost Cause and Civil War History* (Bloomington: Indiana University Press, 2000); David W. Blight, *Beyond the Battlefield: Race, Memory, and the American Civil War* (Amherst: University of Massachusetts Press, 2002); W. Scott Poole, *Never Surrender: Confederate Memory and Conservatism in the South Carolina Upcountry* (Athens: University of Georgia Press, 2004); Anne E. Marshall, *Creating a Confederate Kentucky: The Lost Cause and Civil War Memory in a Border State* (Chapel Hill: University of North Carolina Press, 2010); W. Stuart Towns, *Enduring Legacy: Rhetoric and Ritual of the Lost Cause* (Tuscaloosa: University of Alabama Press, 2012); Alice Fahs and Joan Waugh, *The Memory of the Civil War in American Culture* (Chapel Hill: University of North Carolina Press, 2004).

7. For more on the rise of a Southern nationalism, see Drew Gilpin Faust, *The Creation of Confederate Nationalism: Ideology and Identity in the Civil War South* (Baton Rouge: Louisiana State University Press, 1988); Anne S. Rubin, *A Shattered Nation: The Rise and Fall of the Confederacy, 1861–1868* (Chapel Hill: University of North Carolina Press, 2005); Andre M. Fleche, *The Revolution of 1861: The American Civil War in the Age of Nationalist Conflict* (Chapel Hill: University of North Carolina Press, 2012); Emory M. Thomas, Lesley J. Gordon, and John C. Inscoe, *Inside the Confederate Nation: Essays in Honor of Emory M. Thomas* (Baton Rouge: Louisiana State University Press, 2005).

8. Of the many books about the Battle of New Orleans campaign, a few that particularly highlight the Southern nature of the conflict are Frank Lawrence Owsley, *Struggle for the Gulf*

Borderlands: The Creek War and the Battle of New Orleans, 1812–1815 (Gainesville: University Press of Florida, 1981); Arsène Lacarrière Latour, *Historical Memoir of the War in West Florida and Louisiana in 1814–15: With an Atlas,* ed. Gene A. Smith (Gainesville: University Press of Florida, 1999); Angela Pulley Hudson, *Creek Paths and Federal Roads: Indians, Settlers, and Slaves and the Making of the American South* (Chapel Hill: University of North Carolina Press, 2010).

9. For early uses of the battle as an example of Southern and western states' military prowess, see *Norfolk American Beacon and Commercial Diary,* Dec. 13. 1816; *Baltimore Patriot,* Jan. 8, 1822; *Charlestown (MA) Franklin Monitor,* Mar. 18, 1820; *Boston Patriot and Daily Chronicle,* Feb. 3, 1818. For more on the social implications of the growing militarism in the South, see Jennifer R. Green, *Military Education and the Emerging Middle Class in the Old South* (Cambridge: Cambridge University Press, 2011); Rod Andrew, *Long Gray Lines: The Southern Military School Tradition, 1839–1915* (Chapel Hill: University of North Carolina Press, 2001).

10. For more on the Texas Revolution and its connections to the War of 1812 in general and the Battle of New Orleans specifically, see Stephen L. Hardin, *Texian Iliad: A Military History of the Texas Revolution, 1835–1836* (Austin: University of Texas Press, 1994); Edward L. Miller, *New Orleans and the Texas Revolution* (College Station: Texas A&M University Press, 2004); William C. Davis, *Lone Star Rising: The Revolutionary Birth of the Texas Republic* (New York: Free Press, 2004); H. W. Brands, *Lone Star Nation: How a Ragged Army of Volunteers Won the Battle for Texas Independence, and Changed America* (New York: Doubleday, 2004).

11. Andrew Ewing, *An Oration Delivered on the Occasion of the Inauguration of the Bust Erected to the Memory of Gen. Andrew Jackson, in the City of Memphis, January 8, 1859* (Nashville: E. G. Eastman, 1859).

12. Alexander Hill Everett, *An Address Delivered at Salem on the Eighth of January, 1836, at the Request of the Democratic Young Men of That Place, in Commemoration of the Victory of New Orleans* (Boston: Beals & Greene, 1836).

13. *Concord New Hampshire Patriot and Daily Gazette,* Mar. 7, 1850; *Pittsfield (MA) Sun,* Feb. 28, 1850. For more on the Compromise of 1850, see David Morris Potter and Don E. Fehrenbacher, *The Impending Crisis, 1848–1861* (New York: Harper & Row, 1976); Mark Joseph Stegmaier, *Texas, New Mexico, and the Compromise of 1850: Boundary Dispute and Sectional Crisis* (Kent, OH: Kent State University Press, 1996).

14. William M. Leftwich, *Anniversary Address Delivered by Rev. W. M. Leftwich, in the Capitol of Missouri, on the Eighth Day of January 1859; by Invitation of the General Assembly* (Jefferson City, MO: C. J. Corwin, 1859).

15. Leftwich, *Anniversary Address.* Historians have written copious volumes of work on the secession movement, its origins, and its ideological underpinnings. For a representative sample, see James L. Abrahamson, *The Men of Secession and Civil War, 1859–1861* (Wilmington, DE: SR Books, 2000); Charles B. Dew, *Apostles of Disunion: Southern Secession Commissioners and the Causes of the Civil War* (Charlottesville: University Press of Virginia, 2001); Ralph A. Wooster, *The Secession Conventions of the South* (Princeton, NJ: Princeton University Press, 1962).

16. "Against corruptions" from *Pittsfield Sun* (MA), Jan. 1, 1857; "decorated for the occasion" from *Pittsfield Sun* (MA), Jan. 18, 1855. For more on Northern reaction to the sectional crisis, see Jean H. Baker, *Affairs of Party: The Political Culture of Northern Democrats in the Mid-Nineteenth Century* (Ithaca, NY: Cornell University Press, 1983). For more on Tammany Hall and its influence in Northern politics and the Democratic Party, see Sean Wilentz,

Chants Democratic: New York City and the Rise of the American Working Class, 1788–1850 (New York: Oxford University Press, 1984).

17. "Union-loving citizens" from *New York Herald*, Jan. 7, 1861; remaining quotes from *Milwaukee Daily Sentinel*, Jan. 9, 1861. For more on the Northern reaction to the beginning of the war, see Kenneth M. Stampp, *And the War Came: The North and the Secession Crisis, 1860–1861* (Baton Rouge: Louisiana State University Press, 1950.); Russell McClintock, *Lincoln and the Decision for War: The Northern Response to Secession* (Chapel Hill: University of North Carolina Press, 2008); Melinda Lawson, *Patriot Fires: Forging a New American Nationalism in the Civil War North* (Lawrence: University Press of Kansas, 2002).

18. For more on the Civil War experience of New Orleans, see Chester G. Hearn, *When the Devil Came Down to Dixie: Ben Butler in New Orleans* (Baton Rouge: Louisiana State University Press, 1997); Gerald Mortimer Capers, *Occupied City: New Orleans under the Federals, 1862–1865* (Lexington: University of Kentucky Press, 1965); Michael D. Pierson, *Mutiny at Fort Jackson: The Untold Story of the Fall of New Orleans* (Chapel Hill: University of North Carolina Press, 2008).

19. For more on the pre–Union army service of the regiment of free people of color, see James G. Hollandsworth, *The Louisiana Native Guards: The Black Military Experience during the Civil War* (Baton Rouge: Louisiana State University Press, 1995); Roland C. McConnell, *Negro Troops of Antebellum Louisiana: A History of the Battalion of Free Men of Color* (Baton Rouge: Louisiana State University Press, 1968).

20. For more on the service of the Louisiana regiment of free people of color in the Union army, see Nathan W. Daniels and C. P. Weaver, ed., *Thank God My Regiment an African One: The Civil War Diary of Colonel Nathan W. Daniels* (Baton Rouge: Louisiana State University Press, 1998).

21. For more on the history of the Place d'Armes, see Lawrence N. Powell, *The Accidental City: Improvising New Orleans* (Cambridge, MA: Harvard University Press, 2012); Leonard V. Huber, *Jackson Square through the Years* (New Orleans: Friends of the Cabildo, 1982).

22. *Amherst (NH) Farmer's Cabinet*, July 2, 1863.

23. *Amherst (NH) Farmer's Cabinet*, July 2, 1863. For more on the dispute over Jackson and martial law in New Orleans, see Robert V. Remini, *Andrew Jackson and the Course of American Empire, 1767–1821* (New York: Harper & Row, 1977), 309; Robert V. Remini, *Andrew Jackson and the Course of American Freedom, 1822–1832* (New York: Harper & Row, 1981), 14.

24. For more on Reconstruction and the South's relation to Northern Democrats, see Michael Perman, *Reunion without Compromise: The South and Reconstruction, 1865–1868* (Cambridge: Cambridge University Press, 1973); Eric Foner, *Reconstruction: America's Unfinished Revolution, 1863–1877* (New York: Harper & Row, 1988); Michael Perman, *The Road to Redemption: Southern Politics, 1869–1879* (Chapel Hill: University of North Carolina Press, 1984).

25. G. Volney Dorsey, *An Address on the Character and Services of Andrew Jackson: Delivered by Invitation, Before the General Assembly of Ohio, January 8, 1864* (Columbus, OH: Glenn, Thrall & Heide, 1864).

26. *Las Vegas Daily Gazette*, Jan. 9, 1883, Jan. 17, 1884; *Nashville Republican Banner*, Jan. 6, 1867, Jan. 10, 1868.

27. *San Antonio Express*, Jan. 11, 1868. For more on the reaction of Southerners to the war and their qualms about reconciliation, see Scott Reynolds Nelson and Carol Sheriff, *A People*

at War: Civilians and Soldiers in America's Civil War, 1854–1877 (New York: Oxford University Press, 2007); Nina Silber, *The Romance of Reunion: Northerners and the South, 1865–1900* (Chapel Hill: University of North Carolina Press, 1993).

28. For more on the immigration of slave owners into the Old Southwest, see Adam Rothman, *Slave Country: American Expansion and the Origins of the Deep South* (Cambridge, MA: Harvard University Press, 2005); Thomas Dionysius Clark and John D. W. Guice, *Frontiers in Conflict: The Old Southwest, 1795–1830* (Albuquerque: University of New Mexico Press, 1989).

29. For more on the preponderance of the Civil War in the memory of the South, see Edward L. Ayers, *The Promise of the New South: Life after Reconstruction* (New York: Oxford University Press, 1992), 27–28; Gaines M. Foster, *Ghosts of the Confederacy: Defeat, the Lost Cause, and the Emergence of the New South, 1865 to 1913* (New York: Oxford University Press, 1987); William Alan Blair, *Cities of the Dead: Contesting the Memory of the Civil War in the South, 1865–1914* (Chapel Hill: University of North Carolina Press, 2004); C. Vann Woodward, *Origins of the New South, 1877–1913* (Baton Rouge: Louisiana State University Press, 1951).

30. For more on the history of the monument, see Leonard Victor Huber, *The Battle of New Orleans and Its Monument* (New Orleans: Louisiana Landmarks Society, 1993); Jerome A. Greene, *Historic Resource Study, Chalmette Unit, Jean Lafitte National Historical Park and Preserve* (Denver: US Department of the Interior, National Park Service, 1985).

31. "The monument" from Elisha Stockwell, *Private Elisha Stockwell Sees the Civil War*, ed. Byron R. Abernathy (Norman: University of Oklahoma Press, 1958), 155; "covered with" from W. E. Pedrick, *New Orleans As It Is* (Cleveland: William W. Williams, 1885), 14–15.

32. *New Orleans Times-Democrat*, Aug. 23, 1890. For how the treatment of this monument differed from the growing collection of Civil War monuments and preserved battlefields around the United States, see Thomas J. Brown, *The Public Art of Civil War Commemoration: A Brief History with Documents* (Boston: Bedford / St. Martin's, 2004); Cynthia J. Mills and Pamela H. Simpson, *Monuments to the Lost Cause: Women, Art, and the Landscapes of Southern Memory* (Knoxville: University of Tennessee Press, 2003); Kirk Savage, *Standing Soldiers, Kneeling Slaves: Race, War, and Monument in Nineteenth-Century America* (Princeton, NJ: Princeton University Press, 1997); Timothy B. Smith, *The Golden Age of Battlefield Preservation: The Decade of the 1890s and the Establishment of America's First Five Military Parks* (Knoxville: University of Tennessee Press, 2008).

Chapter 5 · *"True Daughters of the War"*

1. "True daughters" from *New Orleans Times-Picayune*, Jan. 9 1915; "to the memory of" located on the plaque affixed on the observation deck of the Chalmette Monument.

2. For more on the formation of the UDC and their impact on Southern culture and the Lost Cause, see Karen L. Cox, *Dixie's Daughters: The United Daughters of the Confederacy and the Preservation of Confederate Culture* (Gainesville: University Press of Florida, 2003); John A. Simpson, *Edith D. Pope and Her Nashville Friends: Guardians of the Lost Cause in the Confederate Veteran* (Knoxville: University of Tennessee Press, 2003).

3. For excellent works on the history of women's patriotic organizations in general, see Wallace Evan Davies, *Patriotism on Parade: The Story of Veterans' and Hereditary Organizations in America, 1783–1900* (Cambridge, MA: Harvard University Press, 1955). For the Daughters of 1812 specifically, see Frank J. Douglas, Robert Bachman, George Lynn Woodruff, and LeRoy Habenight, *National Society of United States Daughters of 1812, 1892–1989: History* (Metairie, LA: National Society of United States Daughters of 1812, 1989). For the influence in the

South of groups like the Daughters of the Republic of Texas, see Gregg Cantrell, "The Bones of Stephen F. Austin: History and Memory in Progressive-Era Texas," *Southwestern Historical Quarterly* 108, no. 2 (Oct. 2004): 145–78.

4. Louisiana Act No. 8 (Jan. 17, 1894); An Act Providing for the Completion by the Secretary of War of a Monument to the Memory of the American Soldiers who fell in the Battle of New Orleans at Chalmette, Louisiana, and Making the Necessary Appropriation Thereof, 59th Cong., 2nd sess. (Mar. 4, 1907).

5. For more on the trouble concerning administering historic homes, see Sherry Butcher-Younghans, *Historic House Museums: A Practical Handbook for Their Care, Preservation, and Management* (New York: Oxford University Press, 1993); Patricia West, *Domesticating History: The Political Origins of America's House Museums* (Washington, DC: Smithsonian Institution Press, 1999).

6. Charles H. Browning, *The American Historical Register and Monthly Gazette of the Patriotic-Hereditary Societies of the United States of America*, vol. 3 (Philadelphia: Historical Register, Sept. 1895–Feb. 1896), 400, 507.

7. F. Arnemann to United States Daughters, 1776 to 1812, Dec. 6, 1909, United States Daughters of 1812, Chalmette Chapter, Papers, Tulane University Special Collections; House Report No. 81 to accompany House Resolution 2232, An Act in Reference to a National Military Park on the Plains of Chalmette (Nov. 19, 1921).

8. From 1880 to 1915, prominent statues to memorialize the Confederacy appeared all over New Orleans at considerable expense. Famed American sculptor Alexander Doyle produced five of the most famous statues: Washington Artillery Cenotaph (1880), Robert E. Lee Monument (1884), "Calling the Roll" (1886), General Albert Sydney Johnston Equestrian Statue (1887), and General P. G. T. Beauregard Equestrian Statue (1915). Considering the time it took to get Andrew Jackson's statue placed in Jackson Square and to get the Chalmette Monument completed, the Civil War clearly dominated Southern minds and philanthropic donations in this period. For more on the role of statuary in memory and memorialization, see Kirk Savage, *Standing Soldiers, Kneeling Slaves: Race, War, and Monument in Nineteenth-Century America* (Princeton, NJ: Princeton University Press, 1997).

9. Aline Gray Roberts, ed., *Celebrating One Hundred Years of the TN State Society United States Daughters of 1812* (n.p.: s.n., 2009).

10. Mary C. Dorris, *Preservation of the Hermitage 1889–1915—Annals, History, and Stories —the Acquisition, Restoration, and Care of the Home of General Andrew Jackson by the Ladies Hermitage Association for Over a Quarter of a Century* (Nashville, 1915).

11. Dorris, *Preservation of the Hermitage*.

12. Tom Kanon, "Forging the 'Hero of New Orleans': Tennessee Looks at the Centennial of the War of 1812," *Tennessee Historical Quarterly* 71, no. 2 (Summer 2012): 139–40. Kanon's article is an indispensible examination of Tennessee's attitudes toward both the Creek War and the War of 1812 one hundred years later.

13. Quoted in Kanon, "Forging the 'Hero of New Orleans,'" 137.

14. *Nashville Tennessean*, June 21, 1914; *Nashville Banner*, Jan. 9, 1915; *Nashville Tennessean*, July 22, 1914.

15. Ladies Hermitage Association Board of Directors Meeting Minutes, Jan. 1906–Sept. 1914, Collections at the Hermitage (Nashville, TN), 129.

16. Reau E. Folk, *Battle of New Orleans, Its Real Meaning: Exposure of Untruth Being Taught Young America Concerning the Second Most Important Military Event in the Life of the Republic* (Nashville: Ladies Hermitage Association, 1935).

17. *Nashville Tennessean,* Jan. 21, 1917.

18. *Nashville Tennessean,* Apr. 12, 1914. For more on the Ohio monument to the Battle of Lake Erie, see Henry Watterson, *The Perry memorial and centennial celebration under the auspices of the national government and the states of Ohio, Pennsylvania, Michigan, Illinois, Wisconsin, New York, Rhode Island, Kentucky, Minnesota and Indiana* (Cleveland: Interstate Board of the Perry's Victory Centennial Commissioners, 1912).

19. *Nashville Tennessean,* Nov. 29, 1914.

20. *Nashville Tennessean,* Mar. 28, 1912.

21. LHA Meeting Minutes, 141.

22. *Nashville Banner,* Jan. 8, 1915.

23. *Nashville Banner,* Jan. 9, 1915.

24. *Nashville Banner,* Jan. 9, 1915; *Nashville Tennessean,* Jan. 12, 1915.

25. "The Celebration of Jackson Day, January 8, 1915," *Tennessee Historical Magazine* 1 (Mar. 1915). For more on the Battle of Franklin, see James L. McDonough and Thomas Lawrence Connelly, *Five Tragic Hours: The Battle of Franklin* (Knoxville: University of Tennessee Press, 1983). There is also the irony that, during the Battle of New Orleans, Thomas Hart Benton was vehemently anti-Jackson and had shot the general just a year before the British attacked the Gulf Coast. Jackson still carried Benton's bullet in him throughout the New Orleans campaign; however, he did return it to Benton twenty years later, after they became friends again.

26. Quoted in Kanon, "Forging the 'Hero of New Orleans,'" 149.

27. *Nashville American,* Jan. 3, 1915.

28. *Nashville Tennessean,* Dec. 21, 1914; *Nashville Tennessean,* Dec. 27, 1914.

29. *The Battle of New Orleans, Official Programme* (New Orleans: Louisiana Historical Society, 1915), 8.

30. *Official Programme,* 8–9.

31. *Official Programme,* 10.

32. *Official Programme,* 10–11.

33. *Official Programme,* 11–13; *New Orleans Times-Picayune,* Jan. 11, 1913.

34. *Official Programme,* 13–16.

35. *New Orleans Times-Picayune,* Oct. 12, 1914; *New Orleans Times-Picayune,* Oct. 22, 1914; Battle of New Orleans Scrapbook, 1815–1940, Louisiana Historical Center, Louisiana State Museum.

36. *New Orleans Times-Picayune,* Jan. 8–11, 1915.

37. *New Orleans Times-Picayune,* Jan. 9, 1915.

38. *New Orleans Times-Picayune,* Jan. 10, 1915.

39. Robert W. Blythe, *Administrative History of Jean Laffite National Historical Park and Preserve* (Atlanta: Cultural Resources Division, Southeast Regional Office, National Park Service, 2013), 28–29.

40. Report no. 194 to accompany House Resolution 6151; Secretary Hurley quoted in Blythe, *Administrative History of Jean Laffite,* 30.

Chapter 6 · *"Not Pirate . . . Privateer"*

1. Wilson's War Message to Congress, Brigham Young University Library World War I Document Archive, http://wwi.lib.byu.edu/index.php/Wilson's_War_Message_to_Congress.

2. For more on the US entry into World War I, see David M. Kennedy, *Over Here:*

The First World War and American Society (New York: Oxford University Press, 1980); Justus D. Doenecke, *Nothing Less Than War: A New History of America's Entry into World War I* (Lexington: University Press of Kentucky, 2011); Edward M. Coffman, *The War to End All Wars: The American Military Experience in World War I* (New York: Oxford University Press, 1968).

3. For more on American international relations with and shift in public attitude toward Great Britain in the twentieth century, see John E. Moser, *Twisting the Lion's Tail: American Anglophobia between the World Wars* (New York: New York University Press, 1999); Ritchie Ovendale, *Anglo-American Relations in the Twentieth Century* (New York: St. Martin's, 1998); Richard Wevill, *Britain and America after World War II: Bilateral Relations and the Beginnings of the Cold War* (London: I. B. Tauris, 2012).

4. This overt American confidence came to its fullest fruition in American consumer success both domestically and around the globe. The full implications for the consumer impact on memory of the Battle of New Orleans are explored in the next chapter, but one of the most important books to explore the topic is Lizabeth Cohen, *A Consumers' Republic: The Politics of Mass Consumption in Postwar America* (New York: Knopf, 2003). For a different take on the United States' culture of confidence, see Tom Engelhardt, *The End of Victory Culture: Cold War America and the Disillusioning of a Generation* (Amherst: University of Massachusetts Press, 1998).

5. By as late as January 5, 1941, newspapers reported that the Democratic National Committee had failed to set a date for the dinner; *Dallas Morning News*, Jan. 5, 1941. Officially, the reason for delaying the fund-raiser, held on the same date for over 150 years, was "to give the Democrats more time to recover from the recent [presidential] campaign"; *Dallas Morning News*, Nov. 26, 1940. Given that Roosevelt won the election by 449 electoral votes to 82, one questions how taxed the Democratic National Committee really was.

6. For early works that centered on Laffite and the Baratarians, see *Lives, Exploits, and Cruelties of the Most Celebrated Pirates and Sea Robbers: Brought Down to the Latest Period* (London: Milner, 1820); J. H. Ingraham, *Lafitte: The Pirate of the Gulf* (New York: Harper & Brothers, 1836); Prentiss Ingraham, *Lafitte's Legacy; or, The Avenging Son: A Romance of the Gulf* (New York: Beadle & Adams, 1888).

7. For more early examples of Laffite's treatment in American popular culture, see Mary Devereux, *Lafitte of Louisiana* (Boston: Little, Brown, 1902); Alexander E. Powell, *Gentlemen Rovers* (New York: C. Scribner's Sons, 1913). For more on American accusations of British depredations and alliances with unseemly characters, see Joseph Dorris and Jesse Denson, *The Chronicles of Andrew: Containing an Accurate and Brief Account of General Jackson's Victories South, Over the Creeks, Also His Victories Over the British at Orleans with Biographical Sketches of His Life, &c.* (Milledgeville, GA: S&F Grantland, 1815); *Norfolk American Beacon and Commercial Diary*, Dec. 13, 1816.

8. There have been numerous treatments on Laffite and his men, but many are less than reputable popular histories. For scholarly treatments of the Baratarians, see William C. Davis, *The Pirates Laffite: The Treacherous World of the Corsairs of the Gulf* (Orlando, FL: Harcourt, 2005); Robert C. Vogel and Kathleen F. Taylor, *Jean Lafitte in American History: A Bibliographic Guide* (St. Paul, MN: White Pine, 1998); Jane Lucas De Grummond and Ronald R. Morazan, *The Baratarians and the Battle of New Orleans* (Baton Rouge, LA: Legacy, 1979).

9. A reader looking for the definitive scholarly examination of exactly what Laffite and his men were guilty of and their historical treatment should see Robert C. Vogel, "Jean Laf-

fite, the Baratarians, and the Battle of New Orleans: A Reappraisal," *Louisiana History: The Journal of the Louisiana Historical Association* 41, no. 3 (Summer 2000): 261–76.

10. For examples of nineteenth-century romantic treatments of Laffite, see Louisiana State Museum, James Joseph Alcée Fortier, and Charles Gayarré, *The story of Jean and Pierre Lafitte, the pirate-patriots, including a note on the indispensable victory at New Orleans, January 8th, 1815; a publication of the Louisiana State Museum, James J. A. Fortier, editor; and a reprint of Historical sketch of Pierre and Jean Lafitte, the famous smugglers of Louisiana, 1809–1814, by Charles Gayarré, from the Magazine of American history, v.10, July–Dec., 1883, Historical publication co., New York, by courtesy of Howard Memorial Library* (New Orleans, [ca. 1880]); Richard Penn Smith, *Lafitte; or, The Barratarian Chief: An American Tale* (Hamilton, NY: Williams, Orton, 1830).

11. Baroness Orczy, *The Scarlet Pimpernel* (New York: Signet, 2000); Johnston McCulley, *The Curse of Capistrano* (New York: Grosset & Dunlap, 1927); *Don Q, Son of Zorro*, directed by Donald Crisp (Elton Corporation, 1925); *The Elusive Pimpernel*, directed by Maurice Elvey (Stoll Picture Productions, 1919); *The Laughing Cavalier*, directed by A. V. Bramble and Eliot Stannard (Dreadnaught, 1917); *The Mask of Zorro*, directed by Fred Niblo (Douglas Fairbanks Pictures, 1920); *Return of the Scarlet Pimpernel*, directed by Hanns Schwarz (London Film Productions, 1937); *The Scarlet Pimpernel*, directed by Richard Stanton (Fox Film Corporation, 1917); *The Scarlet Pimpernel*, directed by Harold Young (London Film Productions, 1934); *The Triumph of the Scarlet Pimpernel*, directed by T. Hayes Hunter (Cricklewood Studios, 1928).

12. For more on Prohibition and its effects on American attitudes toward criminality, see Daniel Okrent, *Last Call: The Rise and Fall of Prohibition* (New York: Scribner, 2010); Kathleen Morgan Drowne, *Spirits of Defiance: National Prohibition and Jazz Age Literature, 1920–1933* (Columbus: Ohio State University Press, 2005); Norman H. Clark, *Deliver Us from Evil: An Interpretation of American Prohibition* (New York: Norton, 1976).

13. For more on Lyle Saxon, see James W. Thomas, *Lyle Saxon: A Critical Biography* (Birmingham, AL: Summa, 1991); Chance Harvey, ed., *The Life and Selected Letters of Lyle Saxon* (Gretna, LA: Pelican, 2003).

14. Lyle Saxon, *Lafitte the Pirate* (Gretna, LA: Pelican, 1989).

15. *The Buccaneer*, directed by Cecil B. DeMille (Paramount Pictures, 1938); *Dallas Morning News*, Feb. 6, 1928; *New York Times*, Feb. 17, 1938; *New York Times*, Mar. 20, 1938.

16. *Buccaneer* (1938).

17. *Buccaneer* (1938).

18. *Buccaneer* (1938).

19. Scott Eyman, *Empire of Dreams: The Epic Life of Cecil B. DeMille* (New York: Simon & Schuster, 2010); Robert S. Birchard, *Cecil B. DeMille's Hollywood* (Lexington: University Press of Kentucky, 2004); Cecil B. DeMille, *Autobiography* (Englewood Cliffs, NJ: Prentice-Hall, 1959).

20. *The Buccaneer*, directed by Anthony Quinn (Paramount Pictures, 1958).

21. *Buccaneer* (1958).

22. Tim Weiner, *Legacy of Ashes: The History of the CIA* (New York: Doubleday, 2007), 36. DeMille was one of many Hollywood celebrities to take an interest in communism, and the connection between culturally influential Americans and communism was the subject of the notorious McCarthy hearings only years before the release of the remade *Buccaneer*. Richard M. Fried, *Nightmare in Red: The McCarthy Era in Perspective* (New York: Oxford

University Press, 1990); Robert Griffith, *The Politics of Fear: Joseph R. McCarthy and the Senate* (Lexington: Published for the Organization of American Historians [by] University Press of Kentucky, 1970); Thomas Patrick Doherty, *Cold War, Cool Medium: Television, McCarthyism, and American Culture* (New York: Columbia University Press, 2003).

23. *Buccaneer* (1958); Michelangelo Capua, *Yul Brynner: A Biography* (Jefferson, NC: McFarland, 2006); Jhan Robbins, *Yul Brynner: The Inscrutable King* (New York: Dodd, Mead, 1987).

24. *Buccaneer* (1958).

25. *Buccaneer* (1958).

26. *Buccaneer* (1938); *Buccaneer* (1958).

27. *Buccaneer* (1938); *Buccaneer* (1958).

28. Johnny Horton, "The Battle of New Orleans," *The Battle of New Orleans*, 1959 by Columbia Records, 45 rpm. For information on the record's success, see "Billboard Hot 100 50th Anniversary—the Billboard Hot 100 All-Time Top Songs," www.billboard.com/specials/hot100/index.shtml; "Billboard Hot 100 50th Anniversary—Top Billboard Hot 100 Country Songs," www.billboard.com/bbcom/specials/hot100/charts/top-country.shtml.

29. Numerous artists have covered the song over the years, including Johnny Cash (1972), Nitty Gritty Dirt Band (1974), and Dolly Parton (1976). One of the most recent covers was done in 2010 by a British indie rock group of Indian descent known as Cornershop.

30. Richard Kent Streeter, *The Jimmy Driftwood Primer: A Biography* (Calhoun, GA: J. Driftwood Legacy Project, 2003); Ann Davenport, "The Original Music of Jimmy Driftwood: Songs 1964–1979" (PhD diss., Johns Hopkins University, 1983).

31. Robert Cochran, "Remembering Jimmy Driftwood," *Arkansas Historical Quarterly* 57, no. 4 (Winter 1998): 435–38.

32. Jimmy Driftwood, "The Battle of New Orleans," *Jimmie Driftwood Sings Newly Discovered Early American Folk Songs*, 1958 by RCA Records, Victor RPM.

33. For nineteenth-century works that relied on tearing the British down to help build up the Americans, see *Norfolk American Beacon and Commercial Daily*, Dec. 13, 1815; James Ross, *Victoria Neo-Aurelina: Pax Gandavensis*, trans. Michael Fortune (Philadelphia: Lydia R. Bailey, 1816).

34. There was a great deal of interest in reinterpreting America's past in the context of its Cold War present. For a few works on the topic, see Richard M. Fried, *The Russians Are Coming! The Russians Are Coming! Pageantry and Patriotism in Cold-War America* (New York: Oxford University Press, 1998); John E. Bodnar, *Remaking America: Public Memory, Commemoration, and Patriotism in the Twentieth Century* (Princeton, NJ: Princeton University Press, 1991).

35. For more on the promotion of American ideas and patriotism in the 1940s and 1950s, see Laura A. Belmonte, *Selling the American Way: U.S. Propaganda and the Cold War* (Philadelphia: University of Pennsylvania Press, 2008); George H. Roeder, *The Censored War: American Visual Experience during World War Two* (New Haven, CT: Yale University Press, 1993); Kenneth Alan Osgood, *Total Cold War: Eisenhower's Secret Propaganda Battle at Home and Abroad* (Lawrence: University Press of Kansas, 2006).

36. Some excellent books that explore how the Cold War affected the struggle for enhanced civil rights in the United States include Mary L. Dudziak, *Cold War Civil Rights: Race and the Image of American Democracy* (Princeton, NJ: Princeton University Press, 2000); Thomas Borstelmann, *The Cold War and the Color Line: American Race Relations in the Global Arena* (Cambridge, MA: Harvard University Press, 2001).

Chapter 7 · *"Tourism Whetted by the Celebration"*

1. Anthony J. Stanonis, *Creating the Big Easy: New Orleans and the Emergence of Modern Tourism, 1918–1945* (Athens: University of Georgia Press, 2006), 96.

2. Radio conversation between Cecil B. DeMille and Lyle Saxon, Jan. 10, 1938, Lyle Saxon Papers, Tulane University.

3. There has been considerable work done on the topic of New Orleans and tourism's effects on the city. See Stanonis, *Creating the Big Easy*; Jonathan Mark Souther, *New Orleans on Parade: Tourism and the Transformation of the Crescent City* (Baton Rouge: Louisiana State University Press, 2006); Kevin Fox Gotham, *Authentic New Orleans: Tourism, Culture, and Race in the Big Easy* (New York: New York University Press, 2007).

4. Fort McHenry, like Chalmette, is an urban park site situated on valuable waterfront property. Unlike Chalmette, the fort had the benefit of being under the control of the US Army from the start. The army continued to use the grounds surrounding the fort well into World War II, even after the government transferred the property to the NPS in 1925. Harold I. Lessem and George C. Mackenzie, *Fort McHenry National Monument and Historic Shrine, Maryland* (Washington, DC: National Park Service, 1954). Historians have begun to pay a great deal of attention to how battlefield parks develop and what that means for the culture at the time. For representative works, see Timothy B. Smith, *The Golden Age of Battlefield Preservation: The Decade of the 1890s and the Establishment of America's First Five Military Parks* (Knoxville: University of Tennessee Press, 2008); Joan M. Zenzen, *Battling for Manassas: The Fifty-Year Preservation Struggle at Manassas National Battlefield Park* (University Park: Pennsylvania State University Press, 1998); Timothy B. Smith, *A Chickamauga Memorial: The Establishment of America's First Civil War National Military Park* (Knoxville: University of Tennessee Press, 2009).

5. An Act to Authorize the Secretary of War to Assume the Care, Custody, and Control of the Monument to the Memory of the Soldiers who Fell in the Battle of New Orleans, at Chalmette Louisiana, and to Maintain the Monument and Grounds Surrounding it, 71st Cong., 2nd sess. (June 2, 1930); Report no. 194 to Accompany House Resolution 6151.

6. Robert W. Blythe, *Administrative History of Jean Laffite National Historical Park and Preserve* (Atlanta: Cultural Resources Division, Southeast Regional Office, National Park Service, 2013), 29–31. Blythe's work is the best single reference for those trying to understand how the Chalmette park came to be and the intricacies of NPS operations.

7. An Act to Provide for the Study, Investigation and Survey for Commemorative Purposes, of the Battle Field of Chalmette, Louisiana (Feb. 5, 1931); Senate Document no. 27, 72nd Cong., 1st sess. (Dec. 11, 1931).

8. New Orleans Association of Commerce to Interested Organizations and Individuals, June 22, 1931, Jean Laffite National Park vertical files, Tulane University Special Collection; Stanonis, *Creating the Big Easy*, 96–97.

9. Blythe, *Administrative History of Jean Laffite*, 40.

10. *Variety Magazine*, Dec. 9, 22, 1937.

11. *Variety Magazine*, Jan. 4, 8, 1938.

12. Louisiana Act 163, 1938; An Act to Provide for the Establishment of the Chalmette National Historical Park in the State of Louisiana, and for Other Purposes (Aug. 10, 1931); Blythe, *Administrative History of Jean Laffite*, 31.

13. *New Orleans Item*, Dec. 8, 1939.

14. J. Walter Coleman, Superintendent, Vicksburg National Military Park to Director,

National Park Service, Oct. 21, 1939, Jean Laffite National Park and Preserve Archives, Special Collections, Earl K. Long Library, University of New Orleans; Blythe, *Administrative History of Jean Laffite*, 41–42.

15. Works Progress Administration photographs, Jean Laffite National Park and Preserve Archives, Special Collections, Earl K. Long Library, University of New Orleans.

16. National Park Service Plan for Chalmette Comfort Station, Jean Laffite National Park and Preserve Archives, Special Collections, Earl K. Long Library, University of New Orleans; Blythe, *Administrative History of Jean Laffite*, 43.

17. Edwin S. Bres, *Notes on the Establishment and the Development of the Chalmette National Historical Park* (1964), Sesquicentennial of the Battle of New Orleans Collection, Williams Research Center, Historic New Orleans Collection.

18. An Act to Authorize the State Parks Commission of Louisiana to Purchase Additional Lands, Situated in St. Bernard Parish, July 15, 1946; *Chalmette National Historical Park* (Washington, DC: Government Printing Office, 1944).

19. National Park Service Acceptance of Conveyance, June 20, 1950, Jean Laffite National Park and Preserve Archives, Special Collections, Earl K. Long Library, University of New Orleans.

20. *St. Bernard Voice*, Feb. 17, 1951.

21. Quoted in Blythe, *Administrative History of Jean Laffite*, 50.

22. *St. Bernard Voice*, Apr. 11, 1952.

23. *New Orleans States*, Aug. 25, 1953.

24. Martha Robinson to General Edwin S. Bres, Mar. 18, 1955, Records of the Battle of New Orleans Sesquicentennial Celebration Commission, Williams Research Center, Historic New Orleans Collection.

25. *New Orleans Times*, July 12, 1957.

26. *Variety Magazine*, Dec. 17, 1958.

27. *Reading (PA) Eagle*, Dec. 16, 1958; *Daytona Beach (FL) Morning Journal*, Dec. 17, 1958.

28. *New Orleans Times-Picayune*, Apr. 17, 1959.

29. *New Orleans Times-Picayune*, Apr. 17, 1959.

30. Joint Resolution to Establish the Sesquicentennial Commission for the Celebration of the Battle of New Orleans, to Authorize the Secretary to Acquire Certain Properties within the Chalmette National Historic Park, and for other Purposes, 87th Cong., 2nd sess. (Oct. 9, 1962).

31. *St. Bernard Voice*, July 22, 1939.

32. The situation in Chalmette was very similar to that in other cities that experienced white flight in the mid-twentieth century. For more on this, see Richard Moe and Carter Wilke, *Changing Places: Rebuilding Communities in the Age of Sprawl* (New York: Henry Holt, 1997); Andres Duany, Elizabeth Plater-Zyberk, and Jeff Speck, *Suburban Nation: The Rise of Sprawl and the Decline of the American Dream* (New York: North Point, 2000); Martin Anderson, *The Federal Bulldozer: A Critical Analysis of Urban Renewal, 1949–1962* (Cambridge, MA: MIT Press, 1964).

33. Many of the former residents of Fazendeville still reside in the Ninth Ward of New Orleans, even after Hurricane Katrina decimated that area. The Battlefield Baptist Church is the center of what remains of this community. For more on Fazendeville, see Ron Chapman, "Fazendeville," *Louisiana Life*, Winter 2004, www.myneworleans.com/Louisiana-Life/Winter-2004/Fazendeville/.

34. Minutes of the Battle of New Orleans 150th Committee, Jan. 20, 1964, Battle of New Orleans Sesquicentennial Correspondence and Minutes, 1964–71, Williams Research Center, Historic New Orleans Collection.

35. Quote from Martha G. Robinson to Henry Z. Carter, Oct. 26, 1964, Records of the Battle of New Orleans Sesquicentennial Celebration Commission, Record Group 79, National Archives and Records Administration II. See also Deputy Secretary of the Interior George E. Robinson to J. Francis Pohlhaus, Dec. 2, 1964.

36. Battle of New Orleans Sesquicentennial Celebration Committee, "Official Program, 150 Years of Peace, 1815–1965" (New Orleans: The Commission, 1965); *Battle of New Orleans Sesquicentennial Celebration, 1815–1865: Final Report to the United States Congress* (Washington, DC: Government Printing Office, 1966).

37. Menu of the Official Banquet Commemorating the 150th Anniversary of the Battle of New Orleans and 150 Years of Peace between the United States and Great Britain, [Sesquicentennial Commission's Banquet] International Room, Roosevelt Hotel, Williams Research Center, Historic New Orleans Collection; Louisiana Historical Society, "Sesquicentennial of the Battle of New Orleans: Annual Banquet" (New Orleans: The Society, 1965).

38. Income information from "Consumer Income, Income in 1965 of Families and Persons in the United States" (Washington, DC: United States Census Bureau, 1967). Quote from Battle of New Orleans Sesquicentennial Celebration Committee, "Official Program, 150 Years of Peace, 1815–1965" (New Orleans: The Commission, 1965).

39. Battlefield tourism continues to remain a huge industry for small towns in rural America. For more on this topic, see Frances H. Kennedy and Douglas R. Porter, *Dollars and Sense of Battlefield Preservation: The Economic Benefits of Protecting Civil War Battlefields: A Handbook for Community Leaders* (Washington, DC: Preservation Press, 1994). The federal government has even begun trying to aid local communities in understanding the ramifications of their decision to rely on cultural tourism; see *Preserving America: Historic Preservation and Heritage Tourism in Housing and Community Development: A Guide to Using Community Development Block Grant Funds for Historic Preservation and Heritage Tourism in Your Communities* (Washington, DC: US Department of Housing and Urban Development, Community Development Block Grant Program, 2004).

40. For more on the repercussions of Fazendeville, see Allison H. Peña, "Fazendeville: Highlighting Invisible Pasts and Dignifying Present Identities," *Cultural Resources Management* 24, no. 5 (2001): 24–27.

41. The Battle of New Orleans was not the only historic event to feel the effects of segregation and the civil rights movement. The centennial of the Civil War lasted from 1961 to 1965, at the same time that commemorations were under way for the Battle of New Orleans and the War of 1812. For a detailed discussion of the Civil War's memory in this same period, see David W. Blight, *American Oracle: The Civil War in the Civil Rights Era* (Cambridge, MA: Belknap Press of Harvard University Press, 2011).

Chapter 8 · A "Rustic and Factual" Appearance

1. *New Orleans Times-Picayune*, Jan. 16, 2013.

2. *New Orleans Times-Picayune*, Jan. 9, 2004.

3. See www.thehermitage.com/event/the-hermitage-gala/.

4. *New York Times*, Nov. 24, 1968.

5. Author's visit to the Hermitage, Aug. 7, 2012.

6. Newspaper clippings, [Jan. 1965], Battle of New Orleans Scrapbook, 1815–1940, Louisiana Historical Center, Louisiana State Museum; James Moody Papers Relating to the Battle of New Orleans Sesquicentennial Celebration, 1964–65, Tennessee State Archives.

7. *Nashville Tennessean*, Jan. 6, 2015.

8. Quoted in Robert W. Blythe, *Administrative History of Jean Laffite National Historical Park and Preserve* (Atlanta: Cultural Resources Division, Southeast Regional Office, National Park Service, 2013), 70.

9. The *Louisville (KY) Courier*, June 28, 1964, has a colorful full-page layout dedicated to the group which depicts the dresses they wore.

10. Superintendent, Chalmette to Regional Director, Southwest Region, Sept. 16, 1974, Jean Laffite National Park and Preserve Archives, Special Collections, Earl K. Long Library, University of New Orleans.

11. *Reading (PA) Eagle*, Jan. 1, 1975; *Louisville (KY) Courier*, June 28, 1964; *Naples (FL) Daily News*, Mar. 24, 1974. Quote from *Henderson (NV) Home News*, Nov. 5, 1964.

12. *New Orleans Times-Picayune*, Mar. 19, 1973; photographs in the Jean Laffite National Park and Preserve Archives, Special Collections, Earl K. Long Library, University of New Orleans.

13. Photographs in the Jean Laffite National Park and Preserve Archives, Special Collections, Earl K. Long Library, University of New Orleans. These were the same groups that helped when the 1958 *Buccaneer* premiered in New Orleans. *Reading (PA) Eagle*, Dec. 16, 1958; *Daytona Beach (FL) Morning Journal*, Dec. 17, 1958.

14. Site Managers Report, Feb. 1955, Jean Laffite National Park and Preserve Archives, Special Collections, Earl K. Long Library, University of New Orleans; Joyce Marie Jackson, "Declaration of Taking Twice: The Fazendeville Community of the Lower Ninth Ward," *American Anthropologist* 108, no. 4 (Dec. 2006): 7665–80.

15. Jean Laffite National Park and Preserve visitation statistics, https://irma.nps.gov/Stats/ SSRSReports/Park%20Specific%20Reports/Annual%20Park%20Visitation%20Graph%20 (All%20Years)?Park=JELA. These statistics show a decrease in park attendance following the disbanding of the Boy Scout reenactments. The reliability of later park numbers is troublesome for a number of reasons. In 1979, Chalmette Park joined with the larger Jean Laffite Park and Preserve, causing an artificial jump in the statistics. Further, numbers for the Chalmette unit on its own are also complicated by the fact that hundreds of visitors weekly "visit" the site as the *Creole Queen* riverboat docks on its tour of the Mississippi River. These visitors are included in park visitation statistics whether they are actually there to learn about the battlefield or not. Finally, Chalmette Park is an urban green space that attracts numerous joggers and bicyclists. These visitors are also not necessarily in the park to learn the history, and so counting their visitation for purposes of tracking interest in the site from a cultural standpoint presents a further challenge to methodology.

16. For representative histories, see Marquis James, *Andrew Jackson, the Border Captain* (Indianapolis: Bobbs-Merrill, 1933); Robert Tallant, *The Pirate Lafitte and the Battle of New Orleans* (New York: Random House, 1951); Lyle Saxon, *Lafitte, the Pirate* (New York: Century, 1930).

17. Charles B. Brooks, *The Siege of New Orleans* (Seattle: University of Washington Press, 1961); Wilburt S. Brown, *The Amphibious Campaign for West Florida and Louisiana, 1814–1815: A Critical Review of Strategy and Tactics at New Orleans* (Tuscaloosa: University of Alabama Press, 1969).

18. For more on the history of the NPS and its employees, see Ronlad A. Foresta, *America's National Parks and Their Keepers* (Washington, DC: Resources for the Future, 1984). For more on the historiography of the war over time, see Donald R. Hickey, "The War of 1812: Still a Forgotten Conflict?," *Journal of Military History* 65, no. 3 (July 2001): 741–69; Donald R. Hickey, *The War of 1812: A Forgotten Conflict* (Urbana: University of Illinois Press, 1989).

19. Examples of many of these items now exist in the collections of the Louisiana State Museum and the Historic New Orleans Collection.

20. The members of the Louisiana Historical Society have collected items relating to the battle and Louisiana history since the mid-nineteenth century. B. F. French, *Historical Collections of Louisiana, Embracing Translations of Many Rare and Valuable Documents Relating to the Natural, Civil and Political History of That State* (New York: Wiley & Putnam, 1846); Louisiana Historical Society, *Catalogue of the Exhibit of the Historical Society Opened February 20th, 1900, at the Fisk Free Public Library in New Orleans, La* (New Orleans: Palfrey-Dameron, 1900).

21. Historic New Orleans Collection; see www.hnoc.org/visit/aboutus.html.

22. "Interpretive Prospectus for Tour Road in Chalmette National Historic Park," approved Feb. 15, 1962, Jean Laffite National Park and Preserve Archives, Special Collections, Earl K. Long Library, University of New Orleans.

23. J. Fred Roush, *Chalmette National Historical Park* (Washington, DC: National Park Service, 1954).

24. The park did not discover the issue until the mid-2000s. Ted Birkedal and John Coverdale, *The Search for the Lost Riverfront: Historical and Archeological Investigations at the Chalmette Battlefield, Jean Laffite National Historical Park and Preserve* ([New Orleans, LA]: National Park Service, US Department of the Interior, 2005).

25. *Wood Preservation News*, Feb. 1965.

26. General Bres to Regional Director, Southeast Region, Mar. 25, 1964, Records of the Battle of New Orleans Sesquicentennial Commission, Williams Research Center, Historic New Orleans Collection.

27. Edwin S. Bres, *Notes on the Establishment and the Development of the Chalmette National Historical Park* (1964), Sesquicentennial of the Battle of New Orleans Collection, Williams Research Center, Historic New Orleans Collection; Blythe, *Administrative History of Jean Laffite*, 68.

28. Birkedal and Coverdale, *Search for the Lost Riverfront*, 462–63, 472.

29. Jerome A. Greene, *Historic Resource Study: Chalmette Unit, Jean Laffite National Historical Park and Preserve* (Denver: United States Department of the Interior, National Park Service, 1985); Kevin Risk, *Chalmette Battlefield and Chalmette National Cemetery: Cultural Landscape Report* (Atlanta: National Park Service, Southeast Regional Office, Cultural Resources Stewardship Division, 1999).

30. *New Orleans Times-Picayune*, Oct. 24, 1993; Blythe, *Administrative History of Jean Laffite*, 92.

31. National Park Service, Denver Service Center, *Sutibility/Feasability Study, Propsed Jean Laffite National Cultural Park, Louisiana* (Denver: National Park Service, 1973).

32. *St. Bernard Voice*, Oct. 22, 1980; Chalmette Staff Meeting Notes, Feb. 26, 1980, Jean Laffite National Park and Preserve Archives, Special Collections, Earl K. Long Library, University of New Orleans.

33. Concept Sketches, Chalmette Interpretive Center (1984), Jean Laffite National Park and Preserve Archives, Special Collections, Earl K. Long Library, University of New Orleans.

34. John E. Cornelison, Tammy D. Cooper, and David Lowe, *Archeological Survey of the Chalmette Battlefield at Jean Lafitte National Historical Park and Preserve* (Tallahassee: National Park Service, Southeast Archeological Center, 2002).

35. Betsy Swanson to Ted Birkedal, Aug. 25, 2987, Jean Laffite National Park and Preserve Archives, Special Collections, Earl K. Long Library, University of New Orleans.

36. Greene, *Historic Resource Study*; Risk, *Chalmette Battlefield and Chalmette National Cemetery.*

37. *New Orleans Times-Picayune*, Jan. 7, 2011. For more on the archeological work, see Birkedal and Coverdale, *Search for the Lost Riverfront.* Information on the diorama is taken from this author's photographs.

38. Commentary on the exhibit labels is based on the author's visit to the site on March 19, 2012.

39. *New Orleans Times-Picayune*, Jan. 4, 1965. Prior to Hurricane Katrina, the Chalmette unit's office had pictures of these 1960s-era reenactors hanging on the wall. Other photographs of them also exist in the Jean Laffite National Park and Preserve Archives, Special Collections, Earl K. Long Library, University of New Orleans.

40. *Battle of New Orleans Sesquicentennial Celebration, 1815–1865: Final Report to the United States Congress* (Washington, DC: Government Printing Office, 1966).

41. *New Orleans Times-Picayune*, Jan. 7, 2013, Jan. 10, 2013, Apr. 7, 2008, Feb. 7, 2013, Feb. 5, 2009.

42. For more on the hobby of living history, see Iain McCalman and Paul A. Pickering, *Historical Reenactment: From Realism to the Affective Turn* (Basingstoke: Palgrave Macmillan, 2010); Charlie Schroeder, *Man of War: My Adventures in the World of Historical Reenactment* (New York: Hudson Street Press, 2012); Tony Horwitz, *Confederates in the Attic: Dispatches from the Unfinished Civil War* (New York: Pantheon Books, 1998). Commentary on the park being a "white park" is taken from Robert Blythe's interview with former superintendent Geraldine Smith; Blythe, *Administrative History of Jean Laffite*, 89.

43. *New Orleans Times-Picayune*, Jan. 13, 2013, Jan. 6, 2010, Jan. 11, 2013, Jan. 11, 2002; Blythe, *Administrative History of Jean Laffite*, 89.

44. Appointments are made by the governor, the lieutenant governor, the president of the state senate, the speaker of the state house of representatives, congressmen whose districts include the battlefield, the city of New Orleans, the Parish of St. Bernard, the Parish of Jefferson, and the New Orleans Multicultural Tourism Network.

45. Louisiana State Legislature, Boards and Commissions, Battle of New Orleans Bicentennial Commission, www.legis.la.gov/legis/BoardMembers.aspx?boardId=910; Louisiana Division of Administration, Boards and Commissions, Battle of New Orleans Bicentennial Commission, http://doa.louisiana.gov/boardsandcommissions/viewBoard.cfm?board=574.

46. Westley Annis, "Oppose Louisiana House Bill 1287: Battle of New Orleans Bicentennial Commission," www.thecanetruck.com/archives/2010/06/oppose-louisian.html.

47. Pickles quoted in Christian Villere and Christopher Tidmore, "Commemoration of Bicentennial Battle of New Orleans Faces Its Own Battle," *Louisiana Weekly*, Dec. 10, 2012, www.louisianaweekly.com/commemoration-of-bicentennial-battle-of-new-orleans-faces-its-own-battle/.

48. Villere and Tidmore, "Commemoration of Bicentennial."

49. Timothy Pickles, founder and creative director, Louisiana Living History Foundation, e-mail message to author, July 27, 2015.

50. Krisy Wallisch, Public Information Officer, Jean Laffite National Historical Park and Preserve, e-mail message to author, July 27, 2015.

51. *New Orleans Times-Picayune*, Jan. 8, 2015.

52. These comments are based on conversations the author has had with senior leaders in interpretation at the Louisiana State Museum and the Historic New Orleans Collection.

53. See *New Orleans Times-Picayune*, Apr. 7, 2008, Jan. 10, 2013, for examples.

54. For works that explore public history and community involvement, see Jerome De Groot, *Consuming History: Historians and Heritage in Contemporary Popular Culture* (London: Routledge, 2009); Roy Rosenzweig and David P. Thelen, *The Presence of the Past: Popular Uses of History in American Life* (New York: Columbia University Press, 1998).

55. *New Orleans Times-Picayune*, Jan. 13, 2013, Jan. 6, 2010, Jan. 11, 2013, Jan. 11, 2002.

Conclusion · *"What Is Past Is Prologue"*

1. For an updated reappraisal of an old classic that touches on this subject, see Donald R. Hickey, *The War of 1812: A Forgotten Conflict, Bicentennial Edition* (Urbana: University of Illinois Press, 2013).

2. For some views on the role of militia, see Samuel Woodworth, *The Hunters of Kentucky; or, The Battle of New Orleans* (New York: Brown, [1818]); *Boston Patriot and Daily Chronicle*, Feb. 3, 1818.

3. *Boston Patriot and Daily Chronicle*, Feb. 10, 1820; *Independent Chronicle and Boston Patriot*, Feb. 16, 1820; *Charlestown (MA) Franklin Monitor and Middlesex (CT) Republican*, Mar. 18, 1820; *Boston Patriot and Daily Chronicle*, Mar. 23, 1820; *Boston Essex Patriot*, Apr. 1, 1820; *Boston Agricultural Intelligencer*, Mar. 24, 1820; *Portland (ME) Eastern Argus*, Mar. 28, 1820; *Haverville (MA) Essex Patriot*, Apr. 1, 1820. For more on the Hartford Convention and its fallout, see David Hackett Fischer, *The Revolution of American Conservatism: The Federalist Party in the Era of Jeffersonian Democracy* (New York: Harper & Row, 1965), xix; Sean Wilentz, *The Rise of American Democracy: Jefferson to Lincoln* (abr. college ed.; New York: W. W. Norton, 2009), 81–82; George Dangerfield, *The Era of Good Feelings* (New York: Harcourt, Brace, 1952), 88, 98; Shaw Livermore Jr., *The Twilight of Federalism: The Disintegration of the Federalist Party, 1815–1830* (Princeton, NJ: Princeton University Press, 1962), 61; Richard Buel Jr., *America on the Brink: How the Political Struggle over the War of 1812 Almost Destroyed the Young Republic* (New York: Palgrave Macmillan, 2006).

4. For the relationship between westerners, Jackson, and the future of the Democratic Party, see Homer C. Hockett, *Western Influences on Political Parties to 1825: An Essay in Historical Interpretation* (New York: Da Capo, 1970).

5. *Portsmouth (NH) Journal of Literature and Politics*, Jan. 12, 1828; *Keene New Hampshire Sentinel*, Dec. 7, 1828.

6. For early uses of the battle as an example of Southern and western states' military prowess, see *Norfolk American Beacon and Commercial Diary*, Dec. 13, 1816; *Baltimore Patriot*, Jan. 8, 1822; *Charlestown (MA) Franklin Monitor*, Mar. 18, 1820; *Boston Patriot and Daily Chronicle*, Feb. 3, 1818.

7. *Concord New Hampshire Patriot and Daily Gazette*, Mar. 7, 1850; *Pittsfield (MA) Sun*, Feb. 28, 1850.

8. William M. Leftwich, *Anniversary Address Delivered by Rev. W. M. Leftwich, in the Capitol of Missouri, on the Eighth Day of January 1859; by Invitation of the General Assembly* (Jefferson City, MO: C. J. Corwin, 1859).

9. *Nashville Banner*, Jan. 8, 1915.

10. *The Battle of New Orleans, Official Programme* (New Orleans: Louisiana Historical Society, 1915), 8–9. Indeed, the narrative of the happy African American fighting implicitly for the preservation of slavery survived well into the twentieth century, including the sesquicentennial of the battle. See WDSU Special Projects Unit, "The Battle That Missed the War: 150 Years of Peace, 1815–1965," Telecast 7, 1965, narrated, written, and produced by Mel Leavitt and Paul Yacich.

11. *The Buccaneer*, directed by Cecil B. DeMille (Paramount Pictures, 1938); radio conversation between Cecil B. DeMille and Lyle Saxon, Jan. 10, 1938, Lyle Saxon Papers, Tulane University.

12. Harold I. Lessem and George C. Mackenzie, *Fort McHenry National Monument and Historic Shrine, Maryland* (Washington, DC: National Park Service, 1954).

13. Eric Foner, *Give Me Liberty! An American History*, 3rd ed. (New York: W. W. Norton, 2012), 313; George Brown Tindall and David E. Shi, *America: A Narrative History*, 8th ed. (New York: W. W. Norton, 2010).

Manuscript Collections

Battle of New Orleans Scrapbook, 1815–1940. Louisiana Historical Center. Louisiana State Museum.

Battle of New Orleans Sesquicentennial Correspondence and Minutes, 1964–71. Williams Research Center. Historic New Orleans Collection.

Bres, Edwin S. *Notes on the Establishment and the Development of the Chalmette National Historical Park* (1964). Williams Research Center. Historic New Orleans Collection.

James Moody Papers Relating to the Battle of New Orleans Sesquicentennial Celebration, 1964–65. Tennessee State Archives.

Jean Laffite National Park and Preserve Archives. Special Collections. Earl K. Long Library. University of New Orleans.

Jean Laffite National Park vertical files, Tulane University Special Collection.

Ladies Hermitage Association Board of Directors Meeting Minutes, January 1906–September 1914. The Hermitage. Nashville, TN.

Lyle Saxon Papers. Special Collections. Tulane University.

Menu of the Official Banquet Commemorating the 150th Anniversary of the Battle of New Orleans and 150 Years of Peace Between the United States and Great Britain. [Sesquicentennial Commission's Banquet] International Room, Roosevelt Hotel, Williams Research Center. Historic New Orleans Collection.

Record Group 79, National Archives and Records Administration II.

Records of the Battle of New Orleans Sesquicentennial Celebration Commission. Williams Research Center. Historic New Orleans Collection.

Sesquicentennial of the Battle of New Orleans Collection. Williams Research Center. Historic New Orleans Collection.

United States Daughters of 1812. Chalmette Chapter Papers. Tulane University Special Collections.

Published Primary Sources

Aitchison, Robert. *A British Eyewitness at the Battle of New Orleans: The Memoir of Royal Navy Admiral Robert Aitchison, 1808–1827.* Edited by Gene A. Smith. New Orleans: Historic New Orleans Collection, 2004.

Atherton, Charles Gordon. *An Oration, Delivered on the Fourteenth Anniversary of the Battle of New Orleans, at Goffstown, January 8, 1829.* Concord, NH: R. H. Sherburne, 1829.

The Battle of New Orleans, Official Programme. New Orleans: Louisiana Historical Society, 1915.

Battle of New Orleans Sesquicentennial Celebration, 1815–1865: Final Report to the United States Congress. Washington, DC: Government Printing Office, 1966.

Browning, Charles H. *The American Historical Register and Monthly Gazette of the Patriotic-Hereditary Societies of the United States of America.* Vol. 3. Philadelphia: Historical Register, September 1895–February 1896.

Chalmette National Historical Park. Washington, DC: Government Printing Office, 1944.

Claiborne, William C. C. *Militia General Order.* New Orleans, January 26, 1815.

"Consumer Income, Income in 1965 of Families and Persons in the United States." Washington, DC: United States Census Bureau, 1967.

Daniels, Nathan W. *Thank God My Regiment an African One: The Civil War Diary of Colonel Nathan W. Daniels.* Edited by C. P. Weaver. Baton Rouge: Louisiana State University Press, 1998.

DeMille, Cecil B. *Autobiography.* Englewood Cliffs, NJ: Prentice-Hall, 1959.

Devereux, Mary. *Lafitte of Louisiana.* Boston: Little, Brown, 1902.

Dorris, Joseph, and Jesse Denson. *The Chronicles of Andrew: Containing an Accurate and Brief Account of General Jackson's Victories South, Over the Creeks, Also His Victories Over the British at Orleans with Biographical Sketches of His Life, &c.* Milledgeville, GA: S&F Grantland, 1815.

Dorris, Mary C. *Preservation of the Hermitage 1889–1915—Annals, History, and Stories—the Acquisition, Restoration, and Care of the Home of General Andrew Jackson by the Ladies Hermitage Association for Over a Quarter of a Century.* Nashville, 1915.

Dorsey, G. Volney. *An Address on the Character and Services of Andrew Jackson: Delivered by Invitation, Before the General Assembly of Ohio, January 8, 1864.* Columbus, OH: Glenn, Thrall & Heide, 1864.

Everett, Alexander H. *An Address Delivered at Salem on the Eighth of January, 1836, at the Request of the Democratic Young men of that Place, in Commemoration of the Victory of New Orleans.* Boston: Beals & Greene, 1836.

Ewing, Andrew. *An Oration Delivered on the Occasion of the Inauguration of the Bust Erected to the Memory of Gen. Andrew Jackson, in the City of Memphis, January 8, 1859.* Nashville: E. G. Eastman, 1859.

Folk, Reau E. *Battle of New Orleans, Its Real Meaning; Exposure of Untruth Being Taught Young America Concerning the Second Most Important Military Event in the Life of the Republic.* Nashville: Ladies Hermitage Association, 1935.

Fortier, James Joseph Alcée, and Charles Gayarré. *The story of Jean and Pierre Lafitte, the pirate-patriots, including a note on the indispensable victory at New Orleans, January 8th, 1815; a publication of the Louisiana State Museum, James J. A. Fortier, editor; and a reprint of Historical sketch of Pierre and Jean Lafitte, the famous smugglers of Louisiana, 1809–1814, by Charles Gayarré, from the Magazine of American history, v.10, July–Dec., 1883, Historical publication co., New York, by courtesy of Howard Memorial Library.* New Orleans, [ca. 1880].

French, B. F. *Historical Collections of Louisiana, Embracing Translations of Many Rare and Valuable Documents Relating to the Natural, Civil and Political History of That State.* New York: Wiley & Putnam, 1846.

Gilpin, Henry D. *A Speech Delivered at the Union and Harmony Celebration, by the Democratic Citizens of the City and County of Philadelphia, of the Twenty-first Anniversary of the Victory of New Orleans, January 8, 1836.* Boston: Beals & Greene, 1836.

Gleig, G. R. *The Campaigns of the British Army at Washington and New Orleans, 1814–1815*. 1834. Reprint, San Francisco: Lulu Press, 2012.

———. *A Narrative of the Campaigns of the British Army at Washington and New Orleans, Under Generals Ross, Pakenham, and Lambert, in the Years 1814 and 1815: With Some Account of the Countries Visited*. London: J. Murray, 1821.

Greene, Jerome A. *Historic Resource Study: Chalmette Unit, Jean Lafitte National Historical Park and Preserve*. Denver: US Department of the Interior, National Park Service, 1985.

Greenleaf, Abner. "Address Delivered at Jefferson-Hall, Portsmouth, N.H., Jan 8, 1828, Being the Thirteenth Anniversary of Jackson's Victory at New Orleans." Portsmouth, NH, 1828.

Grice, C. E. *The Battle of New Orleans; or, Glory, Love, and Loyalty: An Historical and National Drama*. Baltimore: Commercial Press, 1815.

Hill, Isaac, Nathan Buckman Felton, Joseph M. Harper, and James B. Thornton. *An address, delivered at Concord, N.H. January 8, 1828, being the thirteenth anniversary of Jackson's victory at New Orleans*. Concord, NH: Manahan, Hoag, 1828.

Hunt, Gilbert J. *The Late War Between the United States and Great Britain, From June 1812 to February 1815, Written in the Ancient Historical Style*. New York: David Longworth, 1816.

Ingraham, J. H. *Lafitte: The Pirate of the Gulf*. New York: Harper & Brothers, 1836.

Ingraham, Prentiss. *Lafitte's Legacy; or, The Avenging Son: A Romance of the Gulf*. New York: Beadle & Adams, 1888.

Jackson Banquet at Washington City, January 8, 1854. Washington, DC: Jackson Democratic Association, 1854.

James, Marquis. *Andrew Jackson, the Border Captain*. Indianapolis: Bobbs-Merrill, 1933.

Latour, Arsène Lacarrière. *Historical Memoir of the War in West Florida and Louisiana in 1814–15: With an Atlas*. Edited by Gene A. Smith. Expanded edition. Gainsville: University Press of Florida, 1999.

Leftwich, William M. *Anniversary Address Delivered by Rev. W. M. Leftwich, in the Capitol of Missouri, on the Eighth Day of January 1859; by Invitation of the General Assembly*. Jefferson City, MO: C. J. Corwin, 1859.

Lives, Exploits, and Cruelties of the Most Celebrated Pirates and Sea Robbers: Brought Down to the Latest Period. London: Milner, 1820.

Louisiana Historical Society. *The Battle of New Orleans, Official Programme*. New Orleans: Louisiana Historical Society, 1915.

———. *Catalogue of the Exhibit of the Historical Society Opened February 20th, 1900, at the Fisk Free Public Library in New Orleans, La*. New Orleans: Palfrey-Dameron, 1900.

McCulley, Johnston. *The Curse of Capistrano*. New York: Grosset & Dunlap, 1927.

Monroe, James. *The Papers of James Monroe: A Documentary History of the Presidential Tours of James Monroe, 1817, 1818, 1819*. Edited by Daniel Preston. Vol. 1. Westport, CT: Greenwood, 2003.

National Park Service, Denver Service Center. *Sutibility/Feasability Study, Proposed Jean Lafitte National Cultural Park, Louisiana*. Denver: National Park Service, 1973.

"Official Program, 150 Years of Peace, 1815–1965." New Orleans: The Commission, 1965.

An Oration Delivered at Mr. Days Hotel on Friday, 16th April 1819 on the Rise and Progress of New Orleans Since The Memorable Battle on the 8th of January, 1815: With Observations of Its Future Prospects. New Orleans: John McPherson, 1819.

Orczy, Baroness. *The Scarlet Pimpernel*. New York: Signet, 2000.

Parton, James. *General Butler in New Orleans: Department of the Gulf in the Year 1862: With an Account of the Capture of New Orleans, and a Sketch of the Previous Career of the General, Civil and Military*. New York: Mason Brothers, 1864.

Pedrick, W. E. *New Orleans As It Is*. Cleveland: William W. Williams, 1885.

Powell, Alexander E. *Gentlemen Rovers*. New York: C. Scribner's Sons, 1913.

Proceedings at the Banquet of the Jackson Democratic Association, Washington, Eighth of January, 1852. Washington, DC: Jackson Democratic Association, 1852.

Proceedings of the Democratic Celebration of the Anniversary of the Glorious Battle of New Orleans, by "the Personal and Political Friends" of George Mifflin Dallas . . . the oration . . . by Horn R. Kneas with an Appendix Containing Very Interesting Letters Written by Vice President Dallas in the year 1845. Philadelphia: Office of *The Daily Keystone*, 1846.

Risk, Kevin. *Chalmette Battlefield and Chalmette National Cemetery: Cultural Landscape Report*. Atlanta: National Park Service, Southeast Regional Office, Cultural Resources Stewardship Division, 1999.

Ross, James. *Victoria Neo-Aurelina: Pax Gandavensis*. Translated by Michael Fortune. Philadelphia: Lydia R. Bailey, 1816.

Roush, J. Fred. *Chalmette National Historical Park*. Washington, DC: National Park Service, 1954.

Saxon, Lyle. *Lafitte the Pirate*. Gretna, LA: Pelican, 1989.

Smith, Richard Penn. *Lafitte; or, The Barratarian Chief: An American Tale*. Hamilton, NY: Williams, Orton, 1830.

Stockwell, Elisha. *Private Elisha Stockwell Sees the Civil War*. Edited by Byron R. Abernathy. Norman: University of Oklahoma Press, 1958.

Tallant, Robert. *The Pirate Lafitte and the Battle of New Orleans*. New York: Random House, 1951.

Tatum, Howell. *Major Howell Tatum's Journal While Acting Topographical Engineer (1814) to General Jackson Commanding the Seventh Military District*. Edited by John Spencer Bassett. Northampton, MA: Department of History of Smith College, 1922.

Torrey, Nathan. *Verses on the Signal Victory Obtained over the British Troops at New Orleans, January 8th, 1815 by Gen. Andrew Jackson, and the Brave Troops Under his Command*. Hindsdale, MA, March 24, 1815.

"Unparalleled Victory." Broadside. Boston: Coverly, 1815.

Watterson, Henry. *The Perry memorial and centennial celebration under the auspices of the national government and the states of Ohio, Pennsylvania, Michigan, Illinois, Wisconsin, New York, Rhode Island, Kentucky, Minnesota and Indiana*. Cleveland: Interstate Board of the Perry's Victory Centennial Commissioners, 1912.

White, John Blake. *The Triumph of Liberty; or, Louisiana Preserved: A National Drama*. Charleston, SC: John Hoff, 1819.

Woodworth, Samuel. *The Hunters of Kentucky; or, the Battle of New Orleans*. New York: Brown, [1818].

The Young Democratic Clubs of the District of Columbia Present the Jackson Day Dinner for the Benefit of the Democratic National Committee: To be Held at the Willard on Wednesday, January the Eighth, Nineteen Hundred and Thirty-six at Seven-thirty O'clock. Washington, DC: National Capital Press, 1936.

Yvonnet, Francis V. *An Oration Delivered at the Baptist Church in the City of Troy, on the*

Eighth Day of January, 1828, in Commemoration of the Victory Obtained at New-Orleans, on the Eighth of January, 1815, by Gen. Andrew Jackson, and the forces under his command. Troy, NY: Francis Adancourt, 1828.

Newspapers and Periodicals

Albany Argus
Alexandria (VA) Gazette
American Beacon and Norfolk and Ports-
  mouth Daily Advertiser
Amherst (NH) Farmer's Cabinet
Amherst (NH) Hillsboro Telegraph
Baltimore Patriot
Baltimore Patriot and Evening Advertiser
Baltimore Patriot and Mercantile Advertiser
Barre (MA) Patriot
Bennington Vermont Gazette
Boston Agricultural Intelligencer
Boston Essex Patriot
Boston Independent Chronicle
Boston Patriot and Daily Chronicle
Boston Patriot and Independent Chronicle
Boston Yankee
Brattleboro (VT) American Yeoman
Camden (SC) Gazette
Charlestown (MA) Franklin Monitor
Charlestown (MA) Franklin Monitor and
  Middlesex (CT) Republican
City of Washington (DC) Gazette
Concord New Hampshire Patriot and Daily
  Gazette
Concord New Hampshire Patriot and State
  Gazette
Cooperstown (NY) Watch-Tower
Dallas Morning News
Danville (VT) North Star
Daytona Beach (FL) Morning Journal
Easton (MD) Republican Star and General
  Advertiser
Hallowell (ME) American Advocate and
  Kennebec Advertiser
Hartford American Mercury
Hartford Connecticut Courant
Haverville (MA) Essex Patriot
Henderson (NV) Home News
Independent Chronicle and Boston Patriot
Keene New Hampshire Sentinel

Las Vegas Daily Gazette
Little Rock Arkansas Whig
Louisville (KY) Courier
Middlesex (CT) Gazette
Milwaukee Daily Sentinel
Naples (FL) Daily News
Nashville American
Nashville Banner
Nashville Gazette
Nashville Republican Banner
Nashville Tennessean
New Bern Carolina Centennial
New Orleans Daily Picayune
New Orleans Item
New Orleans Times-Democrat
New Orleans Times-Picayune
Newport (RI) Mercury
New York Columbian
New York Commercial Advertiser
New York Daily Advertiser
New York Herald
New York Mercantile Advertiser
New York National Advocate
New York Spectator
New York Times
New York Weekly Museum
Norfolk American Beacon and Commercial
  Diary
Petersburg (VA) American Star
Philadelphia Franklin Gazette
Pittsfield (MA) Sun
Portland (ME) Eastern Argus
Portsmouth (NH) Journal of Literature and
  Politics
Portsmouth New Hampshire Patriot
Providence (RI) Patriot
Providence (RI) Patriot and Columbian
  Phoenix
Reading (PA) Eagle
Richmond Enquirer
Salem Essex Register

Salem Gazette
San Antonio Express
Springfield (MA) Hampden Patriot
St. Bernard Voice
St. Francisville (LA) Time Piece
St. Louis Enquirer
Stockbridge (MA) Berkshire Star
Troy (NY) Farmer's Register

United States Magazine and Democratic
  Review
Variety Magazine
Washington (DC) Daily Intelligencer
Washington City (DC) Weekly Gazette
Wilmington (DE) American Watchman
Wood Preservation News

Film, Movies, and Television

The Buccaneer. Directed by Cecil B. DeMille. Paramount Pictures, 1938.
The Buccaneer. Directed by Anthony Quinn. Paramount Pictures, 1958.
Don Q, Son of Zorro. Directed by Donald Crisp. Elton Corporation, 1925.
Driftwood, Jimmy. "The Battle of New Orleans." *Jimmie Driftwood Sings Newly Discovered Early American Folk Songs.* RCA Records, 1958.
The Elusive Pimpernel. Directed by Maurice Elvey. Stoll Picture Productions, 1919.
Horton, Johnny. "The Battle of New Orleans." *The Battle of New Orleans.* Columbia Records, 1959.
The Laughing Cavalier. Directed by A. V. Bramble and Eliot Stannard. Dreadnaught, 1917.
The Mask of Zorro. Directed by Fred Niblo. Douglas Fairbanks Pictures, 1920.
Return of the Scarlet Pimpernel. Directed by Hanns Schwarz. London Film Productions, 1937.
The Scarlet Pimpernel. Directed by Richard Stanton. Fox Film Corporation, 1917.
The Scarlet Pimpernel. Directed by Harold Young. London Film Productions, 1934.
The Triumph of the Scarlet Pimpernel. Directed by T. Hayes Hunter. Cricklewood Studios, 1928.

Websites

About the Collection. Historic New Orleans Collection. www.hnoc.org/visit/aboutus.html.
Annis, Westley. "Oppose Louisiana House Bill 1287: Battle of New Orleans Bicentennial Commission." Accessed Apr. 24, 2013. www.thecanetruck.com/archives/2010/06/oppose-louisian.html.
Battle of New Orleans. About. Facebook. Accessed Apr. 24, 2013. www.facebook.com/pages/Battle-of-New-Orleans/526172437424759?id=526172437424759&sk=info.
Battle of New Orleans Bicentennial Commission. Accessed Apr. 24, 2013. www.battleofneworleans2015.com.
Billboard Hot 100 50th Anniversary—the Billboard Hot 100 All-Time Top Songs. Accessed Feb. 7, 2013. www.billboard.com/specials/hot100/index.shtml.
Billboard Hot 100 50th Anniversary—Top Billboard Hot 100 Country Songs. Accessed Feb. 7, 2013. www.billboard.com/bbcom/specials/hot100/charts/top-country.shtml.
Chapman, Ron. "Fazendeville." *Louisiana Life,* Winter 2004. Accessed Mar. 1, 2013. www.myneworleans.com/Louisiana-Life/Winter-2004/Fazendeville/.
The Hermitage. Events Calendar. Accessed Apr. 20, 2013. www.thehermitage.com/events/calendar/2013/04/19/hermitage-gala.580524.
Jean Laffite National Park and Preserve Visitation Statistics. Accessed Apr. 24, 2012. https://irma.nps.gov/Stats/SSRSReports/Park%20Specific%20Reports/Annual%20Park%20Visitation%20Graph%20(All%20Years)?Park=JELA.

Louisiana Division of Administration. Boards and Commissions, Battle of New Orleans
Bicentennial Commission. Accessed Apr. 24, 2013. http://doa.louisiana.gov/boardsand
commissions/viewBoard.cfm?board=574.

Louisiana State Legislature. Boards and Commissions, Battle of New Orleans Bicentennial Commission. Accessed Apr. 24, 2013. www.legis.la.gov/legis/BoardMembers.aspx?
boardId=910.

Star-Spangled 200. Facebook. Accessed Apr. 24, 2013. www.facebook.com/starspangled200.

2015 Bicentennial of the Battle of New Orleans. About. Facebook. www.facebook.com/
2015BattleOfNewOrleans.

United States Army Center for Military History. "Regular Army Special Designation Listing." www.history.army.mil/html/forcestruc/spdes-123–ra_ar.html.

Villere, Christian, and Christopher Tidmore. "Commemoration of Bicentennial Battle
of New Orleans Faces Its Own Battle." *Louisiana Weekly*. Accessed Apr. 24, 2013.
www.louisianaweekly.com/commemoration-of-bicentennial-battle-of-new-orleans
-faces-its-own-battle/.

Wilson's War Message to Congress. Brigham Young University Library World War I Document Archive. http://wwi.lib.byu.edu/index.php/Wilson's_War_Message_to_Congress.

Published Secondary Sources

Abrahamson, James L. *The Men of Secession and Civil War, 1859–1861*. Wilmington, DE: SR
Books, 2000.

Anderson, Martin. *The Federal Bulldozer: A Critical Analysis of Urban Renewal, 1949–1962*.
Cambridge, MA: MIT Press, 1964.

Andrew, Rod. *Long Gray Lines: The Southern Military School Tradition, 1839–1915*. Chapel
Hill: University of North Carolina Press, 2001.

Aron, Stephen. *How the West Was Lost: The Transformation of Kentucky from Daniel Boone to
Henry Clay*. Baltimore: Johns Hopkins University Press, 1996.

Ayers, Edward L. *The Promise of the New South: Life after Reconstruction*. New York: Oxford
University Press, 1992.

Baker, Jean H. *Affairs of Party: The Political Culture of Northern Democrats in the Mid-
Nineteenth Century*. Ithaca, NY: Cornell University Press, 1983.

Barbuto, Richard V. *Niagara 1814: America Invades Canada*. Lawrence: University Press of
Kansas, 2000.

Belmonte, Laura A. *Selling the American Way: U.S. Propaganda and the Cold War*. Philadelphia: University of Pennsylvania Press, 2008.

Birchard, Robert S. *Cecil B. DeMille's Hollywood*. Lexington: University Press of Kentucky,
2004.

Birkedal, Ted, and John Coverdale. *The Search for the Lost Riverfront: Historical and Archeological Investigations at the Chalmette Battlefield, Jean Lafitte National Historical Park and
Preserve*. [New Orleans, LA]: National Park Service, US Department of the Interior, 2005.

Blair, William Alan. *Cities of the Dead: Contesting the Memory of the Civil War in the South,
1865–1914*. Chapel Hill: University of North Carolina Press, 2004.

Blight, David W. *American Oracle: The Civil War in the Civil Rights Era*. Cambridge, MA:
Belknap Press of Harvard University Press, 2011.

———. *Beyond the Battlefield: Race, Memory and the American Civil War*. Amherst: University of Massachusetts Press, 2002.

———. *Race and Reunion: The Civil War in American Memory.* Cambridge, MA: Belknap Press of Harvard University Press, 2001.

Blythe, Robert W. *Administrative History of Jean Laffite National Historical Park and Preserve.* Atlanta: Cultural Resources Division, Southeast Regional Office, National Park Service, 2013.

Bodnar, John E. *Remaking America: Public Memory, Commemoration, and Patriotism in the Twentieth Century.* Princeton, NJ: Princeton University Press, 1991.

Borstelmann, Thomas. *The Cold War and the Color Line: American Race Relations in the Global Arena.* Cambridge, MA: Harvard University Press, 2001.

Brands, H. W. *Lone Star Nation: How a Ragged Army of Volunteers Won the Battle for Texas Independence, and Changed America.* New York: Doubleday, 2004.

Brooks, Charles B. *The Siege of New Orleans.* Seattle: University of Washington Press, 1961.

Brown, Richard D. *Knowledge Is Power: The Diffusion of Information in Early America, 1700–1865.* New York: Oxford University Press, 1989.

Brown, Thomas J. *The Public Art of Civil War Commemoration: A Brief History with Documents.* Boston: Bedford / St. Martin's, 2004.

Brown, Wilburt Scott. *The Amphibious Campaign for West Florida and Louisiana, 1814–1815: A Critical Review of Strategy and Tactics at New Orleans.* Tuscaloosa: University of Alabama Press, 1969.

Buckley-Zistel, Susanne. *Conflict Transformation and Social Change in Uganda: Remembering after Violence.* Basingstoke: Palgrave Macmillan, 2008.

Buel, Richard, Jr.. *America on the Brink: How the Political Struggle over the War of 1812 Almost Destroyed the Young Republic.* New York: Palgrave Macmillan, 2006.

Butcher-Younghans, Sherry. *Historic House Museums: A Practical Handbook for Their Care, Preservation, and Management.* New York: Oxford University Press, 1993.

Cantrell, Gregg. "The Bones of Stephen F. Austin: History and Memory in Progressive-Era Texas." *Southwestern Historical Quarterly* 108, no. 2 (Oct. 2004): 145–78.

Capers, Gerald Mortimer. *Occupied City: New Orleans under the Federals, 1862–1865.* Lexington: University of Kentucky Press, 1965.

Capua, Michelangelo. *Yul Brynner: A Biography.* Jefferson, NC: McFarland, 2006.

Cayton, Andrew R. L. *The Frontier Republic: Ideology and Politics in the Ohio Country.* Kent, OH: Kent University Press, 1986.

"The Celebration of Jackson Day, January 8, 1915." *Tennessee Historical Magazine* 1 (Mar. 1915).

Christensen, Bonnie. *Red Lodge and the Mythic West: Coal Miners to Cowboys.* Lawrence: University Press of Kansas, 2002.

Clark, Norman H. *Deliver Us from Evil: An Interpretation of American Prohibition.* New York: Norton, 1976.

Clark, Thomas Dionysius, and John D. W. Guic. *Frontiers in Conflict: The Old Southwest, 1795–1830.* Albuquerque: University of New Mexico Press, 1989.

Cochran, Robert. "Remembering Jimmy Driftwood." *Arkansas Historical Quarterly* 57, no. 4 (Winter 1998): 435–38.

Coffman, Edward M. *The War to End All Wars: The American Military Experience in World War I.* New York: Oxford University Press, 1968.

Cohen, Lizabeth. *A Consumers' Republic: The Politics of Mass Consumption in Postwar America.* New York: Knopf, 2003.

Cole, Donald B. *Andrew Jackson: The 1828 Election and the Rise of the Two-Party System.* Lawrence: University Press of Kansas, 2009.

———. *A Jackson Man: Amos Kendall and the Rise of American Democracy.* Baton Rouge: Louisiana State University Press, 2004.

———. *Vindicating Andrew Jackson: The 1828 Election and the Rise of the Two-Party System.* Lawrence: University Press of Kansas, 2000.

Cornelison, John E., Tammy D. Cooper, and David Lowe. *Archeological Survey of the Chalmette Battlefield at Jean Lafitte National Historical Park and Preserve.* Tallahassee: National Park Service, Southeast Archeological Center, 2002.

Cox, Karen L. *Dixie's Daughters: The United Daughters of the Confederacy and the Preservation of Confederate Culture.* Gainesville: University Press of Florida, 2003.

Crackel, Theodore J. *Mr. Jefferson's Army: Political and Social Reform of the Military Establishment, 1801–1809.* New York: New York University Press, 1989.

Craven, Avery. *The Growth of Southern Nationalism, 1848–1861.* Baton Rouge: Louisiana State University Press, 1953.

Cress, Lawrence Delbert. *Citizens in Arms: The Army and the Militia in American Society to the War of 1812.* Chapel Hill: University of North Carolina Press, 1982.

Cunliffe, Marcus. *Soldiers and Civilians: The Martial Spirit in America, 1775–1865.* Boston: Little, Brown, 1968.

Dangerfield, George. *The Awakening of American Nationalism, 1815–1828.* New York: Harper & Row, 1965.

———. *The Era of Good Feelings.* New York: Harcourt, Brace, 1952.

Daughan, George C. *1812: The Navy's War.* New York: Basic Books, 2011.

Davies, Wallace Evan. *Patriotism on Parade: The Story of Veterans' and Hereditary Organizations in America, 1783–1900.* Cambridge, MA: Harvard University Press, 1955.

Davis, William C. *Lone Star Rising: The Revolutionary Birth of the Texas Republic.* New York: Free Press, 2004.

———. *The Pirates Laffite: The Treacherous World of the Corsairs of the Gulf.* Orlando, FL: Harcourt, 2005.

De Groot, Jerome. *Consuming History: Historians and Heritage in Contemporary Popular Culture.* London: Routledge, 2009.

De Grummond, Jane Lucas, and Ronald R. Morazan. *The Baratarians and the Battle of New Orleans.* Baton Rouge, LA: Legacy, 1979.

Dew, Charles B. *Apostles of Disunion: Southern Secession Commissioners and the Causes of the Civil War.* Charlottesville: University Press of Virginia, 2001.

Dichtl, John R. *Frontiers of Faith: Bringing Catholicism to the West in the Early Republic.* Lexington: University Press of Kentucky, 2008.

Doenecke, Justus D. *Nothing Less Than War: A New History of America's Entry into World War I.* Lexington: University Press of Kentucky, 2011.

Doherty, Thomas Patrick. *Cold War, Cool Medium: Television, McCarthyism, and American Culture.* New York: Columbia University Press, 2003.

Douglas, Frank J., Robert Bachman, George Lynn Woodruff, and LeRoy Habenight. *National Society of United States Daughters of 1812, 1892–1989: History.* Metairie, LA: National Society of United States Daughters of 1812, 1989.

Drowne, Kathleen Morgan. *Spirits of Defiance: National Prohibition and Jazz Age Literature, 1920–1933.* Columbus: Ohio State University Press, 2005.

Duany, Andres, Elizabeth Plater-Zyberk, and Jeff Speck. *Suburban Nation: The Rise of Sprawl and the Decline of the American Dream.* New York: North Point, 2000.

Dudziak, Mary L. *Cold War Civil Rights: Race and the Image of American Democracy.* Princeton, NJ: Princeton University Press, 2000.

Dufour, Charles L. *The Night the War Was Lost.* Lincoln: University of Nebraska Press, 1994.

Edgerton, Gary R., and Peter C. Rollins, *Television Histories: Shaping Collective Memory in the Media Age.* Lexington: University Press of Kentucky, 2001.

Engelhardt, Tom. *The End of Victory Culture: Cold War America and the Disillusioning of a Generation.* Amherst: University of Massachusetts Press, 1998.

Eyal, Yonatan. *The Young America Movement and the Transformation of the Democratic Party.* Cambridge: Cambridge University Press, 2007.

Eyman, Scott. *Empire of Dreams: The Epic Life of Cecil B. DeMille.* New York: Simon & Schuster, 2010.

Fahs, Alice, and Joan Waugh. *The Memory of the Civil War in American Culture.* Chapel Hill: University of North Carolina Press, 2004.

Faust, Drew Gilpin. *The Creation of Confederate Nationalism: Ideology and Identity in the Civil War South.* Baton Rouge: Louisiana State University Press, 1988.

Findlay, John M. *Magic Lands: Western Cityscapes and American Culture after 1940.* Berkeley: University of California Press, 1992.

Fischer, David Hackett. *The Revolution of American Conservatism: The Federalist Party in the Era of Jeffersonian Democracy.* New York: Harper & Row, 1965.

Fleche, Andre M. *The Revolution of 1861: The American Civil War in the Age of Nationalist Conflict.* Chapel Hill: University of North Carolina Press, 2012.

Foner, Eric. *Give Me Liberty! An American History.* 3rd ed. New York: W. W. Norton, 2012.

———. *Reconstruction: America's Unfinished Revolution, 1863–1877.* New York: Harper & Row, 1988.

Foresta, Ronlad A. *America's National Parks and Their Keepers.* Washington, DC: Resources for the Future, 1984.

Foster, Gaines M. *Ghosts of the Confederacy: Defeat, the Lost Cause, and the Emergence of the New South, 1865 to 1913.* New York: Oxford University Press, 1987.

Fried, Richard M. *Nightmare in Red: The McCarthy Era in Perspective.* New York: Oxford University Press, 1990.

———. *The Russians Are Coming! The Russians Are Coming! Pageantry and Patriotism in Cold-War America.* New York: Oxford University Press, 1998.

Gallagher, Gary W., and Alan T. Nolan. *The Myth of the Lost Cause and Civil War History.* Bloomington: Indiana University Press, 2000.

Goode, James M. *Four Salutes to the Nation: The Equestrian Statues of General Andrew Jackson.* Washington, DC: White House Historical Association, 2010.

Gotham, Kevin Fox. *Authentic New Orleans: Tourism, Culture, and Race in the Big Easy.* New York: New York University Press, 2007.

Grant, Susan-Mary. *North over South: Northern Nationalism and American Identity in the Antebellum Era.* Lawrence: University Press of Kansas, 2000.

Green, Jennifer R. *Military Education and the Emerging Middle Class in the Old South.* Cambridge: Cambridge University Press, 2011.

Griffith, Robert. *The Politics of Fear: Joseph R. McCarthy and the Senate.* Lexington: Published for the Organization of American Historians [by] University Press of Kentucky, 1970.

Hardin, Stephen L. *Texian Iliad: A Military History of the Texas Revolution, 1835–1836.* Austin: University of Texas Press, 1994.

Harvey, Chance, ed. *The Life and Selected Letters of Lyle Saxon.* Gretna, LA: Pelican, 2003.

Heale, M. J. *The Presidential Quest: Candidates and Images in American Political Culture, 1787–1852.* London: Longman, 1982.

Hearn, Chester G. *The Capture of New Orleans, 1862.* Baton Rouge: Louisiana State University Press, 1995.

———. *When the Devil Came Down to Dixie: Ben Butler in New Orleans.* Baton Rouge: Louisiana State University Press, 1997.

Hettle, Wallace. *The Peculiar Democracy: Southern Democrats in Peace and Civil War.* Athens: University of Georgia Press, 2001.

Hickey, Donald R. *The War of 1812: A Forgotten Conflict.* Urbana: University of Illinois Press, 1989.

———. *The War of 1812: A Forgotten Conflict, Bicentennial Edition.* Urbana: University of Illinois Press, 2013.

———. "The War of 1812: Still a Forgotten Conflict?" *Journal of Military History* 65, no. 3 (July 2001): 741–69.

Hockett, Homer C. *Western Influences on Political Parties to 1825: An Essay in Historical Interpretation.* New York: Da Capo, 1970.

Hofstadter, Richard. *The Idea of a Party System: The Rise of Legitimate Opposition in the United States, 1780–1840.* Berkeley: University of California Press, 1969.

Hollandsworth, James G. *The Louisiana Native Guards: The Black Military Experience during the Civil War.* Baton Rouge: Louisiana State University Press, 1995.

Horwitz, Tony. *Confederates in the Attic: Dispatches from the Unfinished Civil War.* New York: Pantheon Books, 1998.

Howe, Daniel Walker. *The Political Culture of the American Whigs.* Chicago: University of Chicago Press, 1979.

———. *What Hath God Wrought: The Transformation of America, 1815–1848.* Oxford: Oxford University Press, 2007.

Huber, Leonard V. *The Battle of New Orleans and Its Monument.* New Orleans: Louisiana Landmarks Society, 1993.

———. *Jackson Square through the Years.* New Orleans: Friends of the Cabildo, 1982.

Hudson, Angela Pulley. *Creek Paths and Federal Roads: Indians, Settlers, and Slaves and the Making of the American South.* Chapel Hill: University of North Carolina Press, 2010.

Hurt, Douglas. *The Ohio Frontier: Crucible of the Old Northwest, 1720–1830.* Bloomington: Indiana University Press, 1996.

Jackson, Joyce Marie. "Declaration of Taking Twice: The Fazendeville Community of the Lower Ninth Ward." *American Anthropologist* 108, no. 4 (Dec. 2006): 7665–80.

Kaiser, Leo M. *Early American Latin Verse, 1625–1825.* Wauconda, IL: Bolchazy-Carducci, 2005.

Kanon, Tom. "Forging the 'Hero of New Orleans': Tennessee Looks at the Centennial of the War of 1812." *Tennessee Historical Quarterly* 71, no. 2 (Summer 2012): 139–40.

Kennedy, David M. *Over Here: The First World War and American Society.* New York: Oxford University Press, 1980.

Kennedy, Frances H., and Douglas R. Porter. *Dollars and Sense of Battlefield Preservation: The Economic Benefits of Protecting Civil War Battlefields: A Handbook for Community Leaders.* Washington, DC: Preservation Press, 1994.

Knudson, Jerry W. *Jefferson and the Press: Crucible of Liberty.* Columbia: University of South Carolina Press, 2006.

Kohl, Lawrence Frederick. *The Politics of Individualism: Parties and the American Character in the Jacksonian Era.* New York: Oxford University Press, 1989.

Kohn, Richard H. *Eagle and Sword: The Federalists and the Creation of the American Military Establishment, 1783–1802.* New York: Free Press, 1975.

Laver, Harry S. *Citizens More Than Soldiers: The Kentucky Militia and Society in the Early Republic.* Lincoln: University of Nebraska Press, 2007.

Lawson, Melinda. *Patriot Fires: Forging a New American Nationalism in the Civil War North.* Lawrence: University Press of Kansas, 2002.

Lessem, Harold I., and George C. Mackenzie. *Fort McHenry National Monument and Historic Shrine, Maryland.* Washington, DC: National Park Service, 1954.

Levine, Bruce C. *Half Slave and Half Free: The Roots of Civil War.* New York: Hill & Wang, 1992.

Linenthal, Edward Tabor. *Sacred Ground: Americans and Their Battlefields.* Urbana: University of Illinois Press, 1991.

Lipstadt, Deborah E. *Denying the Holocaust: The Growing Assault on Truth and Memory.* New York: Free Press, 1993.

Livermore, Shaw, Jr. *The Twilight of Federalism: The Disintegration of the Federalist Party, 1815–1830.* Princeton, NJ: Princeton University Press, 1962.

Marshall, Anne E. *Creating a Confederate Kentucky: The Lost Cause and Civil War Memory in a Border State.* Chapel Hill: University of North Carolina Press, 2010.

McCalman, Iain, and Paul A. Pickering. *Historical Reenactment: From Realism to the Affective Turn.* Basingstoke: Palgrave Macmillan, 2010.

McClintock, Russell. *Lincoln and the Decision for War: The Northern Response to Secession.* Chapel Hill: University of North Carolina Press, 2008.

McConnell, Roland C. *Negro Troops of Antebellum Louisiana: A History of the Battalion of Free Men of Color.* Baton Rouge: Louisiana State University Press, 1968.

McCormick, Richard Patrick. *The Second American Party System: Party Formation in the Jacksonian Era.* Chapel Hill: University of North Carolina Press, 1966.

McDonough, James L., and Thomas Lawrence Connelly. *Five Tragic Hours: The Battle of Franklin.* Knoxville: University of Tennessee Press, 1983.

Middlekauf, Robert. *The Glorious Cause: The American Revolution, 1763–1789.* Oxford: Oxford University Press, 2005.

Miller, Edward L. *New Orleans and the Texas Revolution.* College Station: Texas A&M University Press, 2004.

Mills, Cynthia J., and Pamela H. Simpson. *Monuments to the Lost Cause: Women, Art, and the Landscapes of Southern Memory.* Knoxville: University of Tennessee Press, 2003.

Mintz, Steven, and Susan Kellogg. *Domestic Revolutions: A Social History of American Family Life.* New York: Free Press, 1988.

Moe, Richard, and Carter Wilkie. *Changing Places: Rebuilding Community in the Age of Sprawl.* New York: Henry Holt, 1997.

Moser, John E. *Twisting the Lion's Tail: American Anglophobia between the World Wars.* New York: New York University Press, 1999.

Muller, Charles G. *The Darkest Day: The Washington–Baltimore Campaign during the War of 1812*. Philadelphia: University of Pennsylvania Press, 2003.

Murtagh, William J. *Keeping Time: The History and Theory of Preservation in America*. Pittstown, NJ: Main Street Press, 1988.

Nathans, Heather. *Early American Theater from the Revolution to Thomas Jefferson: Into the Hands of the People*. Cambridge: Cambridge University Press, 2003.

Nelson, Scott Reynolds, and Carol Sheriff. *A People at War: Civilians and Soldiers in America's Civil War, 1854–1877*. New York: Oxford University Press, 2007.

Newman, Simon P. *Parades and the Politics of the Street*. Philadelphia: University of Pennsylvania Press, 1997.

Okrent, Daniel. *Last Call: The Rise and Fall of Prohibition*. New York: Scribner, 2010.

Onuf, Peter S. *Statehood and Union: A History of the Northwest Ordinance*. Bloomington: Indiana University Press, 1987.

Osgood, Kenneth Alan. *Total Cold War: Eisenhower's Secret Propaganda Battle at Home and Abroad*. Lawrence: University Press of Kansas, 2006.

Ovendale, Ritchie. *Anglo-American Relations in the Twentieth Century*. New York: St. Martin's, 1998.

Owsley, Frank Lawrence, Jr. *Struggle for the Gulf Borderlands: The Creek War and the Battle of New Orleans, 1812–1815*. Tuscaloosa: University of Alabama Press, 2000.

Page, Max, and Randall Mason, eds. *Giving Preservation a History: Histories of Historic Preservation in the United States*. New York: Routledge, 2004.

Parsons, Lynn H. *The Birth of Modern Politics: Andrew Jackson, John Quincy Adams, and the Election of 1828*. Oxford: Oxford University Press, 2009.

Pasley, Jeffery L. "The Tyranny of Printers: Newspaper Politics in the Early Republic. Charlottesville: University Press of Virginia, 2001.

Peña, Allison H. "Fazendeville: Highlighting Invisible Pasts and Dignifying Present Identities." *Cultural Resources Management* 24, no. 5 (2001): 24–27.

Perman, Michael. *Reunion without Compromise: The South and Reconstruction, 1865–1868*. Cambridge: Cambridge University Press, 1973.

———. *The Road to Redemption: Southern Politics, 1869–1879*. Chapel Hill: University of North Carolina Press, 1984.

Peskin, Allan. *Winfield Scott and the Profession of Arms*. Kent, OH: Kent State University Press, 2003.

Pierson, Michael D. *Mutiny at Fort Jackson: The Untold Story of the Fall of New Orleans*. Chapel Hill: University of North Carolina Press, 2008.

Poole, W. Scott. *Never Surrender: Confederate Memory and Conservatism in the South Carolina Upcountry*. Athens: University of Georgia Press, 2004.

Potter, David Morris, and Don E. Fehrenbacher. *The Impending Crisis, 1848–1861*. New York: Harper & Row, 1976.

Powell, Lawrence N. *The Accidental City: Improvising New Orleans*. Cambridge, MA: Harvard University Press, 2012.

Preserving America: Historic Preservation and Heritage Tourism in Housing and Community Development: A Guide to Using Community Development Block Grant Funds for Historic Preservation and Heritage Tourism in Your Communities. Washington, DC: US Department of Housing and Urban Development, Community Development Block Grant Program, 2004.

Remini, Robert V. *Andrew Jackson*. New York: Harper Perennial, 1999.

————. *Andrew Jackson and the Course of American Empire, 1767–1821.* New York: Harper & Row, 1977.

————. *Andrew Jackson and the Course of American Freedom, 1822–1832.* New York: Harper & Row, 1981.

————. *Andrew Jackson: The Course of American Democracy, 1833–1845.* Baltimore: Johns Hopkins University Press, 2013.

————. *The Battle of New Orleans: Andrew Jackson and America's First Military Victory.* New York: Viking, 1999.

Richards, Jeffrey H. *Drama, Theatre, and Identity in the American New Republic.* Cambridge: Cambridge University Press, 2005.

Richards, Leonard L. *The Slave Power: The Free North and Southern Domination, 1780–1860.* Baton Rouge: Louisiana State University Press, 2000.

Robbins, Jhan. *Yul Brynner: The Inscrutable King.* New York: Dodd, Mead, 1987.

Roberts, Aline Gray, ed. *Celebrating One Hundred Years of the TN State Society United States Daughters of 1812.* n.p.: s.n., 2009.

Robertson, Andrew W. *The Language of Democracy: Political Rhetoric in the United States and Britain.* Charlottesville: University of Virginia Press, 2005.

Roeder, George H. *The Censored War: American Visual Experience during World War Two.* New Haven, CT: Yale University Press, 1993.

Rollins, Peter C. *Hollywood as Historian: American Film in a Cultural Context.* Lexington: University Press of Kentucky, 1983.

Rollins, Peter C., and John E. O'Connor. *Why We Fought: America's Wars in Film and History.* Lexington: University Press of Kentucky, 2008.

Rosenzweig, Roy, and David P. Thelen. *The Presence of the Past: Popular Uses of History in American Life.* New York: Columbia University Press, 1998.

Rothman, Adam. *Slave Country: American Expansion and the Origins of the Deep South.* Cambridge, MA: Harvard University Press, 2005.

Rothman, Hal. *Devil's Bargains: Tourism in the Twentieth-Century American West.* Lawrence: University Press of Kansas, 1998.

Rowe, Mary Ellen. *Bulwark of the Republic: The American Militia in the Antebellum West.* Westport, CT: Praeger, 2003.

Rubin, Anne S. *A Shattered Nation: The Rise and Fall of the Confederacy, 1861–1868.* Chapel Hill: University of North Carolina Press, 2005.

Sacher, John M. *A Perfect War of Politics: Parties, Politicians, and Democracy in Louisiana, 1824–1861.* Baton Rouge: Louisiana State University Press, 2003.

Savage, Kirk. *Standing Soldiers, Kneeling Slaves: Race, War, and Monument in Nineteenth-Century America.* Princeton, NJ: Princeton University Press, 1997.

Schroeder, Charlie. *Man of War: My Adventures in the World of Historical Reenactment.* New York: Hudson Street Press, 2012.

Seitz, Laura S., and Elaine D. Baxter. *Before the Throne of Grace: An Evangelical Family in the Early Republic.* Franklin, TN: Providence House, 1999.

Sellers, Charles. *The Market Revolution.* New York: Oxford University Press, 1991.

Sewell, Richard H. *A House Divided: Sectionalism and Civil War, 1848–1865.* Baltimore: Johns Hopkins University Press, 1988.

Shaffer, Jason. *Performing Patriotism: National Identity in the Colonial and Revolutionary American Theater.* Philadelphia: University of Pennsylvania Press, 2007.

Silber, Nina. *The Romance of Reunion: Northerners and the South, 1865–1900*. Chapel Hill: University of North Carolina Press, 1993.

Simpson, John A. *Edith D. Pope and Her Nashville Friends: Guardians of the Lost Cause in the Confederate Veteran*. Knoxville: University of Tennessee Press, 2003.

Skaggs, David Curtis, and Gerard T. Altoff. *A Signal Victory: The Lake Erie Campaign, 1812–1813*. Annapolis, MD: Naval Institute Press, 1997.

Skelton, William B. *The American Profession of Arms, 1784–1861*. Lawrence: University Press of Kansas, 1992.

Smith, Gene A. *Thomas ap Catesby Jones: Commodore of Manifest Destiny*. Annapolis, MD: Naval Institute Press, 2000.

Smith, Timothy B. *A Chickamauga Memorial: The Establishment of America's First Civil War National Military Park*. Knoxville: University of Tennessee Press, 2009.

———. *The Golden Age of Battlefield Preservation: The Decade of the 1890s and the Establishment of America's First Five Military Parks*. Knoxville: University of Tennessee Press, 2008.

———. *This Great Battlefield of Shiloh: History, Memory, and the Establishment of a Civil War National Military Park*. Knoxville: University of Tennessee Press, 2004.

Souther, Jonathan Mark. *New Orleans on Parade: Tourism and the Transformation of the Crescent City*. Baton Rouge: Louisiana State University Press, 2006.

Stagg, J. C. A. *Mr. Madison's War: Politics, Diplomacy, and Warfare in the Early American Republic, 1783–1830*. Princeton, NJ: Princeton University Press, 1983.

Stampp, Kenneth M. *And the War Came: The North and the Secession Crisis, 1860–1861*. Baton Rouge: Louisiana State University Press, 1950.

Stanonis, Anthony J. *Creating the Big Easy: New Orleans and the Emergence of Modern Tourism, 1918–1945*. Athens: University of Georgia Press, 2006.

Stegmaier, Mark Joseph. *Texas, New Mexico, and the Compromise of 1850: Boundary Dispute and Sectional Crisis*. Kent, OH: Kent State University Press, 1996.

Stephenson, Michael. *Patriot Battles: How the War of Independence Was Fought*. New York: HarperCollins, 2007.

Stipe, Robert E. *A Richer Heritage: Historic Preservation in the Twenty-First Century*. Chapel Hill: University of North Carolina Press, 2003.

Streeter, Richard Kent. *The Jimmy Driftwood Primer: A Biography*. Calhoun, GA: J. Driftwood Legacy Project, 2003.

Sturken, Marita. *Tangled Memories: The Vietnam War, the AIDS Epidemic, and the Politics of Remembering*. Berkeley: University of California Press, 1997.

———. *Tourists of History: Memory, Kitsch, and Consumerism from Oklahoma City to Ground Zero*. Durham, NC: Duke University Press, 2007.

Suid, Lawrence H. *Guts and Glory: The Making of the American Military Image in Film*. Lexington: University Press of Kentucky, 2002.

Sydnor, Charles S. *The Development of Southern Sectionalism, 1819–1848*. Baton Rouge: Louisiana State University Press, 1948.

Taylor, Alan. *The Civil War of 1812, American Citizens, British Subjects, Irish Rebels, and Indian Allies*. New York: Vintage, 2011.

———. *William Cooper's Town Power and Persuasion on the Frontier of the Early American Republic*. New York: Norton, 1995.

Thomas, Emory M., Lesley J. Gordon, and John C. Inscoe, *Inside the Confederate Nation:*

Essays in Honor of Emory M. Thomas. Baton Rouge: Louisiana State University Press, 2005.

Thomas, James W. *Lyle Saxon: A Critical Biography.* Birmingham, AL: Summa, 1991.

Tindall, George Brown, and David E. Shi. *America: A Narrative History.* 8th ed. New York: W. W. Norton, 2010.

Towns, W. Stuart. *Enduring Legacy: Rhetoric and Ritual of the Lost Cause.* Tuscaloosa: University of Alabama Press, 2012.

Travers, Len. *Celebrating the Fourth: Independence Day and the Rites of Nationalism in the Early Republic.* Amherst: University of Massachusetts Press, 1997.

Tyler, Norman. *Historic Preservation: An Introduction to Its History, Principles, and Practice.* New York: W. W. Norton, 2000.

Vogel, Robert C. "Jean Laffite, the Baratarians, and the Battle of New Orleans: A Reappraisal." *Louisiana History: The Journal of the Louisiana Historical Association* 41, no. 3 (Summer 2000): 261–76.

Vogel, Robert C., and Kathleen F. Taylor. *Jean Laffite in American History: A Bibliographic Guide.* St. Paul, MN: White Pine, 1998.

Waldstreicher, David. *In the Midst of Perpetual Fetes: The Making of American Nationalism, 1776–1820.* Chapel Hill: University of North Carolina Press, 1997.

Ward, John William. *Andrew Jackson: Symbol for an Age.* New York: Oxford University Press, 1955.

Watson, Harry. *Liberty and Power: The Politics of Jacksonian America.* New York: Hill & Wang, 1990.

Weiner, Tim. *Legacy of Ashes: The History of the CIA.* New York: Doubleday, 2007.

Wells, Robert V. *Life Flows On in Endless Songs: Folk Songs and American History.* Urbana: University of Illinois Press, 2009.

West, Patricia. *Domesticating History: The Political Origins of America's House Museums.* Washington, DC: Smithsonian Institution Press, 1999.

Wevill, Richard. *Britain and America after World War II: Bilateral Relations and the Beginnings of the Cold War.* London: I. B. Tauris, 2012.

Wilentz, Sean. *Chants Democratic: New York City and the Rise of the American Working Class, 1788–1850.* New York: Oxford University Press, 1984.

———. *The Rise of American Democracy: Jefferson to Lincoln.* Abr. college ed. New York: W. W. Norton, 2009.

Woodward, C. Vann. *Origins of the New South, 1877–1913.* Baton Rouge: Louisiana State University Press, 1951.

Wooster, Ralph A. *The Secession Conventions of the South.* Princeton, NJ: Princeton University Press, 1962.

Zagarri, Rosemarie. *Revolutionary Backlash: Women and Politics in the Early Republic.* Philadelphia: University of Pennsylvania Press, 2007.

Zenzen, Joan M. *Battling for Manassas: The Fifty-Year Preservation Struggle at Manassas National Battlefield Park.* University Park: Pennsylvania State University Press, 1998.

Unpublished Secondary Sources

Davenport, Ann. "The Original Music of Jimmy Driftwood: Songs 1964–1979." PhD diss., Johns Hopkins University, 1983.